THE EROSION
OF CHILDHOOD

Child oppression in Britain 1860–1918

Lionel Rose

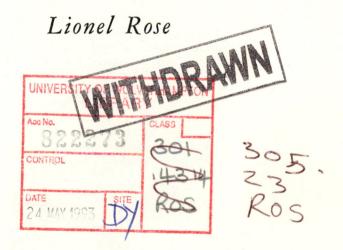

ROUTLEDGE

London and New York

First published 1991
by Routledge
11 New Fetter Lane, London EC4P 4EE

Simultaneously published in the USA and Canada
by Routledge
a division of Routledge, Chapman and Hall, Inc.
29 West 35th Street, New York, NY 1001

Set in 10/12 Garamond by
Columns of Reading
Printed and Bound in Great Britain by
T J Press (Padstow) Ltd,
Padstow, Cornwall

British Library Cataloguing in Publication Data
Rose, Lionel 1944–90
The erosion of childhood: child oppression in Britain, 1860–1918.
1. Great Britain. Children, Social conditions, history
I. Title
305.230941

Library of Congress Cataloging in Publication Data
Rose, Lionel, 1944–90
The erosion of childhood: child oppression in Britain, 1860–1918
Lionel Rose
p. cm.
Includes bibliographical references and index.
1. Children–Great Britain–Social conditions. 2. Children–
Employment–Great Britain–History. 3. Education,
Elementary–Great Britain–History. I. Title.
HQ792.G7R67 1991
305.23'0941–dc20 90–47723
ISBN 0–415–00165–X

CONTENTS

PUBLISHER'S NOTE

Lionel Rose died in August 1990 and sadly did not see the publication of his book. We have endeavoured to check the facts contained in the Bibliography and Notes but must apologize to the reader for a few missing details that we were unable to track down. We apologize, too, for any errors or inconsistencies that may remain in the text.

1

CHILDREN WITHOUT CHILDHOOD: AN INTRODUCTION

British schoolchildren today enjoy a historically unprecedented degree of economic advantage and legal protection. But if they find such protections restrictive and seek to evade them, they can become very vulnerable to exploitation when fending for themselves illicitly in the labour market.

The National Association of Schoolmasters reported in 1987 that 'many tens of thousands of children' were illegally moonlighting. It admitted that 'Children wanted the money, parents wanted them to work, and employers were too ready to break the law', but could point to low wages and blatant disregard for health and safety regulations by employers; thus, between 1975 and 1986, 172 children under 16 were killed while working on farms.[1]

However, it is to the Third World that one must look to see child exploitation at its grossest. A bounding birth rate and dire poverty combine to make children expendable, or valuable only in so far as their appealing qualities are an economic asset, as street sellers, say, beggars and child prostitutes. As urbanization grows apace so the problems of street waifdom, sweatshop slavery and sexual abuse become more widespread.[2]

All this carries echoes of the world described by Dickens, Mayhew, Sims and many others in Victorian Britain. But while we have emerged from the most shocking forms of child exploitation, the tendencies, the potential, are still there. The hidden problem of sexual abuse within the family has come to greater prominence in recent years; homeless youngsters adrift in the big cities can slide into prostitution; and the government's Youth Opportunities Programme can lend itself to the exploitation of semi-conscripted youngsters by unscrupulous employers.

This book examines the status and condition of British children, at work, at school and at home, from the 1860s, a decade of significant public inquiries into child labour and education, to the end of the First World War.

FAMILY SIZES 1860–1918

In 1861 over 7 million of England and Wales's 20 million population were under 15 years old. The birth rate was then at a peak and began to fall slightly only in the later 1870s, and more markedly thereafter.[3] By 1901 the average birth rate was less than half of the 1861 figure, yet the proportion of under-15s in the population had fallen only from just over a third to just under a third during that period.[4] This was due to the sharp decline in the juvenile death rate; for example, among 10–14-year-old boys it fell from 5.1 per cent in the later 1840s to 2.4 per cent in the 1890s.[5] Thus the available supply of cheap juvenile labour did not noticeably decrease, though demand for it did decline in many staple industries owing to technological changes.

The average number of children born to a family fell from over 6 in the 1869s to just over 4 in the 1890s and under 2.5 in 1915.[6] It was the middle classes who took the lead in family limitation from the 1870s, whilst among different occupational groups within the working classes family sizes varied. Lancashire textile workers' families were small, whilst farm labourers were more prolific, though by the Edwardian period there was a noticeable fall in the size of unskilled workers' families.

The extension of child labour laws and the advent of compulsory education are obvious standard accepted motives for the reduction in family size. And one would expect the 'educated' classes to have understood contraceptive techniques earlier. Yet this does not explain why Lancashire mill workers should have kept their families small when there remained opportunities for half-time labour for their children in the mills right up to the end of the period covered by this book.

Despite late Victorian and Edwardian eugenic fears about racial deterioration owing to the faster decline in fertility among the 'quality', a balance in net fertility was in fact maintained by differential death rates. Even as late as 1895 half the children up to 5 would die in the worst slums, compared with 19 per cent in a healthy district like Dulwich.[7] The younger the children the more

2

tenuous their hold on life. The Registrar-General's Annual Report for 1888 shows that of the 511,000 deaths at all ages nearly a quarter (120,000) were infants under 1. (There were about 800,000 births a year at this period.) Survival chances progressively improved after the first year. Among 1–2-year-olds there were under 37,000 deaths, among 2–3-year-olds 15,000 deaths; the figure continuing to decline, so that among 10–14-year-olds inclusive there were under 9,000 deaths.[8] Even at the time of George V's coronation in 1911, in a city with shocking poverty like Glasgow 54.7 per cent of all deaths were of infants and children up to 15. Nearly half of these child deaths were among the under-5s.[9]

A typical Victorian and Edwardian household would have been shifting in composition as little ones died off and new ones were born throughout the fertile period of a marriage, and such was the age span among the brood that at a given time the eldest might already have left home and struck out on their own while the youngest was still a baby.

CHILDREN'S OCCUPATION PATTERNS 1860–1918

Despite the high but falling death rate, and the flow of emigration, the population of England and Wales grew from 20 million in 1861 to 36 million in 1911. We have to visualize streets and tenements, villages and courts, teeming with child life. But how much real childhood youngsters could enjoy, and how soon they were harnessed to the adult treadmill of work and subsistence, may be glimpsed from this brief statistical outline.

Before the industrial revolution children were widely employed in agriculture and domestic production, and the coming of steam power created a great demand for children in textiles in the early nineteenth century.[10] The 1861 census returns would indicate that among boys about a third of the 5–9-year-olds and 55–60 per cent of the 10–14-year-olds were in occupations. For girls, a slightly higher proportion of 5–9-year-olds and just under 50 per cent of the 10–14-year-olds were 'employed'.[11] The government statistician Dr William Farr estimated around this period that a seventh of the child population was 'upper' or 'middle' class,[12] and these would be included among the proportion of non-employed. The census describes 810,000 of the 1,173,000 boys of 5–9 and 778,000 of the 1,171,000 girls of the same age as 'scholars'.

Among 10–14-year-olds, over 480,000 of the 1,060,000 boys and nearly 549,000 of the 1,045,000 girls were 'scholars'. Among the 0–4-year-olds about 16 per cent of boys and girls were so-called 'scholars'. Thus for the majority of working-class children any schooling experience was most common around 5–9 years and rapidly tailed off thereafter.

The census terminology and classifications, not surprisingly for the period, were rather fuzzy. Young half-timers in the mills were, it seems, classed as 'occupied', though they were legally required to attend part-time schooling. We cannot tell whether girls in the so-called 'straw-plait schools' were 'occupied' or 'scholars'. And the census does not distinguish the common childhood combination of intermittent school attendance and odd-jobbing such as street trading, shoeblacking and errand-running. It also seems a little strange, given the priorities of Victorian society, that the proportion of 10–14-year-old girls who were at school (which had to be paid for) and not 'employed' was slightly higher than that of boys. We know that girls were kept at home to help in domestic chores and baby-minding as unpaid labour; such girls were presumably not classed as 'employed' but as 'scholars', simply because, perhaps, they attended Sunday School or a ragged school once or twice a week.

Another ground for caution about the statistics is the over-statement of ages by children and parents to get jobs. The General Report of the 1881 census observed:[13] 'we find reason to believe from careful examination of the age tables that a not inconsiderable number of girls who are not yet fifteen return themselves as being of that or a more advanced age, probably with the view of getting more readily taken as servants.' Correspondingly, parents may have been reluctant to admit that they were putting their under-5s to work. The census records no under-5s as 'employed', yet we know from other sources that chldren as young as 3 were in the straw-plaiting schools or assisting (unpaid) in other domestic employment. However, the Victorian censuses, for all their limitations, do provide the most comprehensive picture of the scale of child labour. In 1861 about 140,000 children up to 14 were employed in 'textiles' (cotton, wool, hosiery, lace, etc.). For girls textiles and domestic service were the two largest single employers. Girls aged 10–14 (inclusive) were 40,000; out of the 259,000 female cotton workers, 65,000 out of the 664,000 general servants and 15,300 out of 68,000 'nurses' (i.e. nursemaids etc.). Boys of 10–14 were

4

nearly 81,500 of the 914,000 male farm workers, 31,300 out of 198,000 male cotton workers and nearly 31,000 out of 247,000 (male) coal miners. The census does record over 27,000 boys as errand boys and messengers, but there were untold thousands of urchins who scavenged a living on the streets.

Whilst there was some fall in the proportion of children in the labour force over the next twenty years, it was the period 1881 to 1901 that witnessed a more rapid decline, as compulsory schooling and advancing labour legislation had their effect. The traditional staple employers like agriculture, domestic service and coal mining employed absolutely no – or relatively fewer – under-15s (though the textiles industry was distinguished by the persistence of the 'half-time' system). Thus girl domestics under 15 had fallen from nearly 100,000 in 1881 to about 67,000 in 1901, and boy farm workers from over 68,000 to about 38,000 over the same period. Boy coal miners had increased in numbers but declined from over 6 per cent to 5 per cent of the mining labour force.[14] Structural changes in the staple industries, like the drift from the land and technological changes in industry, affected these patterns as much as any advance in education and child labour law, for child labour was now diversifying, though quantitatively these increases were more modest; more girls were working as tailoresses and in footwear, for example, and more boys were recorded as messengers, porters, shop, van and office boys.[15] The 'blind-alley' moonlighting jobs of schoolchildren, about which so much concern was being expressed at the time, went unrecorded. In 1901 22 per cent of boys and 12 per cent of girls aged 10–14 were officially 'occupied', and by 1911 this had fallen further to 18.3 per cent and 10.4 per cent respectively.[16] However, we cannot quantify the amount of unrecorded labour, particularly among girls engaged in family chores and assisting in domestic sweated trades. Moreover, the average figures conceal wide regional variations. Thus in 1901 whilst non-mill towns like London, Liverpool, Durham and York recorded well below 1 per cent of 10–13-year-old boys as 'occupied', mill towns like Oldham, Blackburn and Halifax could show anything from 10 per cent to nearly 18 per cent of such boys employed as half-timers. Half-time work was also the dominant outlet for 'occupied' girls under 14. In 1911 of all such girls over a half were in textiles, and a third of the remainder in domestic service, though the 1911 census reported 'a large decline in the number employed in domestic service'.[17]

The early Factory Acts of 1833 and 1844, confined to the textile industry, introduced the principle of part-time schooling for child workers. Following the reports of the Royal Commission on Employment of Children in the 1860s, the Factories Extension Act and the Workshop Regulations Act of 1867 extended this principle to non-textile employment.[18] It was not Parliament's intention to discourage the use of child labour, but to see that child employees received some education. However, while these early statutory responsibilities for employers did not affect child employment in textiles, non-textile employers were finding them too bothersome and began to shed child workers. The 1860 Mines Act (like the 1842 Act) banned boys under 10 from underground work, and it introduced educational conditions for recruitment of boys up to 12 which might oblige mine owners to provide part-time schooling till 12 years old. This too led employers to abandon the employment of boys below 12. A Liverpool factory inspector in the late 1860s noted how parents found their children's half-time factory earnings so meagre 'that on their parts they would rather keep them at home and have no bother with the schooling'.[19] They were left to their own devices while their parents worked, and as one observer commented in 1867: 'They are idling in the streets and wynds; tumbling about in the gutters; selling matches; running errands; working in tobacco shops, cared for by no man.'[20] F. Musgrove points out that the educational and other protective legislation from 1870 was intended not so much to rescue children from exploitation, as to corral them in schools owing to the decline of work for them in industry: 'The economy's diminished scope for juvenile labour was already evident in the sixties; not only was demand decreasing but it was shifting from the important central industries like agriculture to employment more marginal to the economy, like domestic service.'

Thus factory and educational laws were not conceived in a spirit of pure altruism but were interwoven with supply of young hands and the demands of industry. For example, the early motive for the half-time schooling laws was not to broaden children's minds but to 'tame' them as child workers and make them more tractable *in their place of work*. And in the First World War the long-term decline in child labour was reversed by temporary need. Education authorities were then granting exemptions to the 12s and over more freely. Those leaving school between 12 and 14 rose from 197,000 in 1915 to just under 241,000 in 1917. In country districts boys were released from schooling to do farm work. Factory half-timers over 12 (till then in decline) rose from nearly 70,000 in 1914–15 to nearly 74,000 in 1916–17.[21] When the war was over and the men returned, the Fisher Education Act of 1918 locked the under-14s firmly back in school again.

2

FACTORIES AND MINES LEGISLATION

The cotton industry was at the forefront of the new factory system in the early 1800s and became the prime focus in the early exposures of the evils of mass-congregated wage slavery. Textile workers were the first targets of legislation to protect child workers; but the intention was to create sufficiently tolerable conditions for them to prolong their productive lives and to make them more tractable as a massed workforce through rudimentary education. The image of a harsh, callous capitalist profiteering from his child slaves is simplistic. Under the old cottage system of production, where the child was under parental supervision, conditions were at least as bad; children received no wages, and young hand-loom weavers might work in cold, damp cellars. There were, it seems, some indications that factory children were in less bad health than child domestic weavers in the 1830s.[1] The Children's Employment Commission of 1842–3 found that much 'child slavery' lay not between the child and the capitalist, but between the child and the adult employee who took him or her on as an assistant and paid the child out of his or her own earnings; it was the latter who was more given to brutality and ill-treatment than the factory owner. It was common in parts of the Midlands in the 1840s for parents to bond their children to an employer for no wages as payment for debts incurred at work. In 1873 Mr Blenkinsopp, a factory sub-inspector in the Black Country iron trade, observed how parents and adult employees could be more exploitative than employers in evading the factory laws; employers might be unaware of the cheating over ages by parents who falsified Bible entries, or produced the birth certificates of older children. Hours of work were exceeded and the child assistants were taught to run and hide when a factory inspector was in the offing.[2] Nor was it necessarily poverty that drove adults to behave in this way; it might be pure greed. Mr Blenkinsopp cited the case of a father earning £120 a year – an exceptional wage for a working man then. Two older sons together brought in another £54 a year.

> Having discovered that a boy of 12 years was working at night, I went to the house where he lived at 11.30 a.m. and found that he had been working always at night for some time. He had been at work the whole of the previous night, though suffering from a severe burn on the arm. The child worked from six o'clock at night to six in the morning; reached home at 7 a.m.; had to be at school at 2 p.m. [for part-time schooling, then required by law] and back to work at 6 p.m., having only seven hours out of the 24 for meals and rest.

The 1833 Factory Act, as strengthened by Lord Ashley's Act of 1844, set a minimum age for employment in a textile factory (at 8 in 1844), and maximum hours (30 a week) with provision for part-time schooling up to 13 years old for 3 hours each working day, or alternatively full-time on 3 alternate days in the week. No child could start work at all in a textile factory without a health certificate signed by a doctor approved by the factory inspector. Subsequent textile Factory Acts to 1853 regulated the hours of 'young persons' (13–18) at $10\frac{1}{2}$ a day. Of course, cheating and evasion vitiated the law at first but in time the principle of part-time schooling and medical vetting of prospective child employees came to be accepted.[3]

J. R. Clynes, a Lancashire mill boy who was to become a minister in the first Labour government, has left a vivid memoir of conditions amid the clash and clatter of machinery.[4] He was born in 1869, and at 10 became a half-time 'little piecer' from 6 a.m. to noon, for 2s 6d a week, and attending school in the afternoon. Small children were valued, as they could run between the machines, just missing the dangerous moving parts:

> Often the threads on the spindles broke as they were stretched and twisted and spun. The broken ends had to be instantly repaired; the piecer ran forward and joined them swiftly with a deft touch which is an art of its own. This was my job. I performed it, unresting, in my bare feet, since

leather on those oil-soaked floors would have been treacher-ous. Often I fell, rolling instinctively and in terror from beneath the gliding jennies, well aware that horrible mutilation or death would result if the advancing monsters overtook and gripped me. Sometimes splinters as keen as daggers drove through my naked feet, leaving aching wounds from which dribbles of blood oozed forth to add to the slipperiness of the floor .... Running in and out, straining my eyes in the gas-lit gloom to watch for broken threads, my ten-year-old legs soon felt like lead and my head spun faster than the pitiless machinery. But I had to keep on; the dinner whistle would shrill some time soon; then I could rest my aches and regain my breath, ready to run two miles home to dinner and set off for school.

Even so, he considered himself better off than his father had been before legislation reduced the hours of labour. At 12 Clynes started full-time as a piecer at 10*s* a week.

A mill boy of nearly a generation later was George Tomlinson, born in Lancashire in 1890.[5] He too was to rise through the trade union movement to a high rank in the Labour Party. His father had started in the cotton mills at 8, and George began at 12 as a half-timer, earning 2*s* 3*d* for a 30-hour week. For young George, as for so many schoolchildren, the prospect of working in the mill was viewed not with dread but anticipation, as a watershed; now they were earning and were half-way to being grown up. They did not appreciate the long-term physical damage. At 13 George became a full-timer, earning 5*s* for a 56½-hour week.

One should not think that schooling was necessarily welcomed by the children as a relief from labour. They attended either factory schools set up by the employer, dame schools, or the British or National church schools.[6] In the 1840s the worst on the whole were the dame schools, according to factory inspectors' reports; factory schools were better; but the church schools were the best. Competent teachers in the factory schools were, however, lacking. The fees were deducted from the children's wages. Employers provided the premises, which at worst might be some odd corner of the factory where the teaching went on against a background of machine clatter. It was not uncommon for maimed ex-manual workers, themselves barely literate, to be employed as teachers; in effect, lowlier versions of Wackford Squeers, readily resorting to the cane to compensate for a lack of natural authority.

Contemporary comment on the value of this schooling was mixed. Some were more impressed by the fatigue of the pupils; others claimed that their attendance was more regular than full-time 'voluntary' scholars, as it was a legal condition of employment, and that they learned as much as full-timers, since the latter could not digest a full day's mental work. As we shall see, the fatigue issue was to become more insistent later on; it may be that the more favourable comments were coloured by optimism and idealism at this early stage.

The Children's Employment Commission of 1842–3 exposed the horrors of child labour in the mines:[7] children as young as 5 being sent below ground; multiple shifts creating spells of up to 36 hours at a time underground; boys' and girls' cattle-like use as wagon-pullers in narrow shafts; beatings and whippings by older workmen as regular and habitual; injuries from roof falls or wagons rolling over them; and industrial disease of the lungs and skin. Periodic mining disasters had claimed many tragically young lives among the victims. In 1841 the 46 collieries shipping coal from the Tyne employed 7,261 adults and about 2,000 aged 13–18, and *admitted* only to employing nearly 1,500 children below 13. Employers argued that the cheap and plentiful supply of child labour kept costs down and children were useful to work the narrow seams. The 1842 Mines Act banned all females and boys under 10 from underground work, but it was widely evaded, and even in 1860 boys of 6 were worked underground where seams were awkward or thin. The 1860 Mines Act,[8] as well as repeating the ban on under-10s below ground, also made their employment between 10 and 12 conditional upon a certificate of literacy from a schoolmaster, or alternatively required employers to provide part-time schooling for 10–12-year-olds for at least 3 hours a day twice weekly. This applied to underground employees only. Thus while by 1860 major areas of child labour had been publicized in official reports, it was only in textile factories and mines that the principle of minimum wages, maximum hours and educational conditions had been applied.

In 1861 Lord Shaftesbury pressed in Parliament for a new comprehensive study of child employment, as many developments had taken place in industry since the early 1840s, and advances had even worsened some conditions for children.[9] A Royal Commission on Employment of Children was set up and produced six comprehensive Reports between 1863 and 1867, including

11

domestic sweatshops, brickfields, agriculture and chimney-sweeping, which lie outside this chapter.[10] One major area left unconsidered was domestic service; it has been suggested that this was too embarrassingly close to the needs of upper-class legislators, and that this labour was regarded as a useful training for home-making for a woman when she married.[11]

The Reports were a catalogue of long hours, low wages, appalling working conditions, industrial diseases and accidents from dust, heat, fumes, fatigue and poor lighting; and also of widespread ignorance and illiteracy. For example, in the metal trade forges of Staffordshire and Worcestershire children worked night shifts and the same hours as adults – anything from 6 a.m. to 11 p.m.; little girls were working 14 hours a day.[12] Schooling opportunities were very limited; a sample survey of Staffordshire schools showed that only 25 per cent were 10 or over. The investigators were shocked by working children's total ignorance of religion – religious knowledge was then regarded as the criterion of a civilized education. Children's replies to Scripture questions included: 'The devil is a good person; I don't know where he lives', and 'Christ was a wicked man.' One inspector found that of 80 7–16-year-olds at one metalworks 72.5 per cent could not read at all, 13.75 per cent were almost illiterate, and 12.5 per cent could read a little. At a firebricks works a 19-year-old girl moulder responded to questions: 'Have not heard of Scotland. Don't know which way it is from here . . . . Don't know what a whale is.' And from a 12-year-old at the same works: 'Have not heard of France or London. The Queen's name is Mary.'[13]

Accidents were common in the metal trade, where youngsters of 8 worked with pieces of red-hot iron flying about. A nail-maker, William Tetler, told the commission:[14]

> Four years ago my boy, then betwixt 10 and 11, and not having begun long, got two pieces of iron in at the top of his trousers, and before they could be got out they dropped and catched his leg, burning two wounds, each as big as the face of my hammer . . . and the scars are there now and always will be. [This kept him off work for 9 weeks.] He got a dreadful wound on his hand now, from a burn done three weeks ago. If it had been his hammer hand he could not have worked at all.

The grinding trades in the Sheffield cutlery industry were lethal.

Boys started at 9–12 years old, and grinders rarely lived into their forties. The boys worked in very high temperatures and were expected to do overtime. A boy of 9 years old, George Allinsworth, told the commission:[15]

> Came here as a cellar boy last Friday. Next morning we had to begin at 3, so I stopped here all night. Live five miles off. Slept on the floor of the furnace overhead, with an apron under me and a bit of a jacket over me. The two other days I have been here at 6 a.m. Aye! it *is* hot here.

The commission reported the sight of a 14-year-old boy wielding a 22-pound hammer.

In the pottery trade youngsters could work in temperatures of 120–148°F. They served as 'mould-runners', carrying the article fresh out of the mould to the stove room, where the atmosphere was charged with particles of fine clay. This contaminated and overheated atmosphere brought about chest ailments, stunted growth and premature death.[16] In the wallpaper-staining trade children worked from 6 a.m. to 9 or 10 p.m. and were in danger from arsenic poisoning from the green dyes used in colouring. Also, the French chalk or china clay, used to help smooth the brushing of colours over the paper, hung in the air causing respiratory problems. In the match trade youngsters were afflicted with 'phossy jaw' caused by inhaling white phosphorus fumes, though Bryant & May was switching to safer red phosphorus. Hours were long; a 12-year-old girl worked from 7 a.m. sometimes to 9 p.m. for 4s a week. Many witnesses had bad teeth; they felt sick and dizzy at the end of the day, and advanced cases of 'phossy jaw' had to be treated with excision of part of the jawbone in hospital.

Two positive points were, however, brought out in the Reports. The original hostility among textile workers to part-time work had now abated as they saw the benefits to children's health, efficiency and improved output in the time they were working.[17] And compared with the 1840s it was now rare to see children below 6 employed in trades;[18] the lace and straw-plait schools with little girls of 3 or 4 were exceptional. The commission also *claimed* that there was less cruelty and harshness than 20 years before.

The Reports led to the 1867 Factories Extension Act[19] (the Workshops Act passed soon after will be examined in Chapter 3).

Broadly this applied the principles of the textile Factories Acts in regard to minimum ages, health certification, maximum hours and part-time schooling to other types of factory, such as blast furnaces, metalworks, rubber, glass, paper, tobacco, etc. It was hoped to improve the lot of non-textile work-children, but not to remove them from the world of factory labour; however, unlike the textile industry, where part-timers had been increasing in the 1860s, other industries were finding the new obligations uneconomic and began dispensing with child labour, which, as we saw in Chapter 1, was to become progressively marginalized in sweatshop and servicing activities and petty trading, and further constricted by the extension of public schooling from 1870. In the metal trades, for example, the proportion of under-15s employed fell sharply from 7.9 per cent to 3.1 per cent between 1861 and 1881.[20]

The legal protections in the textile trades were being undermined by the early 1870s through new technology and faster rates of production, coupled with incentive schemes which prompted foremen to slave-drive their subordinates.[21] This led to a new (textile) Factory Act of 1874, which raised the minimum age of employment from 8 to 10, and made the part-time ages now run from 10 to the fourteenth birthday. However, a new departure was the opportunity to start full-time at 13 upon production of a certificate of minimum educational attainment. This was the beginning of the 'exemption' system. By this time the 1870 Education Act had empowered local boards of education to make education compulsory in their districts up to 13, and thenceforth there was to be an interrelationship between employment and education law.

The 1874 Act led to demands for its extension to other types of factories and a Royal Commission on Factories and Workshops Acts was appointed in 1876 to consider this. It reported favourably on the effects of earlier legislation:

> The improvement in the sanitary arrangements and ventilation of factories has been most marked in recent years, and the cases in which young children are employed in labour unfitted for their years, or in which young persons and women suffer physically from overwork, are now, we believe, as uncommon as formerly they were common.

Such a statement was relative to its time, and too sanguine. A sample survey of 12-year-olds in 1873 showed an average weight among factory children of 70.57 pounds compared with nearly 79 pounds for middle-class children.[22] Of course we cannot be too certain about Victorian sampling techniques, but the contrast in health and physique between the social classes were to be confirmed by later anthropometric studies. By themselves such figures would not prove unequivocably the ill-effects of early labour; it was agreed justifiably that the working class's poor physique was due at least as much to slum living conditions, and defenders of child labour argued that 'beneficial employment' actually sustained children's health by keeping them away from their disease-ridden habitations and increasing family earnings; this, of course, ignored the multiplicity of occupational diseases children were prey to.

The Royal Commission recommended extension of the 1874 Act and assimilation of workshop and factory law. The 1878 Factories and Workshops Act was a comprehensive and consolidating measure.[23] To some extent the 1876 Education Act had helped towards assimilation by forbidding child employment below 10 and making the employment of 10–13-year-olds conditional upon a certificate of attainment in the three Rs, unless they were to work part-time and continue part-time schooling to 13. Textile factories retained shorter hours under the Act, and though workshop hours were technically assimilated to those of non-textile factories, their physical standards and inspection arrangements were less stringent.

Child labour had by 1890 become a general European concern and an International Labour Conference at Berlin that year recommended a universal minimum working age of 12 (for northern Europe) and even then only if minimum academic standards had been reached; other proposals included a ban on night work under 14, a maximum 6-hour working day for youngsters and stricter safeguards for health and safety.[24] However, the Conservative government did not implement these proposals owing to opposition from its industrialist supporters. In 1891 the minimum working age was raised to 11, and it was not until 1901 that the Berlin recommendations were roughly attained when employment below 12 was prohibited, and this might be extended to 14 in the absence of exemption or labour certificates for full or part-time withdrawal from school. This was supplemented by the Employment of Children Act 1903[25] which empowered local authorities to raise the minimum age for any occupation in their area above 12 and prescribe maximum hours for any child (i.e. up

15

to 14). The Act also barred children outright from any occupation likely to be injurious to health, such as those involving the lifting or carrying of heavy objects. The legislation brings us into the Edwardian era and its energetic concerns for the stamina of the 'race' against the economic challenge to Britain's former industrial primacy, especially from Germany and the USA. The country's future strength was seen increasingly to be in the welfare of children at school and their protection in the workplace. However, the 1903 Act was not energetically enforced. Few local authorities had framed by-laws by 1907 and there was a general reluctance to grapple with the conditions in domestic workshops.[26] Local councillors, drawn mostly from the governing and employing classes, were accused of indifference.[27]

Even the mandatory provisions regarding hazardous occupations seem to have been widely ignored. Industrial accidents were far more common among children than adults; a factory part-timer in 1909 was still twice as likely to be injured at work as a full-time adult colleague.[28] Historically factory children had experienced scalping from machinery, crushed bones, injury and even death from overseers' blows.[29] Many accidents happened on their first day when over-eager in their new job and inadequately supervised. The death of a 13-year-old piecer, Lewis Timmins, on his first day at a mill in Atherton in 1909 prompted Sir Charles Dilke to raise the matter in Parliament.[30] He complained that employers and older workmen alike did not take their responsibilities to young novices seriously and that the 1903 Act was not being enforced properly by the factory inspectors. Timmins had crawled under a mule with a brush and wiper, believing it to be at rest, but it had just paused before the carriage returned, killing the boy.

Parallel with the trends in factory law, mines legislation was tending towards the further restrictions on labour below ground of boys under 12, and limiting the hours of 12–16-year-olds. In 1872 enactments prescribed longer hours of part-time schooling for the under-12s in coal mines and totally banned underground working in metalliferous mines by the under-12s; a similar ban did not apply to coal mines until 1887.[31] However, youngsters of 13 or over could be worked 54 hours a week. Even in the early 1900s boys in some pits continued to work over 10 hours a day though elsewhere the unions had secured reductions to 6 or 7.[32] In the mines, as in the factories, protective legislation was accompanied by a progressive abandonment of child labour; in 1861 11.9 per cent of the male workforce was under 15, but only 5 per cent in 1901.

Key statutory figures in protective legislation, apart from the factory inspectors, were the certifying factory surgeons. They originated under the 1833 Factory Act to certify the probable age of children whose parents wished them to start work in the textile mills, before the era of civil birth registration. The 1844 Factory Act extended this duty to certifying the physical fitness of children for such work, as a compulsory pre-condition of employment. This was extended to all types of factory in 1867, but workshops had not yet entered the ambit of regulation, and it was claimed that the effect of certification was to drive unfit children into the workshops, where conditions were generally worse.[33] The Factories and Workshops Acts of 1878 and 1901 made it optional only for workshop proprietors to require a factory surgeon's certificate of fitness.[34] The result was that certification for workshops remained a dead letter. In 1901, whilst 376,278 children and young persons were screened for factory jobs, only 413 were examined for workshops.[35] Where factory part-timers were concerned, it seems that some employers were more casual about the legal requirement of health certification, and just accepted the teachers' certificates of eligibility.[36]

How 'effective' were the certifying factory surgeons? We must remember that any disqualification of a child from factory employment doubtless doomed the boy or girl to some casual or workshop labour, and it may be that the good work of the doctors was illusory. Surgeons were under great pressure from employers and parents, especially in their earlier history, and they were prey to various dodges by parents to mislead about the child's age; even when birth registration had become general by the 1870s, parents might produce the birth certificate of an older child and falsify the applicant's identity. None the less, when there were calls by employers in 1891 to abolish certifying surgeons as 'superfluous' now that birth certification was universal, their supporters successfully upheld their continuing worth. Each surgeon might examine up to 200 children a week and, claimed the NSPCC in 1891, they uncovered many potentially dangerous defects:

Six cases of syphilitic sores of the mouth have been detected in glass-blowers. Men and boys alternately use the same blowpipe . . . . A girl who had previously lost one eye has been

17

prevented working among dust . . . . A girl in the early stages of consumption has been prevented working in a dusty flax mill. Two epileptics have been prevented working among machinery, in spite of the urgent solicitations of the parents and a foreman.[37]

We can see how dangers and tragedies were averted in individual cases in individual factories; but we do not know the fate of, for example, the aforementioned one-eyed girl and the epileptics. The overall consequence of factory surgeons' service needs a fuller study.

3

SWEATSHOPS, COTTAGE LABOUR AND MOONLIGHTING UP TO THE FIRST WORLD WAR

Whilst it was the 'dark satanic mills' and their impersonal regime of massed labour under a capitalistic boss that received most of the early publicity for child exploitation, in fact, as was said in the last chapter, much of the worst exploitation was inflicted in small workshops often at the hands of the children's own parents. Small workshops were more hidden; their abuses long pre-dated the industrial revolution[1] and it is most unlikely that children's overall lot was worsened by steam technology. One must remember that the homeless city waifs were usually orphans and runaways from the workhouse or grinding 'apprenticeships', so-called, to *small* tradesmen like chimney sweeps and undertakers as exemplified in *Oliver Twist*. And it was the spotlight cast on factory and mines employment by the 1842–3 Children's Employment Commission and the 1863–1 Royal Commission on Employment of Children that also illuminated the conditions in rural domestic industries, such as lace-, glove- and button-making. In the 1860s little girls of 4 to 6 years old were already ruining their eyesight in straw-plaiting and lace-making. In the hosiery trade toddlers under 5 were kept working till past midnight, and mothers were said to pin the children to their knee to keep them working, and slap them to keep them awake.[2] Other small-scale rural crafts employing children included brush- and besom-making, knitting, chair- and hurdle-making and (in fishing areas) net-braiding.[3] In the cities, the situation was similar. In the 1860s the Scottish philanthropist Annie Macpherson exposed the plight of child matchbox-makers in London's East End receiving 3s 4d for a gross of boxes.[4]

At this time, too, in the same district 7-year-olds in cheap tailoring shops were working 12 hours a day for 6d a day, and in

Bethnal Green's White Street there was a twice-weekly 'slave market' where children would present themselves to be hired.[5] Children employed by parents were generally the worse off for pay. They 'earned' either whatever parents were ready to pay them, or nothing at all as 'helpers'.

Those working in the garment and millinery sweatshops were virtually all girls. The workrooms were overcrowded, overheated and stuffy from the gas fires for heating the irons; condensation ran down the walls, and TB and other respiratory disorders were common. Girls often lived on the premises as 'apprentices', sleeping in crowded, damp rooms, up to three in a bed. During the London 'high society' season youngsters could be up till midnight from 6.30 a.m. completing rush orders.[6] But again it was children employed at home who could be worst off. The crowded slum rooms they ate and slept in were crammed with the raw materials of their trade, and they had to suffer 24 hours a day, for example, the noxious glues, the steam of washerwomen's tubs and the damp of clothes hanging to dry, and nasal and adenoidal reactions to feather-sorting and fur-pulling.[7]

The Workshops Act of 1867[8] forbade the employment of children under 8 in workshops (defined as premises employing fewer than 50 people), and restricted the employment of 8–13-year-olds to $6\frac{1}{2}$ hours a day, with a statutory part-time schooling of 10 hours a week. However, permitted shift arrangements were more flexible than for factories; children did not have to be certified as fit by a doctor; and provisions regarding ventilation, fencing of machinery and prohibition from dangerous trades were less stringent. Inspection arrangements were also looser; these were left to local authority sanitary inspectors, and were not transferred to the factory inspectorate till 1871. The discovery, let alone the inspection, of backstreet workshops, was a hopeless task and the act was largely a dead letter.[9]

As we saw in Chapter 2, the 1878 Factories and Workshops Act was intended to assimilate factory and workshop law in regard to minimum ages, academic attainments and part-time schooling, but improved conditions and restricted hours in factories were in practice not matched in workshops. The declining demand for child factory labour was pushing children, when not at school, into marginal and sweatshop trades, where the forces of supply and demand continued to operate adversely on children, notwithstanding safeguards on paper. Even under the law, in regard to ventilation, cleanliness, holidays and mealtimes, workshop children were still worse off, and inspectors' powers were crippled by the requirement of a magistrate's warrant before they could enter home workshops suspected of breaking the law; this concession to an Englishman's right to privacy now made it impossible to catch offenders red-handed, and ensured that workshop law was not worth the paper it was printed on.

Workshop conditions again started coming to the fore in the late 1880s. Awareness of the ineffectiveness of the 1878 Act, coupled with the current influx of Jews from Russia, who were then identified with clothing sweatshops, and whose competition would, it was feared, drive down wage rates, led to the appointment of a House of Lords Select Committee on the Sweated Trades in 1888.[10] The general conditions were substantially the same as twenty years before; for example, in one boot and shoe workshop, a husband, wife and six children slept in the same room where ten men were employed, a not uncommon arrangement in the capital's increasingly crowded tenements. Wages were too low for children to sustain themselves, and the half-time provisions for the under-13s were widely evaded in the Midlands metal workshops. The one improvement since the 1860s was that the starting age in the metal trade was now around 11 or 12 instead of 7 or 8. But in the surviving scattered and uninspectable rural crafts like straw-plaiting, conditions in the 1890s had not changed much since the 1860s.[11]

Nationwide schooling provision from 1870 had made inroads on full-time labour, but parents were illegally keeping their children from school; the 1891 Factory Act raised the minimum age of employment in factories and workshops to 11, but without inspectors' rights to instant entry into domestic workshops, it was of little value on its own. Visits from the school boards' 'truancy men' and an application of the 1889 Children's Act provisions against the wilful ill-treatment or neglect of children by persons having custody of them were important supplements. But the squeeze on full-time labour was to draw closer attention to the problem of 'moonlighting' – child employment out of school hours – in the 1890s. Prior to the late 1890s the government had paid little heed to this problem, except for entertainers and street traders,[12] but in 1897 an article by Mrs Edith Hogg in the *Nineteenth Century*[13] on 'Schoolchildren as wage earners', followed by *Daily Mail* exposés, brought the issue out into the open. A philanthropic lobby, the Joint Committee on Wage Earning Children, was then formed. Traditionally the Education Department had no interest in children beyond the purely pedagogic; it was solely concerned with the three Rs until a Joint Committee deputation convinced the department of the economic wastefulness of teaching exhausted children.[14]

There was to be a spate of books dealing with 'moonlighting', such as Frank Hird's *The Cry of the Children* (2nd edn, 1898), Robert Sherard's *The Child Slaves of Britain* (1905) and works by Mrs Archibald Mackirdy and Clementina Black in 1907. The issue was also part of a wider concern about adult 'sweating'; in 1906 the *Daily News* ran a 'Sweated Industries' Exhibition, visited by 30,000 people;[15] and in 1907 a Select Committee on Home Work was appointed. The economic argument then put forward against cheap sweated labour was that it reduced the incentive for technological innovation. Modern machinery coupled with high wage rates (for adults), so dispensing with the need for children's earnings, was the best way to benefit the greatest number. None the less, official circles were at first slow to respond. It was back-bench parliamentary initiative which prompted a survey in 1899 of the numbers of moonlighting schoolchildren. Its incomplete returns from questionnaires sent to schools yielded an understated figure of 145,000 'moonlighters' out of 5 million schoolchildren.[16] The 1889 Prevention of Cruelty to Children Act addressed itself to the *moral* dangers inherent in the employment of children as street and pub entertainers, and as street sellers and beggars, but neither this nor the 1894 Cruelty Act dealt with indoor moonlighting beyond general provisions against wilful mistreatment or neglect of children. The 1876 and 1880 Education Acts were only indirectly concerned with child labour in so far as it led to absenteeism and truancy. It is true that Scottish Education Acts of 1878 and 1901 expressly prohibited schoolchild employment after dusk, but they were dead letters.[17] This was the extent of legislation when outside lobbying finally pushed the Home Office and the Education Department into a comprehensive interdepartmental inquiry into the Employment of Schoolchildren, in 1901.[18]

Edith Hogg's article had described striking cases of out-of-school odd-jobbing. For example, one boy worked for a greengrocer from 8 to 9.30 a.m.; then he went to school and worked in his lunchtime from noon to 1 p.m., and again after school from 5 to

7 p.m., and did a further 12 hours on Saturdays, all for 3s a week. A 9-year-old worked in a newspaper shop from 6 p.m. to 8 p.m. for a halfpenny a day. Barbers' boys worked notoriously long hours; one schoolboy worked from 5 p.m. to 10 p.m. daily, plus all day Saturday (up to 15 hours) and part of Sunday, for 2s 6d and food. The work was not arduous but a lot of time was spent waiting for customers, and, as Hogg pointed out, the atmosphere was morally insalubrious as the premises frequently served as backstreet betting shops, and the sporting papers were left lying about for the boys to peruse. In the low-class 'penny shaving shops' customers were ready to put up with the ministrations of inexperienced boys, and Joseph Stamper recalled how in the 1890s he saw a lather boy spitting on the shaving brush to bring up a good head of lather before applying it to the customer's face! The long hours did tell on the boys' health. A London County Council (LCC) medical survey of barbers' boys at the turn of the century revealed that 72 per cent of the sample were anaemic, 63 per cent showed nerve strain and 27 per cent 'severe heart affection'. Robert Sherard in 1905 referred to two recent cases of lather boys who died through overwork.[19]

Boys mostly did delivery jobs (newspapers, milk and groceries) and shop-work, for which they might pick up a penny an hour. Less commonly there was street peddling, minding vans and carts and work at private houses like polishing shoes and cutlery. Other jobs included delivering hot dinners to older neighbours and relations in their lunch break (at the cost of the youngsters' own school dinner break), and in the north of England pre-dawn 'knocking up' (tapping on window panes).[20] There was some exceptionally early rising by youngsters; one 9-year-old boy in 1905 carried milk from 5 a.m. to 7 a.m., and then from 4 p.m. to 6 p.m. for 9d per week; such work entailed carrying heavy cans up flights of stairs in tenements.[21] At the same date one 12-year-old girl cleaned ashes from a baking oven before 6 a.m.[22]

In the countryside there were numerous odd jobs, sometimes just seasonal, like beating out grouse, bird-scaring, pea-picking and weeding, as well as domestic work at the local farmhouse or mansion – polishing, window-cleaning, sweeping out kennels and so on; rural delivery boys had long distances to travel and might have to get up as early as 2 a.m. Around 1900, country moonlighters might earn from a farthing to a penny an hour, and their earnings were a welcome supplement to the wages of farm labourers, who then combined the lowest wage levels with the largest-size families. Schooling took second place and during harvesting children absented themselves from school full-time.[23]

The 1899 survey indicated that anything up to 30 hours a week of moonlighting was the rule, occasionally rising to 50 hours a week. Sherard mentions boys at Lowestoft who worked 50 hours a week carrying coal from the colliers. Such children would just flake out at school and doze the lessons away; understanding teachers knew when to turn a blind eye.

Girls were far less employed in shops than boys. They mainly worked at home, helping in domestic chores, looking after baby brothers and sisters, scrubbing doorsteps and running errands for neighbours for odd pennies.[24] Sherard gave some touching pen-portraits of such young skivvies, like 'Maria D—', a 'doorstep girl' who started this work when 6 years old. Her father, a Poplar stevedore, was often unemployed:

> With her broom much taller than herself as she stands up in the huge sack-cloth apron which she made with her own little fingers 'whilst 'opping last summer', or when she kneels amidst the ashes by a side of a heavy pail of water, she is the type of a very large class of little English girls . . . . Let it be known in Poplar, or Stepney, or Bow, that you require the services of a 'doorstep girl' and . . . a horde of tiny ragged matrons will descend upon you, many far too small to reach the bell-pull of your door, yet eager to scrub doorsteps, blacklead ranges and beat mats much bigger than themselves.

When done at home, this work was regarded as natural to a girl and did not figure in the 'moonlighting' statistics. The 1899 return showed 110,000 boy 'moonlighters' as against 35,000 girls. Such work for parents was commonly unpaid, but they might get 2d to 6d a week if they were lucky, so their earnings were substantially below their brothers'. Sometimes little girls were prepared to do jobs for neighbours for a crust of bread; their disparaging nickname, 'hard-crust nannies', carries a wealth of pathos.[25] This view of children's family duties had been open to sentimentalization in the mid-Victorian period. The children's temperance journal the *Band of Hope Review* in 1859[26] carried a sanctimonious article entitled 'Little helpers' allegedly inspired by the sight of a little girl in the Holloway Road at 8 o'clock one morning taking breakfast to her labourer father. The contributor oozed:

Many of the little readers of the *Band of Hope Review* are the children of hard-working men, who leave their homes by five or six o'clock in the dark winter's mornings for their work. I want all of them to be 'LITTLE HELPERS' not only by cheerfully and carefully carrying father's meals but in every other possible way . . . and to be good children, help mother and be industrious at school.

Hogg gave some instances of the harsh realities:

M.B. aged 10 minds a baby for six and a half hours daily and for thirteen hours on Saturday for 6*d* and food. L.N., aged 9, for two hours daily, and eleven hours on Saturday for 2*d* without food . . . . C.D. turns a mangle for three and a half hours daily and for ten hours on Saturday for 2*d* and her food.

So indispensable were girls at home that parents were more reluctant to release them than their brothers for holidays organized by the Children's Country Holiday Fund.[27]

Children in the poorest households had to help at all hours in domestic trades like matchbox-making, button-carding and laundrywork. Their parents worked for a pittance, and the children's contribution was vital to family survival. Around 1907 adult paper-bag makers received 3*d* to 5*d* a thousand, blouse-makers 1*s* 6*d* a dozen, and button-carders 3*s* for a hundred gross of buttons (a week's worth).[28] Mrs Archibald Mackirdy described the plight of little ones in such families. For example, 'Mrs Jennings', whose husband was an idle pub-hunter, made waistcoats at 7*s* 6*d* to 9*s* 3*d* a dozen (less the cost of materials) and her children helped sew on the buttons. They were kept away from school and she received visits from the attendance officer. Then there was the family of box-makers which earned at most 10*s* a week for working 6 days a week making boxes, out of which 4*s* 6*d* was paid in rent. The children worked all hours, 'children who live in foul odours, labouring with tired hands to make pretty boxes to hold sweets and presents for good and happy children'. And she described the tragic 11-year-old crippled boy, John Bench. He was a hunchback with wasted legs. He sat on a stool by a window all day, painting wooden toys and dolls that his mother tried to sell. His father was a brutal drunkard who beat the helpless lad if he did not work fast enough.

There was a wide range of sweatshop products – sacks, tassels, matchboxes, bead trimmings, fur trimmings, furniture, belts, paper flowers, babies' shoes, and toothbrushes, for example.[29] Many carried occupational hazards – varnishes, fur, fluff and steam brought on respiratory conditions;[30] in box-making there was the all-pervasive smell of paste; little children's fingers became raw with the continual stitching of sacks; while the cramped posture and stuffy polluted atmosphere, coupled with the meagre diet, late nights and exhaustion, stunted their growth and increased their susceptibility to TB. They lived amid the mess of their trade. Their beds were often the heaps of sacking or cloth waiting to be made into the finished product. How many of their more fortunate fellow citizens gave any thought to the child slavery that went into the gift box that carried a luxury bonnet, the paintwork on a toy given lovingly to their own children, the trimming on a dress displayed in a fashionable boutique, or the Christmas cracker merrily pulled at the season of goodwill? How many thought of the sweat that was wrung out of little children laboriously turning the mangle for their washerwomen mothers, to produce the finely starched and ironed linen for their customers' social events? They had only to see the skinny children staggering under piles of materials carried between home and the contractors' premises – a common enough street sight – to set them thinking. Take one case described by Frank Hird in 1898 of a rat-poor family of matchbox-makers earning together 1s $\frac{3}{4}d$ for a 16-hour day. When the order was completed,

> the boxes have to be tied up and carried to the shop, which in this instance is two miles away from the small street where these unhappy people live. The younger of the children, the girl, takes the large bundle in all sorts of weather, badly fed and thinly clad [and] frequently has to wait for two or three hours before fresh work is given to her. As this is required by a certain time she must hurry home, where her mother is waiting and they must sit down to earn another pittance, the brother in the meantime either having gone to school or obtained a small job in the neighbourhood. Sometimes the brother carries the boxes to the shop, and it is then the girl's turn to go to school. But there is always the certainty of hours of toil when they return to their miserable home.

Some salved their consciences with the rationalization that 'moonlighting' at least kept children out of the house and away from their parents' squabbles; and that the 'skills' they picked up in domestic work would stand them in good stead later. Edith Hogg refuted this latter notion. Moonlighting work was dead-end and devoid of real training: 'let anyone try a housemaid "trained" in this fashion, or a nursemaid who has been in the habit of "minding baby" and she will not feel that those young persons would have been the worse servants in mind or body for a little more schooling and a little less training.' The earnings made at this early age, she believed, gave children a taste for quick money and disinclined them to train for skilled trades later.

Children in shops were not covered by the factory and workshop laws; and the workshop laws were unavailing to protect little infants – children below 6 were still working in tasks like button-carding at the turn of the century. However, the NSPCC was sometimes able to rescue children slave-driven by fathers earning good wages or brutalized by drink.[31]

The Inter-Departmental Committee of 1901[32] conducted a much more thoroughgoing study than the one of 1899; it concluded that at least 300,000 children divided their time between school and work, of whom 200,000 were hidden economy 'moonlighters' and the remainder statutory factory half-timers. In London an estimated 8 per cent of schoolchildren were moonlighting (this reached 20 per cent in poorer districts) and in Liverpool 12 per cent of schoolboys.

The committee saw no harm in a moderate amount of work as teaching children the virtues of work and the value of money, but condemned excessive amounts that impaired schooling and health. The long hours by no means meant that the youngsters were at continuous labour, as already observed in relation to barbers' boys. But the Report acknowledged that there was some slave-driving, and that the lifting of heavy weights could be injurious. Robert Sherard was to witness instances such as the 'slight girl of thirteen who is found in a tin-plate works carrying 31 [pounds] on her frail arms, and . . . a grocer's boy who "was dragged quite on one side"' as well as youngsters staggering under the heavy shutters they were taking down from shopfronts.

The committee recommended legislation to cover hitherto unprotected areas of child employment, and this led to the 1903 Employment of Children Act,[33] promoted by T. J. Macnamara MP, a former schoolteacher and a keen campaigner for child welfare. It outlawed the employment of children (under 14) in any job involving the lifting of heavy weights or in anything potentially dangerous to the child's health. And it barred children's employment between 9 p.m. and 6 a.m., though local authorities could widen or narrow these prohibited hours under by-laws. For 14- to 16-year-olds local authorities were free to frame their own by-laws regarding permitted hours and conditions of work. This Act, be it remembered, was supplemented by the Prevention of Cruelty to Children Acts regarding the employment of child entertainers, acrobats and pedlars. The street-trading provisions will be examined in Chapter 8.

The 1903 Act was, as we have seen, weakly implemented. There was no political advantage for local councils to frame or enforce by-laws that would restrict the earnings of voters' children, the rural squirearchy regarded their call on the services of farm labourers' children as a patrimonial right, and it was virtually impossible to check on child labour at home.

The Select Committee on Home Work in 1907 was informed that only a limited number of local authorities had framed by-laws under the Act; both Birmingham and Nottingham, where much child labour at home was used, were not even on that list.[34] In 1915 Grace M. Paton reckoned that of the 6,863,000 children in the elementary schools over 304,000 were still moonlighting outside full-time schooling hours, and a further 200,000 were statutory half-timers. The sweating of children as young as 3 at home in the Nottingham lace trade and in carding hooks and eyes and buttons in Birmingham continued to the First World War at least. In 1914 of 329 local authorities 98 still had no by-laws regarding general employment and 198 no restrictions on street trading.[35] In 1914 a 12-year-old boy was charged with attempted suicide (then a criminal offence); the poor lad ran errands from 7.30 to 9 a.m. before school, and worked in a barber's shop from 6 p.m. to 9 p.m. on weekdays and 8.30 a.m. to 9 p.m. on Saturdays.[36]

There was fragmented but growing evidence of the damage by moonlighting to children's health and school performance in this period, though it cannot be entirely separated from the general environment in which the children lived. We have already noted the LCC observations on the health of barbers' boys. The LCC examined 384 wage-earning boys in 14 schools: 233 showed signs of fatigue; 64 had deformities from carrying heavy loads; and 51 showed signs of heart disorder. The same study also showed that wage-earning schoolboys were generally behind in their school Standards for their ages – many were educationally retarded by as much as two to four years.[37] In 1905 of the 27 working boys at the Michael Faraday School in Walworth:

> All except six were in poor health. One had broken down altogether; one had weak circulation; one had fainted in school during the previous week; yet another had defective circulation. In one single week nine boys who worked out of school hours were taken ill in school [and] obliged to suspend lessons for the rest of the afternoon.[38]

Street sellers were prone to pneumonia,[39] and child feather-sorters were kept away from school with adenoids, nasal discharges, tonsillitis and eye troubles, as the feathers were not cleaned before sorting.[40] One northern lad was forbidden by his mother to sell newspapers as she believed it had contributed to his older brother's death. 'She said if it hadn't been for newspapers our Jack would have been here to-day. She said, "You're not going to run your guts round the streets selling newspapers; running your feet off, you're not doing it."'[41]

Bills were introduced in 1912 and 1913 to extend the outright ban on physically injurious occupations to 14- and 15-year-olds but got nowhere; the newspaper interests were opposed to any curbs and invoked a specious 'civil liberties' argument.[42]

It is difficult to form an impression of the trends in moonlighting between 1903 and 1914 as the census returns for working schoolchildren included statutory part-timers. The anti-sweating movement of the period had succeeded through the Trade Boards Act of 1909 in establishing wage-negotiating machinery for adult sweatshop workers. The anti-sweating argument held that only by raising the incomes of the low-paid to a 'national minimum' would families' economic pressure on their children to moonlight ease up. And Frederic Keeling in 1914 criticized the local poor law authorities, when assessing levels of outdoor relief, for taking children's earning potential into account. Such official practices served only to entrench the problem of moonlighting. Far from relieving family poverty, it was argued, child employment worsened it by driving down adult wage levels.

There was a great increase in child employment generally during the First World War; these were the boom years for children when fathers were away fighting and many schools were closed part-time.

But the 1918 Education Act, with its vision of a brighter tomorrow for the nation's youth, banned the employment of children under 12 out of school hours completely (except where local by-laws permitted such employment by parents); for 12- to 14-year-olds the hours were restricted further and by-laws were now to be framed by the local education departments. These provisions appear to have been applied with more will by local authorities, many of whom by 1923 had banned under-15s altogether from barbers' shops, slaughterhouses, billiard saloons and other undesirable places.[43]

4

CHILDREN ON THE LAND AND CHILDREN AT SEA

The herding of children in agricultural gangs first became the subject of inquiry in 1843 by the Poor Law Commission. No legislative action was taken; in a Parliament still dominated by agricultural interests this was not surprising, and the relative healthiness of farm life made rural children less a subject of concern than their industrial counterparts. However, the moral as well as the physical evils of 'ganging' brought the problem within the purview of the Royal Commission on Employment of Children in 1867.[1] Its inquiry was confined to public gangs, that is, gangs of labourers hired out by a ganging master to different farmers (as distinct from 'private' gangs, hired directly by individual farmers). Public gangers were under greater stress because of the long distances they had to travel to different farms in the season. Ganging was traditional in East Anglia and the Fens.[2] Boys and girls as young as 6 mixed with adults of both sexes, working from 8 a.m. to 6 p.m. in the summer, excluding the time it took to travel to and from their villages. A Huntingdonshire farm labourer's wife told how she got her 6-year-old daughter into a gang: 'She walked all the way (8 miles) to her work and worked from 8 to 5.30 and received 4*d*. She was that tired that her sisters had to carry her the best part of the way home ... and she was ill from it for three weeks, and never went again.' Her older daughters had started in gangs at 11 and 13, leaving home at 5 a.m. and not returning till 9 p.m. Occasionally gangers might travel in a cart, but usually they walked, and it was not unusual to see older brothers and sisters carrying the younger ones on their backs.

It was the moral dangers that disturbed Victorian sensitivities in mixing youths of both sexes in the fields, and allowing them unfettered scope for mischief in the long journeys to and from work. The girls worked in light clothing, rolled back for convenience in the damp grass and corn. Males and females performed their private functions in view of each other. The nature of the work made the girls as free and uninhibited as the men, and the whole suggestive combination was enough to identify gang girls as wantons in the public mind. Indeed, such girls were blighted from any prospective employment as domestics in 'respectable' households. It was alleged that girls as young as 13 got pregnant. Dr C. Morris of Spalding told one investigator:

> I have myself witnessed gross indecencies between boys and girls of 14 to 16 years of age. I once saw a young girl insulted by some five or six boys on the roadside. Other older persons were about 20 or 30 yards off, but they took no notice. The girl was calling out, which caused me to stop ... I have also seen boys bathing in the brooks, and girls between 13 and 19 looking on from the banks.[3]

The children were at the mercy of the gang masters who had contracted their collective labour. The men were reputed to take advantage of the gang girls and to be harsh task-masters. Albert Porter of Spalding, who had worked as a boy ganger between 8 and 14 years old, recalled the gang master, 'a man well known for his cruelty; I saw him beat one boy till his wounds had to be dressed. He kept us in the wheat when it was above our waists the whole of a wet day, so that we were working in drenched clothes, and any attempt to leave was met by a beating .... I got 6*d* a day when I was 10; the oldest boy would not get more than 8*d*.' (This does not seem to have been bad pay for the time, however; the commission's Report gives anything from 1*d* to 6*d* a day as the going rates for children in 1867.) William Hill, aged 15, told of a gang master who used to beat the children with a willow stick and push the girls' noses into the ground. He kicked boys and pushed them up to their chests in the water in the dykes when they were not working satisfactorily.[4] All this was happening at home at a time when public opinion was much exercised by the plight of plantation slaves in America and travelling theatres were moving audiences to tears with melodramatic scenes from *Uncle Tom's Cabin*.

The 1867 Gangs Act banned the employment of children under 8 in public gangs and required gang masters to be licensed by magistrates. Mixed-sex public gangs were banned, and females had to be supervised by a gang mistress. However, private gangs were left unregulated, so the Act's only effect was to increase their number at the expense of public gangs; and girls were morally no safer.[5] The 1873 Agricultural Children Act prohibited the employment of children generally in agriculture under 8, and set the minimum age for public gangs at 10. Chldren between 8 and 12 could be employed only if they attended school part-time but if they reached a prescribed Standard before 12 they could start full-time work. The Act also allowed for over-8s to work full-time during harvesting and school holidays. It was a badly drafted measure, and as enforcement depended on the squirearchical magistracy, its frustration was assured. Rural school attendances were poor and patchy, and it was not until the compulsory provisions of the 1880 Education Act that any improvement began to be seen.[6]

Neither agricultural children's legislation nor education laws could by themselves protect rural youngsters from exploitation. The semi-feudal relationship between farmer and farmhand ensured that the latter's children would be available for work when demanded. It was technological change, such as the advent of the mechanical reaper and binder, that probably did more in the long run to reduce the demand for child labour.[7] In 1861 7.6 per cent of the agricultural workforce was under 15; and in 1881 the figure was 5.5 per cent. However, there was still a demand for children well into the twentieth century for seasonal work, and country school holidays were arranged around this annual cycle. Seasonal work, like pea- and hop-picking, drew competition from urban working-class families, not an unmixed blessing for farmers who found the townsfolk more boisterous and insanitary. Ganging in East Anglia was declining but not dead in 1914, but then the main social problems connected with it were the sanitary regulation of slum folk from London's East End and the Fenland towns.[8]

Fishing apprenticeships had been a fairly common way of disposing of workhouse boys. Under the 1844 Poor Law Act, which governed pauper apprenticeships, the boy's consent to an indenture was necessary only if he was over 14. If he was under 16 and his parents were still alive their consent was necessary.[9] The result was that many young boys were bound to fishing-boat owners against their will. Although officialdom believed there were golden opportunities for workhouse boys to make good in the fishing trade, the boys voted with their feet and absconded in large numbers. At Grimsby, which was the leading recipient of such apprentices, a third of the lads absconded between 1881 and 1893. Owners took a severe line, as abscondences held up the sailing of boats. Where caught, the boys were taken before the magistrates and liable to imprisonment. At Ramsgate in 1878 10 per cent of apprentices were imprisoned for some breach of indentures. A Board of Trade inquiry into the problem ascribed the problem to dissatisfaction with shipboard discipline, low pay as apprentices, and restlessness, and called for more welfare provision for the boys when ashore. By 1897 Ramsgate had made great strides in providing fisherboy homes, and a generally more sympathetic approach drastically reduced the numbers of boys appearing before the bench, but abscondence seems to have remained a problem at Grimsby up to the First World War, and lads in their teens were still acquiring futile prison records for 'refusal of obedience' as a result.

The discipline on board was harsh; 'rope-ending' – beating boys with ropes – was practised into the early 1900s.[10] For their part the boat owners complained that the ex-workhouse boys were the dregs who had failed at other trades, and were the lowest and roughest types.

Poor Law boys also went into the Royal Navy and the merchant marine from the age of 14 in the late nineteenth century.[11] The Poor Law, industrial schools, reformatories and voluntary societies ran training ships as 'feeders'. The Royal Navy laid down minimum physical requirements for entry, which the boys, from their deprived backgrounds, often could not meet.[12] Royal Navy discipline was very strict: flogging for boys (up to 12 strokes with the cane or 24 with the birch on the bare behind) was retained in the 1900s, though abolished for the men. In the merchant navy there were the physical dangers of life at sea and the possibility of contracting TB from living in cramped quarters.

It appears that the Royal and merchant navies were not unpopular as a career among the boys, though the rough life on board merchant ships was said to put many of the better types off; the obscene language and the rough, brutal manner of the officers towards the boys, the poor food and the need to share cramped cabins with older men were deterrents. When ashore in the colonies the boys sometimes absconded. At home in the ports there was a lack of decent hostels and welfare, so the boys hung around the sleazy districts mixing with undesirables. None the less by the early 1900s the supply of aspiring merchant sailors was outstripping the demand as the change from sail to steam was reducing the demand for hands on board; whereas in 1870 there had been 18,303 indentures of apprenticeship in the merchant marine, by 1905 this was down to 5,069.[13]

5

YOUNG SLAVES – CHILDREN IN DOMESTIC SERVICE

To start this chapter it would be instructive to look at figures for the proportion of children employed as domestics within the period of this book. The definition of 'domestic servant' is rather elastic, as it may include or exclude, for example, laundresses doing contract washing, waitresses and cleaners in lodging- and eating-houses, charwomen coming in as 'dailies', and 'nurses' who looked after babies or attended the sick or elderly; while the child moonlighters who did paid domestic odd jobs for other households, or served as unpaid 'little mothers' and 'helpers' at home, would not figure in the census classifications as domestics. Despite these limitations, the censuses do provide a good idea of the extent to which child service was employed in the home.

Of the 1,230,000 females in 'general domestic service' (excluding laundresses and charwomen) in 1881 over 98,000 were girls under 15; in 1891 this peaked to 107,000 girls out of 1,386,000 general female domestics, but by 1901 it had fallen to 64,800 out of 1,331,000. This fall reflects the rise in the school-leaving age and the widening alternative opportunities in shop work and light industry. In the earlier Victorian period some paid servants could be surprisingly young; thus in 1861 15,332 10–14-year-old girls were recorded as 'nurses'; and 983 'nurses' were 5–9 years old, while 729 5–9s were given as general domestics.[1] In fact the censuses probably understate the proportion of under-15s, as girls were kown to exaggerate their ages to improve their chances when applying for work.[2]

In 1871 23 per cent of 'nurses' were under 14, and they were on average younger than all other servants; even at their tender years they would have had prior experience of looking after younger siblings at home.[3]

Few boys went into service. In 1891 there were fewer than 7,000 male servants under 15. They worked as gardeners, assistants, pages, hall boys (cleaning silver and boots), stable boys and so forth. Some farm boys were in fact the sons of other farmers who had sent them away to learn to 'rough it'.

Employment outlets varied widely, and service had its own career ladder. One must not assume that there was necessarily a wide *Upstairs Downstairs* class gulf between master and servant. Any 'respectable' family from artisans upwards sought to avail itself of domestic help as a mark of status. As Flora Thompson wrote: 'Even the wives of carpenters and masons paid a girl sixpence to clean the knives and boots and take out the children on Saturday.' Small farmers, clerks and lodging-house proprietors were not 'upper-class', nor were the laundry owners. Girls might start their experience while still infants charring for a neighbour. Mrs Archibald Mackirdy stated in 1907 that they might earn 2*d* for scrubbing a flight of steps, at the age of 6 or 7, and even at that age had to carry their own buckets and implements from house to house and showed early signs of housemaid's knee. The Departmental Committee on the Employment of Schoolchildren estimated in 1902 that there were some 50,000 moonlighting child domestics, the majority being girls; the boys, it believed, tended to get the better-paid jobs like knife-grinding, polishing and so on at the better houses.

The earliest full-time job was most likely to be 'maid-of-all work' (a euphemism for skivvying) in a 'petty place', that is, a single-servant establishment of the likes of a clerk, schoolteacher, shopkeeper, or curate. Country girls were sent away as soon as possible, but boys were kept at home as their potential earnings on the land were valuable.[4] Between 10 and 15, girls left home to live in with their employer. Mothers might be choosy about the first job; a public house and even a farmhouse were considered low status, and a shopkeeper or vicar was much preferred. The jobs may have been advertised in the press, or found through the local grapevine; the village doctor or midwife, for example, might know of a household where extra help was needed, and the vicar might have contacts. But the job could be very far away. Sally Livingstone (1978) mentions a girl of 11 sent from Stiffkey in Norfolk to the Isle of Wight as a kitchen maid with a ticket tied to her coat; she travelled by donkey cart and train. The children were at the mercy of their employers and the place might turn out very different from what they had been led to believe. A girl born in 1891, one of six children of a farm labourer, was sent away at 13, travelling 16 miles on a carrier's cart to her first job working for a widow, her daughter and the latter's two children.[5] She was exploited as a drudge and lived in a freezing room at the top of the house: 'The missis put me in a room that had no window. She said, "Young girls spend too much time dreaming and looking out of windows."' The girl had to be up at 6 a.m. Her mistress was cold and even spiteful, but she dared not leave her place because her recently widowed father needed the money she was sending home. She was allowed one Sunday a month off to visit home. Her father sensed her unhappiness and took her away, finding her another place nearer home. Here her employers were kinder, but she had a 4-mile walk to and from work each day; however, she was much happier as she could be with her father.

Another even starker instance of vulnerability was that told by a Mrs Wrigley, born in 1858, the daughter of a poor Welsh shoemaker.[6] Even before the age of 8 she was employed at home carrying buttermilk from a farm and coal from the pit and doing the family washing by the River Dee. At 8 she was sent to a house near Stockport to work as a nursemaid, but her employer misled her about the job and instead exploited her as a maid of all work. She had to be up at 6 a.m. to clean the rooms and light the fires, and her master would box her ears if he was displeased. The poor girl could not read or write, and so could not communicate with home to explain her distress, until a kindly neighbour did so on her behalf. Her next job as a farm maid near Oswestry earned her 3s a month for which she did milking, cheese- and butter-making, and looked after the animals; here she was happier. At 14 she went to work at a temperance hotel at Oldham for 16s a month; here her employers were good and encouraged her to study.

Wages for young girls were low; in the 1880s perhaps a shilling a week, plus food and 'perks' like discarded clothing. Even so, dutiful girls sent their savings home to eke out the family budget. In London wages were higher. In the mid-1890s a 13-year-old might earn £5 to £6 a year, rising to £7 16s by 16.[7] Wages in 'petty places' were lower, and girls who worked in them tended to come from the poorest homes or workhouses, to be ignorant and unclean and also possibly light-fingered. As it was their first experience, they might prove ill-suited, weepy, or rebellious; the loneliness and boredom of working alone in a single-servant household with the 'missis' breathing down their necks in the kitchen might be too much, and they would just walk out.

The girls were expected to provide their own uniform at their own expense. Even the most modest household might insist on a cap, collar, cuffs and apron as a mark of respectability.[8] Kate Taylor, born in 1891 in Suffolk, started work at 13 for 1s 3d a week as as farm servant. As she had no uniform, her employers, who were tight-fisted, provided her with the materials to make up her own, which had to be paid for out of her wages, so she worked there for the first six months in effect for nothing.[9]

The hours could be very long; the girls were at the employers' beck and call day and night. The subservience of their status rankled, but at least there was the customary one day off a month, which 'with most of them', Charles Booth remarked, 'seems to be the one thing which makes the servant's life worth living'. In the better-class homes they had in addition an evening off each week and up to a fortnight off a year to go home to their families.

If a girl got work in a more prestigious multi-servant household, she would find herself on the bottom rung of the strict servant hierarchy as an 'under servant' ministering to the upper servants. Discipline was strict 'below stairs', and the girl could expect a cuff or blow from pompous irate older servants. As a scullery maid she peeled potatoes, swept and blackleaded the grate and cleared the flues; as an under housemaid she would clean and scrub 'above stairs', and if a nursemaid, she would wash the infants' linen, keep the nursery spick and span and light the fires. As already noted, the girls might only be a few years older than their charges. In a good house there was at least the fellowship of other servants, though the subservience and sharpened awareness of 'knowing one's place' were etched deeper by the servants' hall pecking order where the snobberies aped the airs and graces of the 'quality' folk above stairs. A required outward show of humility and decorum might be emphasized by compulsory attendance at church and/or family prayers before breakfast in the dining-room. Even in her time off a servant girl might need permission to go out, for so small a task as posting a letter.

The companionship of other servants could be a little too cloying when a girl had to share an attic room with two or three others. A good household did offer some opportunity for specialization and advancement. A kitchen girl might be trained up in time as an under cook; and a housemaid with a flair for the needle or hairdressing might in time become a lady's maid. Men were in very short supply in the servants' social milieu. Marriage between servants was in any case taboo in households, and the girl would keep up any courtship by correspondence with the beau she had left behind in her home village. Another avenue of escape was through courtship with the tradesmen who called at the door, or the policeman who stopped for a cup of tea on his beat. But any such romantic dalliances had to be conducted away from the house in the brief time off, as employers frowned on what were demeaningly termed servants' 'followers'.

The experience of Mrs Layton, born in Bethnal Green in 1855, exemplifies the progression and variety of experience of girls in their early years as domestics.[10] At 10 she started as a baby-minder for a shopkeeper at 1s 6d a week working from 8 a.m. to 7 or 8 p.m. At 13 she worked for a 'very kind' mistress in Hampstead, who insisted that she attend church (which she sometimes skipped), but provided only the floor of the cockroach-infested kitchen as a bed-space. At 15 she became a nursery nurse to a widower in Kentish Town with five children including a new-born baby. It throws a curious light on Victorian morals that in this job she still was unaware how babies were conceived and born! By then she was earning 3s a week; though she loved looking after the children, she was so hard-worked she sometimes fell asleep on the stairs. At 17 she went to work for a woman and her daughter under better conditions; her new employer even encouraged her education.

One danger for a lonely girl a long way from home was 'seduction'. She might be led astray by her employer or his son, or by tradesmen or policemen, soldiers, or other young men she met in the street on errands or during her time off; the greatest risk, contrary to popular assumptions, came not from a designing employer but from males of her own social class.[11] Perhaps another misconception is that the girls were always naive and entirely innocent victims. Even leaving out the 'dollymops' – the girls who dabbled in prostitution as a sideline when out of the house – many girls up from the country would have already been sexually experienced, as Victorian inhibitions held less sway over earthy country folk. Indeed, those country mothers who did care for their daughters' chastity evidently thought they were in less moral danger 'in service' away from home. In the 1890s one child asked a 17-year-old servant from the country if she did not miss her family.

The girl replied yes, but her mother would not let her stay at home after leaving school 'because every Miss i' our village has a child'.[12] In the single-servant household, the girl left on her own when her employers were out might be tempted to let acquaintances into the house. This assignation might lead to the girl's moral downfall, or else thefts from the premises for which she was not responsible but would take the blame.[13] Ruin meant dismissal without the all-important references, and a drift into vagrancy or prostitution.

Another form of recruitment into service was the hiring or 'mop' fair which youngsters would attend in country towns waiting to be inspected by prospective hirers, usually farmers of the district. Parents and hirers would haggle over the price, and when the deal was struck a youngster was committed for a term as a 'bondager' and taken off to the farmstead; at the end of the time the bondager was released with a lump sum. Despite the degradation, for the girls it was preferable to field labour – especially as gangers – which would have ruined their reputations for domestic employment thereafter. By 1900 hiring fairs were in rapid decline, except in Ulster. Patrick Macgill's *Children of the Dead End* (1914) gives a vivid account of an Ulster hiring fair. At the age of 12 he was sent from home and joined a party of children of similar age, walking up to 12 miles to the railway station for the train to the Strabane fair, where they stood in the market-place eyed by hirers from Omagh:

> Most of them were fat, angry-looking fellows who kept moving up and down examining us after the manner of men who seek out the good and bad points of horses which they intend to buy . . . . A big man with a heavy stomach came up to me. 'How much do ye want for the six months?' he asked.
> 'Six pounds', I told him.
> 'Shoulders too narrow for the money,' he said . . . and walked on.

Patrick was finally approved by a farmer who in his rough way of inspecting him 'ran his fingers over my shoulder and squeezed the thick of my arm so tightly that I almost roared in his face with the pain of it'. He was hired for £5 10s for 6 months. His bedroom leaked and his blankets got soaked in wet wather. He was overworked and underfed on a diet exclusively of potatoes and buttermilk, and whenever exhaustion slowed him down, the farmer quickened him with a kick. Patrick did ultimately retaliate by kneeing him in the belly, and he was treated more circumspectly therafter, but he was glad to leave at the end of his hiring term.

The custom of hiring fairs and the reputed mistreatment of servants filtered into children's folklore, and formed the theme of a children's singing game of which there were local variants. A West Country version from the 1880s at least as a 'mother' who presents the 'children' for hire to a 'lady'.[14] The children chant:

> Here comes the lady of the land
> With all her children in her hand
> 'Please do you want a servant today?'

The lady asks: 'What can she do?'
The mother replies:

> She can brew, she can bake
> She can make a wedding cake
> Fit for you or any lady in the land.

The lady takes them on. After a make-believe lapse of time the mother returns to see her chldren, to be treated to tales of cruelty:

> Mother: 'What did she do to you, my dear?'
> One child: 'She cut off my nose and made nose pie.'
> Another child: 'She took out my eyes and made a figged pudden and woulden give me none.'

The game ends with the mother and children chasing the lady and putting her in 'prison'.

The extent of sheer cruelty to young servants is impossible to assess; but there is no doubt that workhouse orphans were the most vulnerable group. The Poor Law authorities were only too glad to get the girls off their hands and made no effort to check the sorts of homes the girls were going into. In 1860 there were an estimated 400,000 single-servant households, many of whose employees were of workhouse background.[15]

It was a particular case of cruelty to an ex-workhouse girl in 1850 that led to a change in the law. Jane Wilbred, a 14-year-old orphan, had been placed out to a Mr and Mrs Sloane by the West London Union in 1849. At first she was well treated but the situation changed when Mrs Sloane's pet bird died and Jane was accused of frightening it to death. From then on she was subjected to a regime of starvation and beating and as her condition became visibly worse to neighbours, she was rescued in November 1850, debilitated and marked from the beatings. The Sloanes were tried and sentenced to 2 years' jail.[16] An Act of 1851 resulted from this, empowering workhouse officers to monitor ex-workhouse servant girls and apprentices till 16.[17] However, the Act was ineffective; the relieving officers who were frequently used were already heavily worked, and in any case the girls often found it hard to open up to male officials. There was no uniformity of administration, for different unions used variously the relieving officers, chaplains, or workhouse matrons. The Act in any case applied only to youngsters in their *first* job after leaving the workhouse.[18] A later Act of 1861 also made it an offence to injure the health or endanger the life of a servant or an apprentice by neglect.[19] An official report for the Poor Law by Mrs Nassau Senior in 1874 on the education and training of workhouse girls for domestic service urged the appointment of women volunteers as monitors instead, and an Act of 1876 empowered unions to employ specialist female inspectors, and from 1879 they were permitted to subsidize voluntary associations for this work.

However, such measures, so far as they were implemented, were self-limiting, for only the better employers would take on girls subject to these safeguards, and there is no doubt that ex-workhouse girls (and not *just* workhouse girls) continued to face appalling treatment in extreme cases. In 1891 at South Shields a 14-year-old ex-Poor Law girl, Frances Bellerby, died at the hands of her mistress Mrs Mary Shade. Shade beat the girl mercilessly with a leather belt or stick, tied her hands behind her back, and kicked her about the floor. The medical inspection of her corpse revealed malnutrition, extensive bruising and an abscess on the skull. Shade was committed for trial.[20] In 1892 14-year-old Ellen Cross, a gamekeeper's daughter, was rescued by the NSPCC from her employer, a farmer and his wife: she had been worked from 5 a.m. to midnight, and was made to do the laundry in an unheated washhouse in winter, where she contracted frostbite in her feet; despite this she was still forced to carry wood. 'On one occasion she was deprived of food from six o'clock one evening to six o'clock next evening because she would not eat some pig's lights which had been drawn about the kitchen by the cat.'[21] Her mistress was particularly cruel, and showed no mercy for her crippled feet, kicking and punching her and forcing her to sleep in a stair cupboard where she could not stretch out. Yet at the trial, her master was acquitted, and the mistress was fined £5 and costs!

Even into the Edwardian period such monstrosities could persist. In 1907 a 12-year-old girl was worked and starved to death by her mistress in a jam-packed daily schedule from 6.15 a.m. as nursery-maid, general cleaner and dogsbody. Her mother was employed as cook in the same house but was too frightened to intervene until it was too late.[22] It is interesting to note from such cases that servants' mistresses could be more heartless and vindictive than the masters. The management of servants was more commonly left to the wives; men were remoter employers and probably just took their wives' word about the alleged shortcomings of a servant during the day. One suspects also that this kind of cruelty could occasionally be prompted by female revenge where the husband had been displaying a more-than-paternal interest in a young servant girl.

Notions of what constituted a 'good employer' are relative to the standards of the time. We have seen that some could be kind and paternalistic but this might be mixed with a piety and an enforced religious observance that the girls found difficult to take. The philanthropist Ellen Barlee, with all her sympathies for helpless young servant girls, allowed humanity to slip into sickly condescension when in 1863 she instanced her own housemaid as a shining example of industriousness.[23] She never bothered herself with reading books any more: 'You see I have no time for it now, but then I was born to be a housemaid, and I won't let anybody beat me at that.' Even a 'decent' household would see that the girls were kept 'at it'. Theresa Cox, born in 1894, went into service in 1906 with what she called 'very nice' people. At 12 years old she had to be up at 7 a.m. for duties before her own breakfast at 8.30 a.m. She worked till 10 ot 10.30 at night, and was allowed a day off each month and each Tuesday from 2 to 10 p.m. Her initial wages were 2s 6d a week, out of which she had to supply her own uniform.[24]

Charity girls were regarded just as fodder for domestic service well into this century, and a benevolent institution like Dr Barnardo's saw its role as conditioning the girls at its Barkingside Home to be dutiful, uncomplaining servants when they left. At its annual fête in 1878 the girls sang:

> When I go into service
> I must watch and pray
> That my Heavenly Father

Will direct my way . . .
I must be good-tempered,
Always neat and clean,
Civil in my manners,
Never pert or mean.
And I need not mind it
If I get no praise;
For my Heavenly Father
Will be pleased with me.
With His love and blessing
Happy I shall be.[25]

The reality was that young girls viewed the prospect of service with fatalism or as a hated inevitability. One early scheme to improve their prospects was to arrange emigration through the Poor Law and charities like Barnardo's and the Quarrier Homes in Glasgow. The colonies were short of women; in Britain women outnumbered men, and a placement with a family in Canada (the main outlet for the scheme) was seen as combining advantage for the girl and for Britain's imperial needs. There were obvious dangers for children fostered out on isolated farmsteads, and the Canadian government arranged for inspection.

In good British households the food was plentiful, but the subservience and servility were detested,[26] and where alternative employment beckoned in factories, shops and offices as opportunities began widening at the end of the century, girls gladly turned their backs on domestic service. By 1911 there were under 48,000 girls below 15 in service, plus 57,000 15-year-olds and 71,500 16-year-olds in a total domestic force of 1,340,000. During the First World War there was a wholesale flight of girls from the pantry to the production line in the booming factories; between July 1914 and January 1918 the number of under-18s employed outside domestic service increased by more than a third.[27]

It is no wonder that the bourgeoisie were sensitive about the supply and quality of servants. There were strong prejudices about the worth and proper purpose of girls' education. Ellen Barlee in 1863 firmly believed that the public money spent on academic subjects for schoolgirls was wasted, as their destiny lay almost certainly in household employment. Others went further, and even as late as 1913 there were those who believed that education positively spoiled girls for domestic service by making them more independent spirits.[28] Samuel Smith in 1885[29] complained of the shortage of trained servants, and urged that cookery and homecraft be an essential part of a girl's training at school; apart from meeting a middle-class need, he maintained, it would upgrade the girls coming from slatternly homes as future wives and mothers. Such instruction as they were given in elementary schools, however, was generally bookish and theoretical in the 1880s, and girl school-leavers were said still not to be able to handle a broom or do any practical cookery.[30] The bourgeoisie equated domestic skill for *working-class* girls with female virtue. This had, of course, a strong self-interested element, but it did possess genuine validity, as Mrs Henrietta Barnett, wife of Canon Barnett of Whitechapel, discovered. She found among decent mothers in this poor parish an earnest wish that their daughters could get places in good-class households as a step up from their slum origins. From 1873 Mrs Barnett began trying to find suitable placements for such girls, but found they were a rough lot; some had to be cleansed of vermin first! Decent employers could find them difficult servants. One girl, Kate Withers, felt so 'riled' by her mistress that she picked up the latter's baby by its long clothes and swung it round her head ready to throw at her mistress just because it 'was 'andy' as a projectile; another girl threw a knife at her mistress; another started a fire in her attic room from lifted floorboards; and yet another was in the habit of 'borrowing' her mistress's clothes.[31]

Ex-workhouse girls proved particularly problematical in holding down a job. They were by common repute sullen, short-tempered and incapable of initiative; and because they owned nothing of their own in the workhouse, they had no sense of private property and were allegedly given to pilfering.[32] But their mentally stultifying upbringing in a cold, rule-ridden institution was not the only cause of the problem; Mrs Emmeline Way told the 1861 Select Committee on Poor Relief that loneliness and a feeling that nobody cared for them outside made them wayward, too.[33] Mrs Way was one of that band of philanthropists who had begun taking workhouse girls under their wing to train them more adequately for domestic service and find them jobs in the better households, for once they were stuck as drudges in a mean 'petty place' or low lodging-house they were trapped by the inability to get worthwhile references.[34] If they ran away they ended up on the streets or back in the workhouse where they received a frosty, even punitive reception as 'recalcitrants'.

Louisa Twining pioneered the domestic training of workhouse girls through her Workhouse Visiting Society, and in 1861 opened a Home for girls who had left the workhouse but were now unemployed. However, it closed in 1862 through lack of funds. Other similar refuges existed; Ellen Barlee mentions, for example, the Dudley Street Refuge off the Edgware Road in London which had opened a special 'Home for Girls' because of the large numbers of homeless girls coming its way. Mrs Way stressed the vital importance of a sense of being cared about, which could transform a girl's conduct. She told of one former institution girl with a background of running away and falling into petty crime. Mrs Way befriended her, and claimed in 1861 that she was a reformed character and had now held down a job in service for a year. She told Mrs Way: 'Until you spoke to me, I had never felt that anyone cared for me. I have been in the workhouse school but I never felt that I had a friend; when I went wrong, I had no one to go to to advise me and I could not help myself.'[35] This is of course Mrs Way's own version. What remain unrecorded are the inner feelings of hapless girls made to feel appreciative of the patronizing kindness shown them by amateur upper-class social workers.

An early awareness of the depressing and institutionalizing effects of life in a general mixed workhouse for a child had led in the 1844 Poor Law Act to a provision for the creation of district schools where workhouse children from several unions could be congregated, away from adult paupers. Though seen as an enlightened development at the time, these schools, where they were set up (primarily in London), drew the criticism over the next generation that they were over-large, regimented 'barracks'. In 1874 the Local Government Board commissioned Mrs Nassau Senior to report on the suitability of metropolitan workhouse education for girls.[36] Mrs Senior attacked district schools as psychologically damaging to girls, and preferred smaller 'separate' schools, belonging to a single Poor Law union; but her ideal was 'boarding out', where the child would be fostered with a family and raised and educated outside the Poor Law ambience altogether. She adduced figures from a sample survey to 'prove' that graduates of district schools were relative failures in domestic service. Of those sent into service from the London district schools only 11.42 per cent were classed as 'good', 26.12 per cent 'fair', 43.26 per cent 'unsatisfactory' and 19.02 per cent 'bad'. Of those sent from the allegedly less impersonal 'separate' schools 20.81 per cent were 'good', 33.06 per cent 'satisfactory' and the remainder unsatis-factory or bad.[37] An example of an 'unsatisfactory' district school product was cited. A 16-year-old girl was said to be 'curiously and unconquerably' apathetic by her mistress: 'Temper so thoroughly perverse that the mistress has sometimes tried the experiment of telling her *not* to do the thing she wants to have done, and always with success.' Her work was sloppy and she refused to use a needle. Although she had been taught religion she 'showed no feeling, and tore up her Bible to light a fire'. (But was this a reaction perhaps to religion being rammed down her throat by a well-meaning but piously condescending employer?) A 'bad' case would involve downright lying, dishonesty and even violence; and unapproved association with the opposite sex.

Mrs Senior's report did not seal the fate of the district schools, which had staunch defenders, but one proposal she made did bear fruit, as already observed: that a voluntary agency of women should oversee the welfare of servant girls in their early years out of the workhouse. This was to lead shortly afterwards to the formation of the Metropolitan Association for Befriending Young Servants (MABYS), and its provincial counterpart the Girls' Friendly Society (GFS).

The so-called domestic training girls received in the district schools in the 1870s was crudely geared to running the schools on unpaid labour; the laundries contained institution-sized boilers, unrelated to the domestic scale and the refinements of ironing fancy clothes; and cook-house potato-peeling was no preparation for a middle-class cuisine. A parliamentary enquiry into Metropolitan Poor Law Schools in 1896 was damning about the district schools twenty years after Mrs Senior, but their defenders, like William Chance, attacked the Report as biased and selective in its evidence.[38] Chance maintained in 1897 that there had been great improvements in the schools over the previous twenty years, and that the domestic training now offered in the best of them placed their products in high demand among better-class employers. Some schools were giving girls practical training in child care in the infant blocks; needlework and more refined cooking were being taught, and at Forest Gate girls were allowed out to do shopping on their own initiative. The Report had ignored the evidence of Miss Poole of MABYS; she had told the inquiry the findings of a survey on 3,654 ex-Poor Law girls in 1895 which returned 91 per cent as 'good' servants. Many mistresses, she claimed, now preferred Poor Law girls to non-pauper girls as employees owing to their specialized training.

Chance's defence of the schools was vindicated by a later Report in 1908 by T. J. Macnamara, a junior minister for the Local Government Board.[39] He concluded that, contrary to widely held prejudice, the schools did attempt to train girls on a domestic not an institutional scale, and that the board's own statistics for the 10 years to 1906 showed that of 12,829 children (that is, *all* children) sent out to jobs by the metropolitan district schools only 75 had returned to the Poor Law; while a MABYS report on 3,223 girls under its wing in 1906 showed that 1,729 were 'satisfactory' and 777 were 'fairly satisfactory'.

But if the metropolitan district schools' training had improved, the same could not be said of the smaller and more rural Poor Law unions. Dorothy Hatcher, the illegitimate daughter of a Kent farm girl, was entrusted to the Tenterden guardians just before and during the First World War. She benefited from the now standard practice of fostering, and was happy with her foster-parents. When she was old enough, however, the authorities removed her to a small training home for servants, accommodating only eight girls near Maidstone. Despite its small, intimate size, the girls were treated impersonally and strictly by the matron. There was a repressive ultra-High Church religious atmosphere and attendance at chapel and confession were compulsory. Dorothy was unimpressed by the 'training'. She was earmarked to become a parlourmaid because of her height:

> None of the work we did could really be called training. Monday was wash day. We all worked as a team, some washing, some mangling, and others hanging out .... Tuesday was baking day. Matron did the baking and no one was allowed to help her, only with the washing up or fetching and carrying. There was one girl who would have loved to do cooking, but that didn't come into the training.[40]

Twice a week she was allowed out to gain direct experience at a local house. The resident servants there gave her odd jobs like chopping wood and polishing to do, but 'I didn't learn much except how to talk about my employer behind her back.'

By 1896 MABYS had 1,000 lady volunteers and nearly 7,500 girls under its care in London. It then ran lodging-houses for unemployed young servants and also a training Home, and had extended its work from ex-Poor Law girls to country girls coming up to the capital for work in service, and also by the early 1900s to girls discharged from industrial schools. Outside London the GFS did similar work, and some cities like Sheffield and Bristol had their own associations.[41] At its peak, around 1910, the GFS had nearly 5,000 girl servants under its wing, but declined thereafter as opportunities outside service were widening for girls, and alternative respectable lodging-houses like the YWCA could accommodate them. The GFS had tried since its earlier days to bring factory girls within its fold and its failure here demonstrated the great shortcoming both of MABYS and the GFS: the volunteers were patronizing Lady Bountifuls who expected their *protégées* to feel grateful; factory girls were more independent and would not put up with this. Employers took on young servants on the understanding that the latter would be visited by MABYS and GFS volunteers for counselling and to take up complaints about their conditions. Many householders, though, had a rooted objection to this kind of intrusion in their homes. The girls received birthday cards and invitations to tea, and MABYS ran clubs for the girls' limited leisure time, but the activities there largely consisted of sewing, and the atmosphere was pious and restrained. The GFS, as a denominational Church of England foundation, was particularly prissy, and would only take on morally 'chaste' girls; even up to 1936 it rejected unmarried mothers. Nigel Middleton tells us that some girls were so sick of being patronized by MABYS that they even changed jobs to escape its watching eye, despite the risk of ending up with a bad employer. He goes as far as to maintain that the 'apparent good work of MABYS was largely an illusion created by and for the Local Government Board's Annual Reports'.[42] MABYS can, however, be credited with compassion for the plight of feeble-minded girls who could not hold a permanent job and would inevitably vegetate in the workhouse. In 1887 it opened its first training Home cum shelter for such girls. The aim was to find them day jobs in service and allow them to return to the shelter each evening. Between 1892 and 1908 its special Home at Hitchin had received 114 girls, so the scale of this work was not large. Nor did the girls always prove capable of keeping their posts, and some returned to the Poor Law. For those who did achieve a measure of self-sufficiency MABYS was particularly concerned lest their low intelligence made them easy sexual prey.[43]

6

BRICKYARD AND CANAL BOAT CHILDREN AND CHIMNEY SWEEPS

Whilst public attention in the early Victorian period focused on the toil of children in textile factories and mines, the labours of thousands of little boys and girls in the brickyards of Staffordshire, Leicestershire, Derbyshire and other parts of Britain went unobserved. Their plight was to be taken up by George Smith, born in 1831 the son of a Staffordshire brickyard worker. He had started in a brickyard at the age of 7, experiencing the commonplace 'abuse' at the hands of brutalized older workers. As he wrote later of conditions prevailing in the 1860s for brickyard children:

> Kicks, cuffs, over-hastening and oaths and curses enough to make the flesh creep, are too frequent modes of impelling to work. The old-men, monkey-like faces, the shrunken, shivering, cowering scared looks of many of the children, are things not to be imagined. I myself have seen, over and over again, the black eye, the unhealed sore, the swollen head, the bruised body in little, very little children, that proclaimed sorrowfully their experience to be filled up by cruelty, murderous violence . . . and punishment within not an inch but a hair's breadth of life.[1]

George himself was an industrious and devout Methodist. He rose to become manager of a brickworks at Coalville in Leicestershire, where his compassion for children inspired him to run a 'model' yard, excluding boys under 12 and girls altogether. A factory inspector, Robert Baker, became an ally and produced a report on brickyards in 1864; this was followed by a report by Inspector H. W. Lord for the Royal Commission on Employment of Children in 1866.[2] Boys and girls as young as 4 were employed in carrying heavy loads of clay or bricks across the yard all day; hot bricks had to be caught straight from the kiln and stacked in the barrows, and young 'puggers' trod the clay until it became more paste-like.[3] In the 1860s the children worked from 5 a.m. to 8 p.m. or even longer, and young girls were coarsened and defeminized by the arduous labour; typically, Inspector Lord expressed moral concern that the girls displayed themselves in minimal rags, exposing their legs in the quagmire of clay. He told of a 12-year-old girl seen staggering along with a barrow stacked with over 200 pounds of bricks along saturated ground. Children carried huge lumps of clay on their heads backwards and forwards all day; in 1870 Smith displayed at a publicity meeting a 43-pound lump of clay that a 9-year-old boy had been carrying on his head. Baker's report put the total distances covered daily by these little beasts of burden at anything from 8 to 18 miles, 6 days a week.

George Smith was disappointed when the 1867 Factories Act, which at last brought some regulation of hours for brickyard children, was confined to yards employing 50 or more employees. He wanted stronger protection and an extension of the provisions to smaller yards. His campaign made a real impact after the publication of his book *The Cry of the Children from the Brickyards of England* in 1871. He claimed there were up to 30,000 children under 16 employed in brickyards. Lord Shaftesbury was moved to visit a yard and told the House of Lords how he had been struck by the sight of pillars of clay there: 'On walking up, I found to my astonishment that the pillars were living beings.'[4] The children, he found, were cold and clammy from the wet clay running down them, and suffered from the extremes of temperature as they approached and left the kilns. An Act of 1871 barred boys under 10 and girls under 16 from working in the yards. Legislation, together with long-term changes in the pattern of labour demand, combined to reduce the percentage of the labour force under 15 in brick-making and quarrying from 7.3 per cent in 1861 to 3.8 per cent in 1881.[5] But the 1871 Act does not seem to have completely stopped the employment of young teenage girls, even into the early 1900s. One Buckinghamshire girl, born in 1889, started in the yards at 14, working from 6 a.m. to 6 p.m. for 9s a week.[6] And boys just out of school were carrying loads as heavy as any in the 1860s. A 1903 factory inspector's report instanced a boy weighing 77 pounds who carried a 69-pound piece of clay, and in the two years since he had increased his own bulk by only 4 pounds.[7] The 'cry from the brickyards' had by no means ceased.

From 1872 George Smith had begun turning his attention to the condition of Britain's canal children, and resigned his job to devote himself full-time to the cause. There were then over 25,000 canal boats, and the rough 'water gypsy' population lived in tiny cramped cabins. Smith told in 1873 of one cabin where a man, his wife and six children lived in 202 cubic feet of space: three children slept on the table, two slept underneath the parents' bed, and one slept in a cupboard overhead. The children rarely saw the inside of a school, and bargees were nearly all illiterate. The parents were notoriously drunken; when they tied up, they would go off to the pubs leaving the children on the barges; next day it was the children who had to do all the heavy labour while the parents slept the drink off. Smith told of many boats he had seen where 'the man who had charge of the boat would be sleeping and snoring his time away, while a bare-footed, half-naked boat child, of some seven or eight summers, would be trudging after the horse, scarcely able to get one foot before the other.' A mother's duties on board precluded proper care of her brood; no cooked meals or washing, and children might be left all day without food. The little ones were beaten and overworked, opening and closing lock gates and guiding the horses on the tow path up to 30 miles a day.[8]

Smith undertook his tour of the canals at considerable personal risk, as the bargees detested him. In 1877 an Act provided for the registration of barges, the regulation of conditions on board, and education of the children, but there was no effective enforcement and it became a dead letter. Smith's journeyings and exposé in *Our Canal Population* (1879) with intensive lobbying secured a stronger measure, the Canal Boats Amendment Act in 1884, which created an inspector of canal boats to see that government regulations regarding hygiene and crowding on board were followed. School attendance had become technically compulsory since 1880. The school board for the registration district of a canal boat was supposedly responsible for the children's schooling; children were meant to attend local schools wherever the boats were tied up, and keep an attendance record card.

How many canal boat children were there? Smith in the 1870s offered an estimate of 30,000–40,000, but in 1894 Gertrude Tuckwell gave a figure of 9,000–10,000. However, one government report in 1898 indicated well under 2,000.[9] All the indications are, therefore, that the numbers of children afloat were declining and that barges were tending more and more to house their families ashore.[10] The increasing use of motor-powered barges by the more prosperous bargees by the early 1900s was also reducing the demand for child labour.[11] It is questionable how far the 1884 Act was responsible for the trend, for although the local sanitary authorities had been obliged to enforce standards on board since 1884, there was only one overall canal boat inspector for the whole country; local inspections were perfunctory, and, said Tuckwell, exploitation of children and dirty conditions still persisted in the 1890s. The predominant view also is that the local education authorities were either apathetic or just plain outwitted in securing school attendances.[12]

In the late Victorian and Edwardian period conditions for canal children were almost as bad as in George Smith's day, albeit for a much-reduced number.[13] Complaints of evasions of the law and gross overwork of children were being voiced[14] when the NSPCC began looking into the question in 1906. A study by the Northwich and Mid-Cheshire branch of the society in 1906–7 revealed widespread evasion of the sanitary and education laws by bargees, and ineffective legal pursuit. The same branch reported in 1908: 'We find that parents are, for the most part, perfectly callous about the danger to life and limb, and, regarding the lack of education, arguing that they themselves grew up under the same conditions.' In 1905 a 10-year-old boy died when he got dragged along a tow path by an excited horse; girls of 8 and 9 were steering boats; there was at least one contemporary instance of a father 'selling' his children to boatmen; in 1910 in separate accidents a boy of 18 months and a girl of 3 were burned to death in their cabins. The 1908 Children's Act had overlooked them; administratively they fell between the stools of government departments and remained an ill-considered marginal group of will-o'-the-wisps.

The NSPCC's director, Robert Parr, published a booklet on canal children in 1910; but a NSPCC-sponsored bill that year banning under-14s from the barges got nowhere. Late into the 1920s the NSPCC was promoting similar bills but with equal futility,[15] and school-age children were still being employed on barges and growing up illiterate in the inter-war years.[16]

Of all the types of child slave, the figure of the little chimney sweep has stood most vividly in the public imagination down the generations. His pathos has inspired more sentimental literature than any other single type of child worker. The skinny, blackened little mite crossing the threshold of genteel folk to struggle up their crooked flues became a folk figure, yet hypocritically people availed themselves of his services while regretting the need for them.

The scandal of boy sweeps was aired in the eighteenth century by the philanthropist Jonas Hanway. An ineffective Act was passed in 1778 barring the use of children under 8. In the early nineteenth century a society was formed to press for further legislation and promote the invention and adoption of mechanical sweepers. William Blake had contributed poetically to the cause in his *Songs of Innocence* and *Songs of Experience*, so launching the little sweep in verse and prose as a tragic folk figure;[17] but while upright citizens could fulminate over the plight of the black slave in America, they shut their eyes to the tribulations of sooty slaves at home. Though sweeping brushes were available in the early Victorian period, the master sweeps' own conservatism and the public's preference ensured that boy sweeps would continue in demand for the difficult flues. Good people would salve their consciences by dropping the boy some tip, or helping to organize the annual 'Sweeps' Day' on 1 May when the boys were given a treat. Around 1850 a girl called Jamesina Waller, who lived at Hunstanton Hall, Norfolk, was moved at the site of the little sweep in their mansion, and later recalled 'the half terror of the poor sooty boy standing on a dust sheet on the floor and Mother holding my hand while she led me up to him and obliged me to put a thick piece of Bread and Butter into his hand, then my astonishment at his thanking us and devouring it'.[18]

A parliamentary inquiry of 1817–18 was to catalogue the same horrors and abuses to be retailed again by the Royal Commission on Employment of Children in 1863 and 1866. Enactments of 1834 and 1840 with their provisions for the boys' approval of their indenture terms before magistrates and raising of minimum ages (to 16 in 1840) were failures; the magistrates entrusted to protect prospective apprentices and enforce the law were owners of the very rambling mansions that begged the sweeps' employment. And the 1834 provisions relating to future flue design had no effect on existing flues. In some districts, like Birmingham and North Staffordshire, local vigilantes formed societies to stamp out the illegal employment of boy sweeps, but in rural areas it continued to flourish. In 1856 a periodical, the *Climbing Boys' Advocate*, was

started to highlight the continuing abuses. In the capital the trade
was persistent as Lord Shaftesbury, a long-standing campaigner,
complained in 1854, but his attempt to get a stronger measure
passed that year failed; the peers' vested interests militated against
it.

Boys were traditionally sold to master sweeps by their parents;
or occasionally they were kidnapped. In 1861 at Leicester a couple
were prosecuted for conspiring to obtain two illegitimate boys of 6
and 8 from a workhouse by false pretences. The boys had been then
sold to a sweep, but were subsequently rescued. Until the early
Victorian legal restrictions, workhouses apprenticed them out
directly, as happened to Oliver Twist when Mr Gamfield, the
master sweep, assured the officials of the humane expediency of
lighting fires in the grate to bring boys down: 'Boys is wery
obstinite, and wery lazy, gen'lmen, and there's nothink like a good
hot blaze to make 'em come down vith a run. It's humane, too,
gen'lmen, acause, even if they've stuck in the chimbley, roasting
their feet makes 'em struggle to hextricate theirselves.' The realities
were only too shocking: the hapless boys were savagely beaten by
sweeps, and kept half-starved to fit up the flue; they struggled up,
sometimes naked so their clothes did not impede their passage;
soot rubbed into their raw, bleeding flesh, and mouthfuls of it were
swallowed. 'Sooty cancer' of the scrotum, an occupational disease,
might necessitate castration. Boys got stuck and died of
suffocation, or were stifled by the smoke of the fires lit by their
masters to bring them down. Those that did not end up deformed
and maimed and proved wiry and agile might be hired out by
sweeps as cat-burglars; another profitable sideline was to send them
down cesspits to retrieve valuables that had fallen in.

The Royal Commission on Employment of Children was
informed in 1863 of widespread evasion of the 1840 Act.[19] A
Nottingham sweep, Mr Ruff, explained that he had lost business
by not using boys; even magistrates had turned him away. Boys as
young as 6 were prepared by hardening the flesh:

> This is done by rubbing it, chiefly on the elbows and knees,
> with the strongest brine, close by a hot fire. You must stand
> over them with a cane, or coax them by a promise of a
> halfpenny &c if they will stand a few more rubs. At first they
> will come back from their work looking as if the caps had

been pulled off; then they must be rubbed with brine again.[20]

Another sweep, Mr Clark, told of his own searing experiences when being 'broken in' as a 6-year-old apprentice. He showed a scar across his calf made by his master with an ash stick; he was 'cut to the bone, which had to be scraped to heal the wound', and he had 'marks of nailed boots &c on other parts'.

Where boys were stuck in the chimney methods of extrication included pouring water down the chimney, attaching a rope to the boy's leg, if exposed, and pulling, or pushing down from above with a pole, and, as a last resort, breaking open the chimney-breast. The Royal Commission's Report in 1863 recommended the compulsory modification of flues to make them amenable to brushes, the licensing of sweeps, and stiffer penalties for the illegal employment of children.

What were the numbers of child sweeps? Lord Shaftesbury in 1854 claimed there were some 4,000 nationwide. The Royal Commission in 1866 reckoned 2,000, chiefly 5–10 years old.[21] The 1861 census gave a grossly understated return of child sweeps at 67 under 9 and 569 aged 10–14, probably because their illegality at those ages inhibited disclosure to the enumerators.

The publication of Charles Kingsley's *The Water Babies* in 1863 with its depiction of the pathetic boy sweep Tom at the mercy of his master Grimes helped to jolt the public conscience, and Lord Shaftesbury sponsored another Act in 1964 to prohibit altogether the employment of boy assistants under 16 (even if not sent up chimneys), though it contained no licensing provision.[22] Again, however, magistrates ignored it.

Punch magazine joined the campaign, addressing itself to the public hypocrisy and blatant persistence of illegal practices. Lord Shaftesbury and the *Climbing Boys' Advocate* continued to expose cases of cruelty and suffocation into the early 1870s, but it was the George Brewster case in 1875 that proved the final catalyst. Brewster had been illegally apprenticed to his master, William Wyer, at the age of 12. The boy had been sent up a chimney at Fulbourn Hospital at Cambridge, and got stuck in a flue 6 inches by 12. Wyer finally extricated him, but the boy died soon after from congestion of the lungs and windpipe with soot. Wyer was jailed for 6 months for employing an under-age boy. Shaftesbury cited this case (which had been reported in the Establishment newspaper *The Times*) when promoting his 1875 Act which now required certificates from the police for all practising sweeps and their employees, and expressly imposed on the police the duty of enforcing the 1840 and 1864 Acts.

This measure, combined with improvements in the flue design, was to kill off the horrors of the boy sweep system. In the 1890s Charles Booth could say that apprenticeship (which in any case was confined to lads of 16 and over) was now virtually obsolete in London though surviving in the north;[23] for the demand for sweeps generally had declined with the use of gas and paraffin.

7

THEATRICAL, CIRCUS AND FAIRGROUND CHILDREN

When Dickens introduced his readers to the child actress Ninetta Crummles as the bogus 'Infant Phenomenon' in *Nicholas Nickleby*,[1] he was caricaturing the use that would have been well known to him as a keen amateur actor, of the drawing power of precocious child performers. Edmund Kean and Sarah Siddons had started as child actors. William Betty (1791–1874) was starring in adult roles as a child prodigy in the early 1800s; at 13 he was playing Hamlet, Romeo and Richard III![2] Around fifty years later Ellen Terry played the Duke of York in *Richard III* when only 6, and her sister Kate played Arthur in *King John* before she was 10.[3]

The 1861 census records as actors, acrobats, dancers and so on about 30 5–9-year-olds and 100 10–14-year-olds in England and Wales, but this is certainly a gross understatement; there was a very high seasonal demand for children in pantomime; perhaps the migratory nature of theatrical companies caused them to slip through the enumeration net. In the 1880s it was reckoned that there were 'as many as' 1,000 theatrical children in London alone.[4]

Lord Shaftesbury was to raise the specific issue of cruelty and physical danger to child acrobats from the early 1870s, and the moral dangers to and alleged exploitation of children in theatrical work were to be canvassed in the 1880s by the emerging child protection movement.

There was then no restriction at all on the employment of children at any age for any hours in theatrical work, except for the requirements of school attendance under the 1870 and 1880 Education Acts. However, parents and theatrical managers found a loophole in the law: children who were sent to fee-paying 'private adventure' schools could be trained and rehearsed under the veil of a sham education.[5] Ellen Barlee's *Pantomime Waifs* (1884) was an emotional plea on behalf of stage children. Pantomime children rehearsed for months without pay in the season, and might perform up to midnight. The raffish, bohemian atmosphere of theatre life, and prancing in scanty clothes on stage, loosened girls' morals. Youngsters were introduced to drink, and the irregular hours and sudden transitions from hot theatres to cold night-time air outside led to ill-health. Out of season the youngsters, perniciously hooked on the tawdry glamour of stage life, kept themselves going with filling-in work such as match- or flower-making, busking before racecourse crowds, or even, Miss Barlee alleged, posing nude for photographers. When in their juvenile prime they could conceivably pick up a handsome 15s to 30s a week on stage. This spoiled them for regular employment elsewhere, and when too 'old' they were thrown on the scrap-heap.

These views were largely echoed by William Mitchell in *Rescue the Children* (1886) and by Mrs Henry Fawcett before the Royal Commission on Education in 1887. Mrs Fawcett, in seeking to rebut the defenders of child-performing, denied that the children's earnings were necessary to poor families; the children did not come from the poorest homes, since theatre producers wanted attractive, alert youngsters. But in so saying she contradicts Ellen Barlee's assertion that pantomime children came mainly from the lowest ranks of society, pushed into the work by mercenary parents. Mrs Fawcett did allude to the dangers to youngsters from undesirable 'stage-door Johnnie' types, and from being left to travel home long distances across London unaccompanied after late-night performances.[6]

Benjamin Waugh of the London Society for the Prevention of Cruelty to Children was personally convinced, however, that Barlee's allegations of cruelty were exaggerated; it was impossible to get sparkling performances by dragooning youngsters.[7] However, the society's own organ, the *Child's Guardian*, featured a number of cases of cruelty and exploitation in theatre work; in April 1888 it cited cases of children as young as 5 travelling unaccompanied by train from Crystal Palace at 10 p.m. and not reaching home till 11.30. The *Daily Telegraph* in 1888 called for a ban on very young children, and commented: 'It is a cruel shame that tiny urchins, only recently emancipated from perambulators or from their nurses' arms, should be dressed up in fantastic costumes, and rouged and whitened and drilled into capering and grimacing and flinging their little arms about, to elicit the applause of unthinking playgoers.'[8]

Gertrude Tuckwell's *The State and its Children* in 1894 gave a lower figure than Barlee's for children's earnings, ranging from 4s a week in East End theatres to £1 (for 'stars') in the West End. But she was far more favourable to the principle of child performers. Physically, she said, they were far better off than the 'haggard half-timer "doffing" in the mill'. The children liked to perform, and in circuses were often carrying on a family tradition, while those performing in 'legitimate' higher-class theatres might be receiving a valuable training for an adult career 'on the boards'. The most reputable theatrical schools and the best circuses, like 'Lord' George Sanger's, did make genuine educational provision. However, she did admit a degree of exploitation. Children in low touring companies, playing pantomime in the cheap gaffs, were worst off, 'dragged in misery and discomfort from town to town', vagrant-like, and made to beg from audiences.[9] They were often sold off by drunken mothers to anyone in the company prepared to take charge of them at the cheapest price. Miss Tuckwell cited a recent case of two children dumped and left stranded in Scotland with no money by a company that no longer needed them.

Ellen Terry (1848–1906) came from a superior theatrical family and served an infant apprenticeship in pantomime, before graduating to Shakespearean child roles at 6. Even for a dedicated young trouper the life was gruelling. She wrote later:

> Rehearsals lasted all day, Sundays included, and when there was no play running at night, until four or five next morning! I don't think any actor in those days dreamed of luncheon. How my poor little legs used to ache! Sometimes I could hardly keep my eyes open when I was on stage, and often when my scene was over, I used to creep into the green room and forget my troubles and my art . . . in delicious sleep.

But she insisted, at the turn of the century, when child performances were being condemned, that she was 'a very strong, happy, healthy child'.[10] However, she had had the support of caring parents, and was being trained for an adult career.

The arguments surrounding the exploitation issue swung to and fro. The 1887 Royal Commission on Education recommended that all public performances below 10 years old be banned, and that child performers above that age be subject to Factory Act hours (which would exclude late night performances). These proposals, as incorporated in the Prevention of Cruelty to Children Bill in 1889, were the most controversial and extensively debated parts of the bill in both Houses of Parliament.[11] The Home Office had already received deputations from groups supporting and groups opposing a ban; the latter included Bram Stoker and Henry Irving, who insisted that the stage had been 'both a nursery and a schoolroom' to some of our most distinguished actresses while of tender years.[12]

Within the House, MPs who otherwise supported the bill as a whole, and who, like Sir Richard Webster and Major Rasch, were members of the NSPCC, opposed such a sweeping ban. One MP riposted to those who seemed to think that theatre work was uniquely objectionable in compelling late nights, that they had only to visit the slums, and they would find 'hundreds of children between 11 and 12 o'clock, or even later, drifting about the doors of the gin-shops, or grovelling in the gutters with oaths and curses ringing in their ears'.[13] In the Lords the Earl of Dunraven dismissed the objections to interference with children's schooling: 'Education is not entirely an affair of blackboards and the rule of three. There is a good deal in practical example, and the kindness with which the little ones are treated in the theatre, the discipline, order and cleanliness forced upon them.'[14]

The Act in its modified final form kept a total ban on the under-7s; those between 7 and 10 required a magistrate's licence. Older children (up to 14 for boys and 16 for girls) were not to work between 10 p.m. and 5 a.m. but local authorities could narrow the prohibited hours. The question of child performers again arose around 1900 in the context of 'moonlighting' concerns, as discussed in Chapter 3. The tussle over further restrictions on theatre work on the Employment of Children Bill in 1903 was a modified repeat of 1889, but the 'high society' lobby which did not want its enjoyment of evening theatre spoiled, prevailed.[15] The Act raised the minimum age for performances to 10, and local authorities could, under the general provisions, raise the minimum to 14, but again the statutory prohibited hours could be reduced by the local authorities. There was to be continuing criticism of magistrates' varying practices in issuing performing licences, and the 1918 Education Act transferred this function to the education authorities.

A more sensitive matter in connection with theatre children was their recruitment for performances abroad. In the early 1900s there began a public scare over an alleged 'white slave traffic'; girls, it was rumoured, were being decoyed or kidnapped and ending up in brothels and harems overseas. The Children (Employment Abroad) Act of 1913 banned such recruitment under 14, and required a magistrate's licence for 14s to 16s.[16] The Act effectively put a stop to employment abroad; between 1913 and 1923 only 35 girls and 3 boys had gone abroad under licence, 29 of the girls to the Paris Folies Bergères alone.[17]

Unlike young singers, dancers and actors, child acrobats were exposed not only to far greater physical risks but also potentially to some harrowing cruelties in their training. It was alleged in the late 1880s that such abuses were increasing, because blasé audiences demanded ever more daring stunts. From infancy youngsters had their limbs 'trained' by harsh strapping, causing deformity and stunting; aching limbs and headaches were an occupational disorder. Sometimes there were serious accidents, even fatalities. One trainer forced his trainees' heads backwards through their knees by progressively shortening a strap running from a belt round their necks; a boy broke his spine as a result.[18] The master of a girl trapeze artist who had been worked to death was murdered by her incensed father. The case was reported in 1889.[19] The girl had complained before her death that whenever she became sleepy through exhaustion, her master threatened to hit her. During one performance she felt so ill that three times she dropped the little boy she was supposed to balance on her shoulders. She herself had fallen off her master's shoulders and her sister had to stand in for her when she was too ill to perform.

Lord Shaftesbury had managed, after several efforts, to get a Children's Dangerous Performances Act passed in 1879.[20] It was made illegal to employ a child under 14 to take part in any 'public exhibition or performance' which might endanger its life or limb. However, the Act was ineffective, as it was open to magistrates to interpret what constituted a potential danger; and the Act related to *performances*, not the training which preceded it. A complaint raised with the Home Secretary in 1883 revealed just how weak the Act was. A little girl in a 'human serpent' performance at Eastbourne had to bend backwards so her head passed between her knees; but the Home Secretary said this did not seem to contravene the 1879 Act.[21]

The plight of child acrobats continued to cause concern; public-spirited individuals tried to bring private prosecutions under the 1879 Act, and Lord Shaftesbury, Ellen Barlee and the NSPCC called for stronger measures. Children were being sold off by parents to trainers; professional procurers, it was alleged, were obtaining such children, and then selling them off to foreign trainers, so removing them from British jurisdiction. In one case, reported in 1894, the father of two illegitimate children had sold them to a professional baby-farmer for £150; she then sold them to a Belgian acrobat for 18s.[22] Not all parents who 'sold' or contracted their children with acrobats were necessarily uncaring and mercenary. They may have genuinely thought that this was a good opportunity for their children in a glamorous-seeming career, and may have been misled about the type of training their chldren would receive. In 1890 one Stephen Etheridge of the 'Ethardos' acrobatic troupe comprising three girls aged 10–12, was prosecuted for ill-treating the 10-year-old, who had a heart condition. She had to balance on her sister's head, turn somersaults and do the splits. The girls' father, a plumber, claimed in court that Etheridge had agreed to teach the girls dancing, music and calisthenics, not contortions.[23]

To some extent the 1889 Prevention of Cruelty to Children Act could be called in aid. Thus in that year the NSPCC was able to use the new Act against the Kimbo troupe of cyclists at Westminster Aquarium; the youngest member was 5 and she worked till 11 p.m. The law was greatly strengthened by the Prevention of Cruelty to Children Act of 1894. This now forbade the *training* of children under 16 as acrobats, contortionists and circus performers, subject to a magistrate's licence so long as they were over 7. However, no licences were needed where the children were directly employed by their parents, as would be common among circus families.[24] In 1897 dangerous *performances* were banned for boys under 16 and girls under 17.[25]

Fairground children were also at risk from serious accidents from the fairground machinery. 'Lord' George Sanger recalled how, when a boy before 1850, he was working a roundabout in his father's fair on Romney Marshes when he tore the flesh off his calf – which his father promptly sewed back on 'with a curved needle and some thick white silk thread' without anaesthetics; the graft 'took'![26]

Sanger was an exponent of the freak show, for which there had always been a grisly public taste. People flocked to see dwarfs and midgets, 'living skeletons', microcephalic imbeciles, those born without arms or legs, misshapen grotesques of every shape displayed in booths. The only alternatives for such unfortunates were the workhouse, the lunatic asylum, or incarceration in the family home where they were kept hidden away in shame. At venues like Bartholomew Fair and Greenwich Fair they were once a great attraction.[27] And a permanent freak-show exhibition in Piccadilly in 1840 was branded by *Punch* magazine as 'Deformito-mania' (though interestingly, it adopted its own name from the hunchback caricature who appeared as its cartoon symbol). Childhood was no bar to being exhibited. In 1844 Phineas T. Barnum exhibited a 25-inch-high, 12-year-old midget as 'General Tom Thumb Junior' on his visit to Britain.[28] One family butcher was recorded in 1892 as stationing his poor cretinous son outside his shop to call the prices and attract custom with his gross appearance![29] A tragic case was Joseph Merrick, the 'Elephant Man', born in Leicester in 1862. When he started work at 12 he could not hold down a job because of his distressing appearance, now diagnosed as probably an extreme form of neurofibromatosis. He entered a workhouse in 1879 but left it to drift into freak shows and it was his exhibition in a shop in Whitechapel in 1884 opposite the London Hospital that brought him to the attention of the surgeon William Treves.[30]

By the turn of the century it would seem that the public appetite for freak shows was waning. Medical advances and improved living conditions had probably been reducing the supply anyway. For example, by 1901 cretinism was found to be alleviated by treatment with thyroid extract.[31] The writer Kenneth Grahame stated in 1925: 'Perhaps the greatest change that has taken place in show life in our generation is the disappearance of freaks and monstrosities.' The last 'fat lady' he had seen was twenty years before in the West Country.[32]

8

JUVENILE STREET TRADERS

Children were so prevalent as street traders in the mid-nineteenth century that Henry Mayhew devoted a whole section of his *London Labour and the London Poor* to the subject in 1851.[1] Of course, when over a third of the population was then under 15 and there was no national compulsory schooling, it was inevitable that children should appear so conspicuously in street life. They were sent out by parents to contribute to the family income however they could, or if mistreatment by parents or employers was unbearable they ran away to fend for themselves. In the absence of a home life, they banded together for companionship, living in sordid common lodging-houses, where, before regulatory legislation, both sexes and all ages mixed promiscuously in the foetid kitchens and dormitories.[2] Those that could not afford the price of a bed slept in the streets, under arches, in doorways, or under the barrows in Covent Garden Market.

The range of articles they hawked was legion: fruit and vegetables (costermongers' leftovers sold off cheaply to the youngsters), firewood, matches, pen nibs, buttons, laces, clothes-pegs, glassware, cheap toys and flowers, to mention just a selection. In addition there were the sellers of services – the errand-runners, cab-hailers, distributors of hand-bills, crossing-sweepers, luggage touts at railway stations and shoeshine boys. Eager eyes were constantly on the watch for a chance to earn an opportunistic penny.

Their wares were often of poor quality and tricked-up for sale: sponges and vegetables might be rotten, and 'silk' braces were really cotton, for example. Children lived by their quick wits in the urban jungle. They 'grew up' precociously, though their life expectations would have been short. Inside they had been hardened

66

by their tough fate, and they were emotionally stunted. Mayhew shrewdly observed that although they formed companionships with their like, they rarely formed true friendships. As a type they were dissipated; they did not attempt to save their meagre earnings; any windfall from a good day was frittered away on binges, tobacco, beer, gambling, penny gaffs and the low girls they consorted with in the lodging-houses.

Boys greatly outnumbered girls, who were less inclined to cut and run from an unhappy home. In flower-selling, though, girls predominated. Mayhew distinguished between true flower-sellers and the crypto-prostitutes. Girls were less ragged than boys, he found (raggedness gave boys an appealing pathos to passers-by), but girls had their own wheedling ways of coaxing custom: 'please, gentleman, do buy my flowers. Poor little girl ... '

Such scenes inspired themes for parlour songs, suitably sanitized and sentimentalized to mask the real desperation of such an existence. A twee ditty of 1854 ran:

> I'm a little Flow'r Girl, Roving Wild and free,
> All the pretty maidens Far and wide know me.
> I for some have Roses, some the Lily pale;
> All with glee, do welcome me, Tripping down the vale.
> Tho' my lot be humble, I have little care;
> Cheerful and contented, All life's ills I bear.[3]

The crossing-sweeper that little Evelyn Sharp used to see from her nursery window in the 1880s could hardly have been 'cheerful and contented'; she saw the boy day after day still at his pitch when she looked out of the window in the morning and when she went to bed at 7 p.m. And the Devonshire girl Jane whose story was told by Ellen Barlee in 1863 was scarcely capable of bearing all life's ills. When her stepmother wanted to be rid of her, she tramped all the way to London at the age of 12, and took up work as a crossing-sweeper; she managed to earn anything from 6d to 3s a day but exposure undermined her health and she had to give it up after 9 months. Her fate would have been dire indeed, had not a refuge for the destitute taken her under its wing.

Coster children formed a distinct sub-group; they helped sell their parents' fruit and vegetables as they trundled their donkey carts through the streets. Unlike the ragged street urchins, they liked to dress 'flash' in emulation of their parents: cord jackets, trousers tight at the knee, good boots, a showy kingsman (a large handkerchief), and a plush skull cap were *de rigueur*. At 13, Mayhew said, a boy knew enough about the trade to strike out on his own account, and at 14 might start cohabiting with a girl.

Young pedlars were in modern parlance 'street-wise'; they knew the best pitches; they knew how to bargain with their suppliers and to trick the police. Though their lives were precarious they were not self-pitying. Their education was sparse, perhaps a rudimentary literacy picked up at the ragged school. One lad acknowledged he had heard of God and 'a book called the Bible' but 'didn't know what it was all about' and 'didn't mind to know'. He did not think the Queen had as much power as the Lord Mayor 'or as Mr Norton, as was the Lambeth beak, and perhaps still is'.

A fair proportion of the street sellers were of ethnic minority origin. Mayhew mentions Irish fruit-sellers, Jewish clothes-dealers, Italian organ boys and Dutch girl broom-sellers. Britain had been absorbing a huge wave of Irish immigrant refugees from the potato famine, and young 'Irish Cockneys', born in Britain, subsequently appear to have figured disproportionately as delinquents, vagrants and thieves.[4] The far smaller numbers of Italian children formed an entirely different problem as the slaves of *padroni* ('masters'), brought over from southern Italy, to be exploited in a strange country as exotic street entertainers and organ-grinders,[5] as we shall see in the next chapter. By the early 1900s English youths had moved in on organ-grinding, though ice-cream-selling remained an Italian preserve.[6]

Conflicting impressions are given of the extent of street selling by Jewish children. Mayhew certainly has references to young Jews in street trading; however, he notes that even amid the squalor of Whitechapel and Petticoat Lane the Jews had strong family bonds and children seldom became outcasts from the home. In contrast to the Irish and costermongers, Jewish girls rarely went in for street trading. Robert Sherard in 1905, writing at a time of fresh waves of Jewish immigration from Russia, noted that destitute new arrivals sent their children out to peddle in Whitechapel and Stepney to help support the family. However, it seems that the Jews were thrifty; the children's earnings went towards the purchase of a barrow, the first step up for the family. Against these impressions, however, Robert Peacock, the Chief Constable of Manchester, stated in 1902 that in his city – another great centre of Jewish immigration – very few Jewish children were sent out as street traders.[7] Though it is fairly certain that Jews on the whole took more care of their children in early childhood than their Gentile neighbours, possibly the youngsters were employed more in Jewish-owned sweatshops as they got older rather than in street trading. A significant point also is that Jews were not drunkards; parental drink-money as a motive for sending children on to the streets would not have existed in their case.

A distinctive facet of street trading was the appearance from 1851 of philanthropically organized 'brigades'. This originated as an offshoot of the ragged schools. John Macgregor, a barrister and ragged school teacher, came up with an idea in 1850 for employing young street-Arabs to their own advantage during the coming Great Exhibition, when tens of thousands of visitors would be coming to London. In 1851 he set up the Shoeblack Society. Urchins were selected and allotted to pitches, and had to wear a uniform in place of their rags. Some of the raw recruits at the start were rough indeed. One was assigned to give the others a demonstration, and, says Macgregor's biographer: 'This first professor of the black art did his work well, notwithstanding the fact that he had a bullet in his neck which he got in a juvenile burglary.'[8]

As it developed, the society established a hostel for the boys, to which they contributed out of their earnings. Profits went into personal bank accounts, and the hostel was governed by strict rules regarding cleanliness, manners, punctuality, religious observance and so forth. The object was to recondition the boys through regulated habits of thrift and smartness, so that when they outgrew the brigade they would be in a better position to hold down respectable jobs as adults. The scheme even included a competitive element by promotion to and demotion from the more lucrative pitches. An auction scheme for pitches was introduced, it seems, to stop the boys lying about their earnings.[9] The brigades were approved by the Home Office and the Metropolitan Police, who favoured brigade boys and harassed independents. Among these 'freebooters' there was universal resentment, and brigade boys were looked on as class renegades: they were jeered at, pelted and had their equipment sabotaged with flour. But the idea caught on and spread to other cities. In Glasgow, the businessman and philanthropist William Quarrier copied the London scheme in 1864, having first entertained a party of tatterdemalion prospects to a grand tea at his home.[10] In Liverpool, the Catholic priests did not like the idea of Catholic boys living in non-Catholic hostels, and the Church set up its own brigades.

The brigades flourished for about half a century. Around 1856–7 they were earning nearly £3,000 a year in London;[11] by the early 1890s this stood at £12,000 in London, and nearly £76,000 nationwide.[12] Dr Barnardo copied the idea and set up his own Shoeblack Brigade for boys resident in his Limehouse Home.[13] In London around 1904 there were different brigades for different parts of London, each with its own distinctive uniform; the Central London Society's hostel could accommodate 44 boys and had a schoolroom for 100.[14]

The schemes were extended to other street trades. In Glasgow Quarrier set up brigades for newsboys and railway parcel-carriers.[15] A Newsboys Home had existed in Liverpool since the 1870s, and in 1900 one in London's Grays Inn Road was charging 2d per night.[16]

The expanding number of boy newsvendors at the end of the last century, created by the development of the cheap popular dailies, starting with the *Daily Mail* in 1896,[17] had made them much more conspicuous in the streets. By the Edwardian period they were to become by far the biggest single group of young street traders, employing some 23,000 lads in England and Wales in 1911.[18] Suburban schoolboys earning pocket money by delivering papers were not seen as a social problem; the 'Arab' types of the city centres, who made a living at it, were a different proposition. Newsvending was a dead-end job, seen as exposing its practitioners to a seedy life of common lodging-houses, drinking and petty gambling.

Before the age of the telephone there was a demand for boy messengers, and commercial companies were set up to employ them. This too was obviously dead-end work, and the companies took no further interest in the lads once they were old enough to start demanding more adult wages, and they were dismissed.[19] This, too, prompted philanthropic brigade schemes, which by 1900 now included waste paper collection and wood-chopping (both Barnardo projects), 'brooming' (sweeping pavements in front of shops) and for girls 'stepping' (sweeping steps).

How successful were the brigades in helping their lads make good later on? The ragged school movement which had spawned them offered some hope of assisted emigration and a fresh start in the colonies, as did Dr Barnardo's, Quarrier's and other orphanage charities later. In 1902 Arthur Maddison of the Reformatory and Refuge Union acknowledged that the Shoeblack Brigades had 'started many a lad on a useful career';[20] one former shoeblack, Mark Knowles, rose to become a barrister and temperance campaigner.[21] However, an expert on juvenile employment problems, J. H. Whitehouse, stated in 1908 of the London Homes for shoeblacks: 'We cannot find that the boys which [sic] pass through these Homes are helped to a satisfactory career in their later lives.' Some emigrated or went into the armed forces but 'there is a great number of whom no satisfactory account can be given'.[22]

By the turn of the century the brigades were past their peak, except perhaps for newsvendors.[23] The shoeblacks in particular had gone into steep decline. The multiplication of initially well-paid dead-end jobs for school-leavers in the late nineteenth century, the extension of compulsory schooling, the industrial schools and orphanage movement which had been taking urchins off the streets, not to mention the rival attractions of newsvending, all conspired to stifle the shoeblacks. The 9 London shoeblacks' hostels of the late 1870s had dwindled to 2 by 1904, and one of those was for the adult handicapped.[24] The 1910 Departmental Committee on the Employment of Children numbered only 12 shoeblacks in urban centres outside the LCC and did not even bother to list it as a contemporary children's street trade.[25]

The brigades in general were now being superseded by more sophisticated approaches to youth training. The very strong street-Arabs of Mayhew's day were now the 'moonlighters' outside school but did not depend for a complete livelihood on street selling; the homeless ones were now more extensively housed in institutions or were being sent on emigration schemes. It was the older ones who still needed the help – those recently discharged from orphanages, for example. Industrial Homes were now being established by charity where such youths could be trained in specific skills, such as cookery, leatherwork and tailoring. The brigades in their earlier form had merely provided rudimentary work-relief and a hoped-for civilizing experience. In 1911 in London there were 40 Industrial Homes, accommodating some 2,000 youngsters of 14 and over; the Edinburgh Industrial Brigade Home for Working Lads accommodated 142 boys and arranged apprenticeships for 14–22-year-olds.[26] Even where such youths had regular jobs it was necessary to steer them towards respectable shelter and by the 1890s philanthropy had stepped into this area, too, with model lodgings for working boys, though they were insufficient to meet the demand.[27]

Mayhew had posed the question: if street waifs were legally barred from trading, how else would they survive? The life-style was long recognized to be closely associated with begging, delinquency and prostitution. In 1881 two-thirds of the children committed to industrial schools and reformatories at the instance of the Manchester School Board had a street trading background.[28] A miscellany of restrictive laws was to aim at reinforcing school attendance requirements and protecting youngsters from parental exploitation, exposure and undesirable associations on the streets at night; but they failed to address Mayhew's question and were to prove only partially effective in the long run. The first measure appears to have been the Scottish Education Act of 1878 which banned street trading by the under-10s altogether, but it proved a dead letter.[29] In England there was a succession of local Acts applying to different boroughs, starting with the Manchester Corporation Act of 1882.[30] This barred the under-14s from trading after dusk, unless they had a minimum education standard. Since education became compulsory in 1880, trading by schoolchildren in school hours would have been illegal anyway, but this measure recognized that out-of-school trading would persist and merely sought to ban it when children ought to have been in bed. Other local Acts in the 1880s, for example those for Birmingham and Sheffield, empowered the municipalities to set permitted hours and ages by by-laws.

The 1889 Prevention of Cruelty to Children Act was the first national law; it banned street trading altogether below 10 years old, and excluded the hours from 10 p.m. to 5 a.m. for boys of 10–13 and girls of 10–15. But child street trading had its strong defenders among those who argued that children's earnings were a necessary supplement for poor families and, as a concession, the Act allowed local authorities to modify the prohibited hours. A great weakness, however, was that as the Act was directed against adult exploiters, not the children themselves, child infractors could not be prosecuted, only those who 'caused or procured' their trading; and this was very difficult to prove if parents stoutly insisted that they were ignorant of their child's activities in the street. The 1894 Cruelty Act raised the minimum prohibited age to 11, extended the prohibited hours and now made parents liable who merely 'allowed' their children to trade illegally.

However, throughout the 1880s and 1890s legislation was virtually a dead letter, except for a few towns like Manchester, Cardiff and Salford where the authorities enforced it vigorously.

Edith Hogg's article on 'Schoolchildren as wage earners' in 1897[31] again rekindled the issue, which was now linked to the growing concern about the effect on the country's economic efficiency of large numbers of school-leavers drifting into initially attractively paid but unskilled dead-end jobs. Liverpool was seen as a microcosm of the problem. In the early 1880s Samuel Smith, the city's MP and popularly known as the 'Arabs' MP' reckoned that of Liverpool's 80,000 children of school age 10,000 were inadequately clothed, housed and fed.[32] Notorious for its swarms of ragged street traders and beggars, the city had established the country's first local Society for the Prevention of Cruelty to Children in 1884. It lacked the legal power under existing local Acts to frame by-laws against street trading, but in the 1890s local private initiatives began to address the problem. A short-lived Newsboys Home between 1892 and 1895 was found to make no impression on the problem. Then in 1895 a charitable Clothing Association was formed, in imitation of schemes recently introduced in Edinburgh and Birmingham.[33] The police acted as agents reporting to the association cases of street children in need. The clothes were specially marked and pawnbrokers were enjoined not to accept them as pledges. However, this benevolent intent to relieve the plight of shivering street traders went wide of the mark; for the young gamins, the cultivated pathos of rags was an aid to trade and they resisted this charity. In 1898 and 1902 Liverpool obtained new Corporation Acts which empowered it to license street traders.[34] However, the Home Office was very chary about giving local authorities free discretion in withholding licences. By-laws had to be approved by the Home Secretary, and when conditions were met, licences were to be granted automatically; they must not be used to put the squeeze on child street trading. Evidently the government accepted that trading was a *symptom* of family need and could not be legislated away. Liverpool banned trading under the age of 11, and licensed boys under 14 and girls under 16 were banned after dusk. Children might be required to reside in approved hostels as a condition; this failed owing to resentment among the children and opposition from Catholics to the possibility of Catholic children being made to reside in homes of other denominations. Licensed traders had to wear special badges, and raggedness was banned; if in genuine need they must accept clothes from the Clothing Association. Manchester also acquired licensing powers in 1901, even though Liverpool seemed to be making no headway then with its new powers.[35] In 1901 Liverpool's Chief Constable spoke before the 1901 Inter-Departmental Committee on the Employment of Schoolchildren about the 'positive scandal' of children being 'sent round at all hours of the night, selling papers half-clothed, up to ... ten o'clock' and how over the last three years an annual average of 1,144 children were picked up for trading outside the hours permitted under the 1894 Cruelty Act.[36] There were insufficient inspectors to police the by-laws, and most traders were still unlicensed. Until 1911 London had a poor record in enforcing its own by-laws; in 1908 there were said to be 12,000–20,000 child traders in the capital, many of them ragged and dirty.[37] From 1911 a stricter clampdown was claimed to have driven some 10,000 boys and 785 girls off the streets.[38] Various nationwide estimates of the number of street traders were mooted before 1914, but they can only be guesses, owing to the unknown extent of illegal trading. The 1901 committee gave an underestimated figure of 25,000 of school age in England and Wales; Frederic Keeling suggested up to 27,000 *licensed* traders for 1912. The 1911 census[39] returned 16,174 boys and 267 girls under 17 selling newspapers alone but this is bound to be an understatement as 'illegals' would have been less likely to admit it.

The 1903 Employment of Children Act which arose out of recommendations of the Inter-Departmental Committee broadly gave all local authorities similar (permissive) powers to those already enjoyed by cities like Liverpool and Manchester. Street trading under 11 was totally banned, and licensing conditions applied to youths from 11 to 16. In the case of boys the Home Office disapproved of any selectivity in licensing.[40] For example, licences could not be withheld on the grounds of a boy's bad character, as street trading might be his only chance to start making an honest living. There was still a central government caution about restricting the right to trade, where boys were driven to it by necessity; the 1903 Act[41] empowered local authorities to narrow the statutory prescribed night-time hours. However, it did provide for a wide range of penalties against the child offenders (fines, industrial schools, or committal to the custody of a 'fit person', such as an orphanage) and also against the adults who encouraged them; parents could be held liable for failing to take due care that the children did not trade. Where girls were concerned, local authorities were encouraged to use more discretion in awarding licences as they were considered at greater moral risk on the streets.[42]

The assumption that juvenile street trading was a matter of survival for poor families was challenged by some. It was common knowledge that children were put out by the most dissolute parents to earn drink-money, with a threat of a beating if they did not bring enough home. In 1905 Robert Sherard was shown a barber's strap with brass hooks attached; this had been used on a 9-year-old Manchester girl who had not sold enough matches in the street, blinding her as a result.[43]

Whilst the parental income of street traders could be as low as 12s a week around 1900,[44] Grace Paton pointed out on the other hand in 1912 that only 11 per cent of licensed street traders in Leeds, and 10 per cent in Birmingham, were the children of widows; this indicated to her a parallel with the practice of comparatively well-paid northern textile workers of sending their children as half-timers into the mills. Witnesses before the 1910 Departmental Committee on the working of the 1903 Act also gave varying impressions of the degree of family need. A Belfast observer found that many came from homes that were very poor, intemperate, or indifferent, but that an 'unduly large' number had parents earning 30s–40s a week (then a very good wage).[45] Glasgow and Liverpool observers tended to emphasize the genuine poverty of the parents.[46] School board officers at Glasgow found that three-quarters of the 12–14-year-olds were handing their earnings over to their parents,[47] but an Edinburgh day industrial school superintendent stated that the extent of sharing earnings with parents varied from home to home. There were many cases where parents initially sent out their children, only to lose control of them as they turned wild and kept their earnings for cigarettes, sweets and the music-halls.[48]

The Edwardian boy street trader had many characteristics in common with his counterpart of Mayhew's day. George Haw, a sympathetic observer, characterized the street boy as a survivor in 1910:

> He is full of amazing resource, the London boy. Let him lose
> a job in the morning and he turns light-heartedly to selling

matches or newspapers in the afternoon. He will hawk for a coster, mind a low shop, keep watch at a corner of a street where a bookmaker takes bets ... and think nothing of beginning the next week by riding an advertising tricycle through the streets for twopence an hour. If all else fails and he happens to be full grown, he will try the Army.

Haw gives too jaunty an impression; for such a youngster's life was destined to be one of insecurity, aimless drift and seediness; a common lodging-house bed when he had the money, and a railway arch when he hadn't. For some time it was a life of ill-health. Sherard recalled in 1905 seeing 'a little boy of nine who had a chocolate box slung round his neck, offering cough lozenges for sale under the dripping wall of the East India Dock Road at one o'clock in the morning. By the irony of things he was coughing in the most distressing manner'.

However, a minority of shrewder ones might cut their teeth in entrepreneurship. Margaret McMillan the educationalist observed how some northern children, still too young to become mill half-timers, were employing other children to sell newspapers for them.[49] 'They take risks and chances with their small capital, keep accounts after their own fashion, and are in fact genuine employers of labour.' McMillan found that street vendors were quicker and brighter at school than the factory half-timers, as the latter were dulled by the monotony of machine labour; however, other opinions were held by teachers who found that the long, irregular hours in the streets affected children's health and concentration at school, and made them recalcitrant, restless, artful dodgers.[50] Olive Hargreaves of Sheffield told the 1910 inquiry of the boys' unwholesome precocity:

> Each boy has his own gang and they take a pride in dodging the police and living a life of lawlessness .... They are highly organized in their own way. There is a private gambling club run by street traders behind a certain ice-cream shop well known to me. Through a regular system of insurance, fines for gambling, theft &c are met out of the common fund. Many 'books' are made in coppers by young bookmakers.

One boy, she said, had been given 10s by a kind-hearted but misguided man to buy fruit as stock for selling, but the money had straightaway gone on betting.[51] The moral dangers might lie in the stock-in-trade; the sporting papers sold by many boys introduced them to gambling; and they learned how to cheat the public with shoddy goods or short-change tricks. The practice of entering bars at night to peddle accustomed youngsters to the pub atmosphere and was feared to hold dangers of prostitution for girls. This loophole in trading law was finally closed by the 1908 Children's Act, barring children under 14 from entering pub bars.

The descent to a criminal record was easy. Railway baggage and parcel touts were frequently had up before the courts for obstruction and railway trespass.[52] In just one case from Leeds during 1912–13 a 15-year-old street trader who had already infringed his licence six times, and had a record for gambling and begging, was convicted of larceny by finding a lady's handbag containing money and valuables. He had distributed the money among his family and other traders, and squandered the rest on himself.[53]

Young Edwardian street traders remained overwhelmingly male.[54] The degree of raggedness seems to have varied from town to town, according to how vigilantly the by-laws and licence conditions were enforced. Manchester was said in 1910 to have a good record in watchfulness, and its police force had a special plain-clothes squad to look out for offenders; its traders were said to have both declined in numbers and improved in dress as a result.[55] Earnings are a difficult thing to generalize about; 5s to 6s a week appears to have been standard, but it was said that in Manchester around 1902 the full-time newsvendors could pick up anything from 10s to 18s a week.[56] So much would have depended on the siting of any pitch, the hours worked, the season, the weather and the passing appeal of the individual vendor and his articles. Hours also varied widely. There were disturbing cases of children working to midnight or beyond, but a limited survey reproduced by the 1910 Departmental Committee[57] suggested that the bulk traded 20 hours or less a week; presumably these were still at school, but we cannot tell from this whether the same children were *also* engaged in other forms of non-street-trade moonlighting. Trade specialities depended in part on physical capabilities. Stronger, older lads would go in for parcel- and suitcase-carrying, or dragging barrel-organs around the streets,[58] match- and flower-selling tended to be for the weak or crippled, and in the juvenile street sub-culture match-selling was despised as the lowest form of selling; Sherard stated that match-sellers could pick up only a shilling a day, working on the streets till midnight. As in Mayhew's day, flower-selling remained a girls' speciality.

By 1908 the 1903 Act was seen by concerned groups to have been too weak to check street trading. At the time that the great Children's Bill of 1908 was passing through Parliament, the government felt that it had too much on its plate to incorporate stronger street-trading provisions, and referred the matter subsequently to the aforementioned Departmental Committee, which reported in 1910. Its findings confirmed the failings of the Act's permissiveness. Where by-laws had been framed, this was generally in the larger urban centres where the problem was more serious; thus 50 of the 74 county boroughs in England and Wales had by-laws, but only a quarter of the smaller boroughs. Even where by-laws existed they were, with honourable exceptions like Manchester, poorly enforced. Local middle-class councillors were not that concerned; and working-class residents were hostile to restrictive regulation.[59] The underlying social concerns about delinquency and 'blind-alley' employment permeate the inquiry, but one bright spot was that for the majority of youngsters street vending was an adolescent phase, and fell off after 14 when they had left school and were able to start full-time jobs. Thus, in England and Wales, outside London, there were 15,321 licensees below 14 and 6,704 aged 14–16.[60] However, it is possible that the street-vending experience was a contributory factor in inclining many school-leavers to take the first easy-money but blind-alley job that came along.

There were defenders of street trading. Newspaper proprietors were a vocal lobby against curbing boy newsvendors; and a minority view on the committee itself believed that street selling was a lesser evil than the stuffy sweatshops poorer children would otherwise be forced into – and that it *kept* lads out of mischief and vagrancy! (This despite the obvious link between street selling and outright begging.) The Majority Report called for the 1903 Act to be made mandatory, with a definite ban on boys to 17 and girls to at least 18. The Minority Report was less sweeping; such bans should apply only when alternative work was available, and from 14 a condition of a licence should be attendance at a continuation school (that is, part-time further education).

A succession of bills between 1910 and 1913 variously followed elements of both sets of recommendations, but they were all 'crowded out' or abandoned in the face of intense opposition, most notably from the newspaper interests.[61] In the idealistic aftermath of the First World War, when it was hoped to improve prospects and widen opportunities for the masses, there was another attack on juvenile street trading. Youngsters' energies were to be channelled exclusively into schooling. The 1918 Education Act banned street trading under 14 altogether; and local education authorities were made responsible for by-laws under the 1903 Act.[62] Subsequent inter-war legislation seems to have brought about the virtual extinction of the juvenile street-Arab by the 1930s.[63]

9

WAIFS AND BEGGARS

Closely bound up with the question of street trading was the perennial problem of child begging. Victorian figures and definitions in this area are imprecise but the 1851 census indicated that over 800,000 of the 4 million or so 3–12-year-olds in England and Wales were neither at work nor receiving any schooling; and many of those 'at school' were intermittent attenders. This large shadowy group would have formed the urchin population of street pedlars, beggars, scavengers and pilferers.[1] In 1848 Lord Ashley (later, Lord Shaftesbury) compassed a figure of 30,000 *shelterless* street-Arabs in London's population of 2.5 million.[2] Assuming that each one begged at some time, this still leaves out of account those child beggars living in common lodging-houses or slum tenements. Nearly thirty years later Dr Barnardo could still estimate some 30,000 homeless youngsters in the capital.[3] Child beggars in fact formed a high proportion of all beggars in the country. Just how eagle-eyed and rampant they were can be gauged from Charles Dickens's account in *The Uncommercial Traveller* (1865).[4] Walking through the street, he once bumped into and knocked over a ragged little scrap. When he stopped to help him up and give him some money out of sympathy, fifty similar ragamuffins

> were about me in a moment, begging, tumbling, fighting, clamouring, yelling, shivering in their nakedness and hunger. The piece of money I had put into the claw of the child I had overturned was clawed out of it, and was again clawed out of that wolfish grip, and again out of that, and soon I had no notion in what part of the obscene scuffle in the mud of rags and legs and dirt, the money might be.

Parental drunkenness, neglect and brutality were common

reasons for staying out, or fleeing from home altogether. The *Child's Guardian* of March 1887, for example, contained a series of cases under the heading 'Eleven drunkards' drudges', about children sent out to beg by their parents. In one case a 13-year-old boy who had been forced to this extremity by a father who was generally in work, told those who had charge of him when arrested, 'I dare not go home till I get a shilling. Father knocks me about sometimes with a poker.' Subsequent investigation proved this to be true.

At a time when mortality rates were high, the premature death of a parent might soon lead to replacement by a step-parent, and this was often another source of misery, through the step-parent's direct cruelty or pernicious influence on the surviving parent. Henry Mayhew was told by one 18-year-old runaway that it was after his widowed father remarried that he began mistreating the boy – chaining him to a shed and to his bed, and feeding him on bread and water for a month.[5] Even children from comfortable backgrounds could be reduced to beggary in this way. At Leeds Assizes in 1887 a prosperous Barnsley man was convicted of causing the death of his son by neglect. When, as a widower, he had remarried, his new wife did not want his three children. He put them out of the home into a squalid hovel, supplying the oldest child with herrings to sell in the street as sole income. It was the death of her younger brother from consumption, aggravated by the father's callous indifference, that prompted the latter's arrest.[6]

From 1866 Dr Thomas John Barnardo began his nightly excursions in London's East End, picking up waifs to take them to his refuge in Stepney. According to his own account, he had first been alerted to the problem of juvenile homelessness by a boy at the ragged school where he had been teaching. The boy had been hanging about after school closed, and when Barnardo asked him why, the lad said that he had no home to go to. He took his intrigued teacher to Houndsditch, where Barnardo met a whole group of lads who slept rough there. The story bears a curious resemblance to an episode at Deansgate in Manchester, where in 1869 two little boys lingered after a ragged school meeting, and confessed to the enquiring teacher that they were homeless; one slept under a railway arch and the other up an old staircase.[7] This discovery was to lead to the foundations of the Boys' and Girls' Refuges and Homes in Manchester and Salford just as Barnardo's Houndsditch encounter was to inspire him to found the Barnardo

Home. Dr Barnardo told in 1871 of two brothers, Arthur and Bobbie, whom he found sleeping in the hallway of a slum tenement. They told him they had run away from a villainous older brother who had used them in his criminal enterprises. They fled from their brother at a tramps' kitchen in Brighton, tramping all the way to London and surviving by begging and eating garbage. Barnardo took them to his refuge, and later, to save them from the clutches of their brother who had learned of their whereabouts, they were sent out to Canada where they both did well.[8]

The degradation that could lead parents to desert their offspring was captured by Evelyn Sharp when as a London girl in the 1880s, watching the street scene from her nursery window, she once saw a tramping family. The slatternly mother was clutching a wailing baby, while behind a ragged toddler was trying to keep up with her parents, who, 'dehumanized by physical wretchedness' paid no heed to her. Though the child tried to catch up, the gap got wider, and the panic-stricken child, powerless to ward off the calamity that seemed inevitable, appeared to be outstripped by the time they vanished from sight.'[9] James Runciman, a Southwark elementary school teacher, described in 1885 the physical condition of the poorest children arriving at school in winter mostly without breakfast. Of a limping girl: 'Her frock was made of rotten-looking brown material; it was split from neck to ankle, but a piece of string tied it round the waist. Two flapping segments fell apart and showed that the child had no underclothing, and her legs were red and raw.' A bareheaded lad followed the girl: 'His bony shanks were thrust into large boots that squelched and made sucking noises on the pavement; his arms were fairly wrung together in an agony of cold, and the crooked limpness of his gait made him seem a cripple.'

The sight of so much child pathos inspired an extensive popular literature to prick the consciences of the more fortunate. At the poetic level, Elizabeth Barrett Browning's 'The Cry of the Children' reads into the souls of the mites, 'Spilt like blots about the city', a premature world-weariness:

> 'Your old earth,' they say, 'is very dreary';
> 'Our young feet,' they say, 'are very weak.'
> Few paces have we taken, yet are weary —
> Our grave-rest is very far to seek.'

Adelaide Proctor's 'Homeless' contrasts the plight of homeless children with the comforts of cosseted pet animals:

> My dogs sleep warm in their blankets
> Safe from the dark and wind;
> All the beasts in our Christian England
> Find pity where they go;
> Those are only the homeless children
> Who are wandering to and fro.

Mawkish parlour songs were infused with the same sentiment. One mid-Victorian example, 'The Children's Home',[10] tells of a bond between a well-off but sickly boy in his garden, and a beggar girl outside the railings. One day she finds that he has passed away and the song ends on the (comforting?) theme that high-born or low, we end up alike with the angels:

> And the high-born child and the beggar
> Passed homeward side by side
> For the ways of men are narrow,
> But the gates of Heav'n are wide.

'Won't You Buy My Pretty Flow'r?'[11] of the same period tells of the little flower-seller appealing to self-intent passers-by:

> Not a loving word to cheer her
> From the passers-by is heard.
> Not a friend to linger near her
> With a heart by pity stirr'd.
> Homeward goes the tide of fashion
> Seeking pleasure's pleasant bow'rs.
> None to hear with sad compassion
> 'Won't you buy my pretty flow'rs?'

In prose, Charles Dickens's *Oliver Twist*, of course, comes immediately to mind as a depiction of the life of the feral gangs of boy thieves who infested the streets of Georgian and early Victorian cities. James Greenwood's *The Little Raggamuffins* (first published in 1866) incorporates common origins of waifdom and delinquency. The subject of the story has been brought up in a notorious slum district, Frying Pan Alley, Clerkenwell. He detests his stepmother, a bibulous Irish woman who on one occasion drinks away some money left by the father in the house for food. She persuades the boy to take the blame for accidentally losing the money in the street, and promises to vouch for him when the father returns. However, she lets him down, and the boy is severely beaten by the father. His stepmother maltreats him and repeatedly accuses him of stealing his younger sister's food. Finally, he walks out and becomes a barrow boy's assistant. The rest of the story is about his life as a street boy; how he descends to thieving and ends up in a reformatory.

There was also a plethora of 'street-Arab' literature aimed specifically at the young. It was maudlin, pious and strongly Christian in tone, often disseminated through Sunday School, Bible classes and the Band of Hope as recommended reading and as prizes. Little waifs were portrayed as idealized models of virtue, spiritually overcoming their hardships to achieve sublimation on earth or into heaven; and on their way bringing out the better natures of adults by their example. The Society for Promoting Christian Knowledge (SPCK) and the Religious Tract Society (RTS) produced a great deal of this literature, and it was the latter that published the archetypal story of this genre, Hesba Stretton's *Jessica's First Prayer* in 1855. Jessica is a little waif who hangs about a coffee stall. The stallholder gives her morsel out of pity and befriends her. She is drawn to a church where he is an attendant, and is captivated by the spiritual atmosphere. She becomes very devout but cannot attend the services in her rags, until the minister, who is deeply touched by her piety, gives her decent clothes. Jessica falls very ill in her hovel and her parents are uncaring. But she is visited by the stallholder who adopts her when she recovers, and she eagerly and regularly attends church thereafter.

Mary Sewell, a prolific writer of verse, included in her *Ballads for Children* (1868) 'Mother's Last Words'. A dying mother enjoins her two sons, Christy and John, to keep faith with God. They are left orphans and survive as crossing-sweepers. They remain true to the church, despite the mockery of other street children. With the onset of winter their earnings as crossing-sweepers fall off. Christy's feet suffer badly and John desperately steals a pair of shoes for him, but their Christian consciences compel them to return them. A kindly lady rescues them from their misery and takes them under her wing. John is apprenticed and saved from poverty, but Christy weakens and dies:

> He left behind his wasted form;
> He rose above the toiling folk,

Above the cross upon St. Paul's,
Above the fog, above the smoke.

This sentimentality and this moralism even found their way into elementary school readers. Nelson's *New Royal Reader* of 1884[12] has a passage on kindness to a beggar and a parable about two young crossing-sweepers who foraged for scraps. One found a bruised apple, but passed it to his younger friend for the first bite, and the homily concludes:

A noble lesson this should teach
Dear children unto you,
Do unto others as you would
That they to you should do.

Even as late as the 1890s the publishers Frederick Warne & Co. considered it profitable to print a series of street-Arab stories with titles like *Old Joe, Poor Mike* and *Chips*. But the multiplication of orphanages and refuges since the 1860s, the work of the NSPCC, and more enlightened policies of fostering out by the Poor Law were by the early 1900s to provide practical ways of assisting waifs and strays that outmoded the mawkish wallowing in 'street-Arab' literature. None the less, in Birmingham around 1910–11 there were still an estimated 15,000 street boys.[13] At Liverpool at the same date, though the ragged, barefoot urchins had been swept off the landing-stages by the begging and street-trading ordinances, they still thronged the backstreets where 'a child with shoes or stockings is the exception'.[14]

Of course the real-life flesh and blood (or should one say, skin and bone?) street urchins were not the spiritual souls depicted in literature. They had to be quick, cunning and unscrupulous to survive and collectively there was a mischievous animal vitality about them. When Henry Mayhew assembled 150 6–9-year-old Arabs to a meeting to hear their views on the idea of a Home for them, he found them rumbustiously uncontrollable at first.[15] They catcalled and interrupted with 'witticisms'. 'Swe-ee-p,' they yelled when a negro boy joined their ranks, followed by peals of laughter. Over half the group had been to prison; some had been flogged but this had served only to enhance their status within their circle and hardened them in their ways. Mayhew did not find them any more unhealthy than youngsters with indoor occupations, as street life kept them exposed to the open air. And despite the foetidness and noise of the common lodging-houses, they slept soundly, exhausted by the day's foraging. Their diet, though, was unhealthy, for on the occasions that they were in funds, they splashed out on binges of innutritious luxuries, like cake and pastries. Despite Mayhew, one can hardly accept that street-Arabs, for all their transient jollities, had any stamina or much of a life-expectation. Genetically they came from debased stock, and must have been congenitally prone to deformity, stunted growth and TB. Their life-style could be killing from the bitter weather and infections picked up in scavenging. An officer of the Shaftesbury Society shelters recalled in Newcastle in the early 1870s: 'When we commenced our night shelter for boys, a boy was discovered in the portico of the Central Railway Station nearly frozen to death, and I have known little children being found in the ash-pit by Corporation scavengers, the children having spent the night there.'[16]

The pathos of child waifs made them very lucrative aids to adult professional beggars. Beggars even hired youngsters from their parents by the day to parade as bogus distressed families.[17] Sometimes parents sold them outright, a practice lasting into the early part of this century. 'Emma Smith' was a Cornish 'workhouse bastard' at the turn of the century, who was handed over by her mother at Plymouth to an itinerant organ-player and his wife.[18] She had to share a bed in a bug-infested hovel with a 13–14-year-old downtrodden boy employed by the organ-grinder. Their job was to sing hymns and pick up coins. Emma was kept deliberately ragged and unkempt to make her more pitiable. Their employers were harsh task-masters; the wife's meals consisted of a mess of bacon bits and cheese cooked together; and from the husband the 6-year-old girl experienced sexual molestation. Though sent to a Sunday School, Emma suspected that this was to enable her to learn a repertoire of hymns for street begging. When the boy, Charlie, was becoming too old to be of further use as a child beggar, the organ-grinder became increasingly indifferent to him, and he finally ran away.

Organ-grinding had been mostly associated with Italian immigrants, the *padroni* and parents of dark, picturesque children who were forced to perform and play in the streets. A whole colony inhabited London's 'Little Italy' in Clerkenwell, and elsewhere they were found in common lodging-houses. From the later 1870s, after the formation of the Italian Benevolent Society (under the auspices of the Italian Embassy), there were greater official efforts to check the abuse of these children. In 1877 a concentrated drive was made to remove them from the clutches of *padroni*, and return them to Italy or get them into London schools; the Home Office encouraged stricter enforcement of the Vagrancy and Industrial Schools Acts to check their use as street entertainers and beggars. However, the effect seems to have been to disperse the *padroni* and their hapless charges to the provinces, away from the metropolitan drive. The problem lingered on into the twentieth century. Emma Smith recalled meeting many Italians in the lodging-houses she stayed in. In 1912 an NSPCC booklet, *The Cruelty Man*, told of an Italian father with five children, all of whom were hired out to exploiters. The NSPCC dealt with his 8-year-old daughter, Mary Sergius, hired out to an Italian organ-grinder and dragged about by him to perform; she had had to share the same bed with him in the lodging-houses, and when rescued was found to be 'verminous, dazed and distressed'.

There was another side of the picture, though. Decent Italian immigrants had close family bonds and, like the Jews, treated their children well. George Sims observed in 1907 how among London's 'Little Italy' child population 'you will find few pinched pale faces, sunken lack-lustre eyes or attenuated frames'.[19]

Children were trained up professionally for particular begging dodges. Some were made up to look tuberculous and sickly; others were taught an appealing 'spiel' to reel off; and others turned on the tears, pretending that some newly purchased article had been stolen from them in the street, and they could expect a thrashing when they got home. Ellen Barlee was taken in by a crippled boy who told her that his new broom had been snatched away from him. She gave him 6*d*, only to be told later that this was his regular begging dodge.[20]

Sometimes revolting cruelties were perpetrated on children to make them more pitiable; into the early years of this century, the deliberate blinding and the starvation of infants as begging ploys were not yet extinct.[21] Even if the children were not deliberately maimed, degraded beggars would readily exploit their accidental afflictions. Early records of the Invalid Children's Aid Association from the late nineteenth century tell of one father whose 6-year-old boy had had one leg amputated through disease of the knee joint. His vile, drunken father would carry the poor boy from pub to pub, exposing his wound to raise drink-money. He was violent to the boy when intoxicated, but the lad was rescued and placed with a charity.[22] Such stories were once regular currency in the *Child's Guardian*; in 1908, for example, it reported a Manchester beggar who exposed the withered legs of a crippled 2-year-old to prompt charity,[23] and in 1910 told of a 3-year-old blind boy used for begging and of a Lincoln woman who kept her 8–9-year-old son stupefied on opium, carrying him from door to door to beg money to take the 'sick' boy to hospital.[24]

In the early days of compulsory education from 1880, blind beggar children would still be seen in schooltime singing, reciting, or playing instruments, as they were excluded from schooling. Though private charities were increasingly providing for trade training for such children, by the late 1880s youngsters were still found to be reverting to begging afterwards as being more profitable.[25]

We observed in Chapter 8 how street selling was often a cover for begging, and raggedness was deliberately contrived. Parents sent their offspring out with articles like matches or laces, but they were not expected to *sell* them. They were primed to cadge from soup kitchens or get credit from shopkeepers with tales of family woe. Opportunistic cadging became second nature to survive; young urchins would hang about shop doorways, begging food from emerging customers, or outside factory gates, hoping that lunchtime left-overs might come their way.[26] Where Jews resided, money could be made by doing odd jobs for pious Jews on the Sabbath. One little tyke cited by Ellen Barlee used to throw a dead cat in a Jew's hallway. The Jew would not touch it on the Sabbath, and then the boy would appear and offer to remove it for a penny. He would carry the dead cat away and repeat the dodge at some other Jew's apartment.[27] Poorer children would beg from slightly better-off neighbours. Joseph Stamper recalled how in Lancashire in the 1890s: 'All children were not as fortunate as we were. Sometimes little starvelings would knock at the door and when mother went: "Can you spare a bit of bread missus?" Mother would come in and cut a butty and take it to the child. The child would eat the butty there and then to make sure nobody stole it.'[28] The law of the jungle applied when hunger pinched. Children would snatch food from others in the street, gobbling it up as they ran, even though they knew they would receive a good hiding when caught.

There were legal penalties for child beggars: the Vagrancy Act of 1824 outlawed begging, 'sleeping out' and peddling without a licence. The Industrial Schools Act of 1857 included child beggars among the morally endangered children who might be committed to those institutions. The Education Acts from 1876 established truant schools and day industrial schools for non-attenders. The Vagrancy Act penalized adults who instigated children to beg on the highway, and the Prevention of Cruelty to Children Acts from 1889 also made it an offence for adults who 'caused' or 'procured' (and from 1894, merely 'allowed')[29] their children to beg, or perform as a cover for begging.

The police co-operated from the start with the NSPCC in enforcing the new cruelty legislation, but seem to have held back in implementing the begging clauses, especially where children were singing; they appeared not to treat singing as a cover for begging, and where the money was taken up by the adult, not the child directly, then they took the curious view that it was not the child who was soliciting the money, so the adult could not be prosecuted under the Cruelty Act provisions.[30] Adults soon learned other dodges to evade the Acts; by ensuring the children were decently dressed, for example, they could avoid charges of cruelty. How effective were the Acts in the 1890s against begging? We noted in the last chapter that they had little effect on street trading by themselves, and the same appears to apply to begging.[31] Gertrude Tuckwell, however, claimed in 1894 that since the 1889 Act 'child-begging has been greatly diminished', but considering the problems surrounding the words 'causes' and 'procures' under the Act, this was an optimistic assertion. The Industrial Schools Acts were not effectively enforced to remove child beggars from their parents. Magistrates were reluctant to commit ratepayers' money to support transients' children in the institutions, and tended to discharge the children on the parents' promise that they would leave the area forthwith.[32] In 1910 the NSPCC could still report the persistence of begging.[33] The judicial statistics cannot be taken as a pointer to the true incidence of juvenile begging, owing to the authorities' reluctance to prosecute or convict, or the bracketing of such cases within other offences, like truancy from school. The commonest juvenile convictions were for theft, malicious damage, gaming and other breaches of police regulations. In 1911, 798 juveniles were convicted of begging and sleeping out. Such a figure leaves out of account the unnumbered cases of youngsters simply warned off by the police or given the proverbial clip round the ear without arrest.

Industrial schools committals show that of the 3,402 boys and 948 girls sent in 1911, about 40 per cent were for Education Act offences; 532 boys and 205 girls were sent as 'found wandering', and 274 boys and 21 girls were sent for begging.[34] Of course many of the Education Act offenders could have been begging while off school, but were not convicted for this.

Considering the sizeable numbers of Edwardian child street traders and crypto-beggars, their relative paucity in NSPCC figures is surprising. In the year ending March 1905 the NSPCC had looked into 375 cases of parents allowing their children to hawk or beg, but had prosecuted in only 6. This was out of a total of 105,926 cases investigated by the NSPCC that year.[35] Again, the statistics may be reduced by the incorporation of many such cases within other forms of cruelty and neglect.

During the First World War there was a rise in juvenile delinquency associated with the disruption of family life, but juvenile begging formed little or no part of this. Perhaps with parents earning good wages in munitions factories there was less occasion for it. A social study conducted during 1917 to 1919 showed that of 7,000 youngsters convicted in a sample of four juvenile courts, the majority were for larceny and house-breaking, and only 396 for vagrancy and begging.[36] In the post-war period, one of the causes of child begging, namely the financing of parents' drinking habits, would have been weakened by the steep decline in alcoholism in the 1920s.

10

VAGRANCY

Child vagrants were at some times the local homeless, sticking to a particular neighbourhood; or at other times long-distance rovers, variously seasonal migrants hop- and pea-picking, gipsies and tinkers, and the unfortunate dependants of adult nomadic beggars. For them it was a life of 'dossing' in the fields and streets, the common lodging-houses and brothels, or the casual wards (that is, the overnight wards) of the workhouses. Children formed a conspicuous proportion of the tramp population of mid-Victorian Britain. The Judicial Statistics for 1868/9 indicate that of the 33,000 or more tramps known to the police in England and Wales 17 per cent were under 16. In 1876 Dr Barnardo reckoned that 6,000–7,000 out of the 27,000 or so dossers in London's *registered* common lodging-houses were under 16. They appeared less commonly in the casual wards, though; in the period 1866–80 under-16s formed between 1 in 13 and 1 in 17 of the workhouse transients.[1]

Some young tramps were independent; young orphans and runaways surviving on their own account. Others were in the custody of parents or some other adult who had assumed proprietorial rights over the child, having acquired it, perhaps by purchase from a desperate or uncaring parent, to drag about as a begging aid. By the Edwardian period the picture had changed markedly for the better in England. The expansion of industrial schools and orphanages like Dr Barnardo's and the Waifs and Strays Society, the improved treatment of children by the Poor Law, which made the workhouse runaway of Mayhew's and Dickens's era a thing of the past, the mechanization of farming which reduced the demand for seasonal labour, the fall in the birth rate after the 1870s which would have cut the numbers of children to trail about, and the vigilance of the NSPCC, all must have played their part in reducing child vagrancy. Estimates of the numbers of child tramps at this time varied. A police census in 1905 suggested 4.5 per cent of all tramps were children; the NSPCC in 1906 gave it as 3 per cent of the country's 30,000-odd 'tramps'. Other figures ranged from a few hundred to at least 5,000. The 1906 Departmental Committee on Vagrancy was satisfied that there had been a long-term decline in child vagrancy.[2] By the early 1900s the numbers of children found in London County Council's (admittedly narrow) tramp censuses sleeping rough or walking the streets were being counted in tens.

Scotland's child vagrant problem was traditionally more severe and persisted as England's improved, despite the efforts of the Scottish SPCC. Before 1914 about one-sixth or one-seventh of Scotland's vagrants were under 14.[3] Scotland had a conspicuous class of tinkers whose high birth rate made children up to a quarter of their population into the 1930s; but even among Scotland's non-tinkers the proportion of child tramps was still over one-seventh between the wars.[4]

The lives of tramp children were miserable and fraught with danger. We saw in the last chapter how poor 'Emma Smith' was exploited and abused by the barrel-organist. It is interesting in her autobiography how 'tied' she felt as an infant to her employers, for when they were based in Plymouth they were able to stop her visiting her grandparents who lived nearby. At the age of 7 she had to carry sacks of coal to her lodging-home and witness the squabbles and drunken fights there. When her employers sub-let their room to a fairground sword-swallower she had to share her bed with him. Emma did receive acts of kindness from strangers on her tramping and begging excursions, and even from fellow lodgers in the doss houses – perhaps an indication of the relative rarity of children in such places by the early 1900s. At 9 she was thrown out to fend for herself, but her family was not able to care for her for long, and after a spell in a Salvation Army Home and a foster home, circumstances brought her back to the barrel-organist and her old way of life. In 1906, now around 12, Emma was independent enough to run away, but the family contact for which she yearned had been ruptured by the death of her grandparents, and she spent the rest of her childhood in a religious shelter for 'fallen' girls. She was in fact still a virgin, though her moral spoilage was assumed from her earlier life-style. Her poignant story is perhaps the most detailed factual account of the experiences of countless children unlucky enough to be born of degraded parents, or as unwanted illegitimates. In 1888 the NSPCC told of a little girl given to four tramps to drag around the country and beg. Near Tamworth a tramp strapped and kicked her viciously, leaving her unconscious; in this state she was found and removed to a local workhouse.[5] The NSPCC's very first prosecution under the 1889 Cruelty Act was that of a tramp who had walked from Nottingham to London with two children under 12, both in agony; one had an eye infection and the other was ruptured, and both died subsequently.[6] A NSPCC inspector – 'The Cruelty Man' – in 1912 recalled instances of callous disposal of children to vagrants. One women, a casual farm labourer, had unconcernedly handed over her child, 'this little cuss', she called it, to some itinerant musicians; and a man gave away his 3-year-old daughter to a canal boatman in exchange for a blanket.[7] The authorities by now had long been co-operating with the NSPCC to nail such cases. In 1899 the Poor Law authorities were officially encouraged to report to the NSPCC all cases of vagrants entering the casual wards accompanied by children.[8] (This probably helps to account for the extremely small numbers of casual ward children by the early 1900s; on 1 January 1907 there were only 98 such children counted in England and Wales.) Where police arrested child tramps under the Vagrancy Act, they notified the NSPCC who would be present in court to bail them out.[9] Interestingly, the NSPCC was not keen to make mere wandering with a child a specific criminal offence, without evidence of actual cruelty.[10] The NSPCC took no action where there was no evident mistreatment. It would be misleading to think that cruelty and tramping were invariably associated. Apart from the asperities of the life-style, many tramp children were reasonably cared for; a well-looked-after child was a useful begging aid. In fact during 1901–4 only 12 to 17 NSPCC prosecutions a year arose out of the mistreatment of tramp children, and in the year ending March 1905, of nearly 106,000 cases looked into by the NSPCC, only 375 involved tramp children. Thus Emma Smith was thankfully one of a diminishing band of unfortunates.

Gipsies were Britain's native-born exotics, forming a distinct caste who in the public mind combined romanticism and dishonesty. True gipsies, with their Romany tongue, their colourful dress, horse-sense and mystique, distinguished themselves from the tinker riff-raff, and in the 1850s George Borrow, the writer and linguist, lyricized the gipsy life in his writings; he estimated their population in Britain then at 10,000. However, George Smith, the campaigner for brickyard and canal children whose work was described in Chapter 6, was to present a very different picture of gipsy life. He had often seen gipsy encampments in the waste land beyond the brickyards and it was a natural extension of his interest in the travelling life of canal children to study that of land-based itinerants – gipsies, tinkers and van folk in travelling circuses and menageries. In 1889 he claimed there were 30,000 such children in England and 20,000 in Scotland, which then had about a seventh of England's population. In 1880 he published his first account of them, *Gipsy Life*, and in 1889 his last, *Gipsy Children*.[11] His aim was a Moveable Dwellings Act to get caravans registered in the same way as canal boats, and made subject to sanitary inspection. Travellers should also have to carry documentation showing that their children had attended school in the district of their encampment. Smith found nothing romantic in their life-style. They were prolific breeders, each couple producing from 8 to 16 children, but the death rate was high. In Epping Forest he entered one hut in a gipsy encampment containing 'five children as ragged as wild goats, as filthy as pigs and quite as ignorant'. There was only one bed, teeming with vermin, and the floor was thick with dirt and mud. An 18-year-old youth was eating a hash of 'meat, soup, fish, broth, roast and fry, thickened with bones and flavoured with snails and bread', while a 'mere girl' was breast-feeding a baby. In another shelter was a family with six children who were 'partially dressed in filthy rags . . . which seem to have been picked out of the ashes upon Hackney Marshes'. In the last two days the family had lived on one loaf and half an ounce of tea. The father was nearly blind: he had been involved in numerous fights and had received a kick over the eyes. They lived by selling oranges and begging. Sometimes they ate rabbits and hedgehogs, and in summer went nest-hunting for eggs. A child at that moment brought in some blackbird's eggs he had found. The mother promptly cracked them open and poured the raw contents 'half-hatched as they were', into the children's mouths – and one child nearly choked on the unhatched fledgling as it fell into its gullet. All the children had been born on straw in a tent in Epping Forest. One child did not even know his own name and he thought that God was a chap who had once lived in the forest and had since gone 'hopping' to Kent.[12]

Travelling children, Smith found, were raised to beg, cheat, steal and peddle. At race meetings and fairs they could be up till midnight helping at the booths; their 'beds' were just piles of rags under caravans, under stalls, in barns, or out in the open.

Smith made several visits to Scotland, and claimed that the children's condition there was even more shocking than in England. One tent on the Border reeked inside of a mixture of rotten hare and rabbit skins, cooking smells and bad herrings. The family slept together in one bed: 'The children were ill in bed with a few dirty old rags to cover them. The man said that "One or two of them had got inflammation on the brain".'[13] There was scarcely a travelling family in Scotland without consumption. The fevers and ill-health so commonly encountered were due not only to the filth but the flimsy nature of their shelters – fabric 'bender tents' – in severe weather.[14] The birth rate was prodigious – one family he met had nineteen children – and babies were born on the road. Gipsies' diet included diseased pork, hedgehogs, hares and snails. Drunkenness was endemic among the adults and the children were maltreated. The prevalence of tinkers in Scotland made them the subject of a Departmental Committee inquiry in 1895. One witness wanted the tinkers' children compulsorily removed and sent to industrial schools.[15] This was rejected by the committee on libertarian grounds; in any case, as I have already noted, magistrates were loath to enforce the industrial school laws on behalf of transients' children, and though the committee recommended that parishes be combined for such purposes to spread the financial burden, Scotland's tinker problem was not 'solved'.

In 1902 John Macdonald of the Scottish SPCC described the situation much as George Smith had in the 1880s.[16] Gipsies, he said, were of a higher order, and in winter they settled in houses and sent their children to school. Tinkers lived in their flimsy tents all year round. They appeared fond of their children when sober, for without them, 'they would be as helpless as a poacher without his dog'. But maltreatment when their parents were drunk, and exposure, led to a high infant mortality rate. Their life-style persisted because of a high degree of public tolerance; the police found them beggars rather than thieves and often ignored them; while sentimentalists viewed them as a colourful part of the local scene and were blind to the real squalor. The tinker problem remained in Scotland well beyond the period of this book.

George Smith's campaign for a Moveable Dwellings Act was strongly opposed by fairground folk who regarded it as intrusive, farmers who benefited from gipsy seasonal labour, romantics who wanted to preserve the gipsy way of life untouched, and those who feared a forced invasion by wild gipsy and tinker children into local schools. Bills introduced between 1885 and 1892 all failed, and virtually the only legislative achievement was a clause in the 1885 Housing of the Working Classes Act providing for the sanitary inspection of caravans but no scheme of registration.[17]

The law in relation to child vagrancy was unsatisfactorily applied. The Vagrancy Act of 1824 provided for short prison terms for vagrants of all ages,[18] and the practice was to sentence tramping youths for a week or so in jail. In 1887 J. W. Horsley, the chaplain to Clerkenwell Jail, had protested that this had no reformative effect and only made the youngsters more antisocial.[19] He told of the case of two children of 6 and 7 who had no parents and were found wandering shelterless. They were remanded in jail for a week pending a hearing under the Vagrancy Act.

> These small children were locked up in a solitary cell for the seven days with absolutely nothing to do and with no human being to speak to them but the turnkeys who brought them their meals. And this frightful punishment ... was inflicted upon these poor children for the crime of poverty.

Charles Russell in 1905 could still write of penniless boys with pathetic backgrounds being sent to jail for sleeping out or begging.[20] In 1900, 310 16–21-year-olds were convicted of begging in England and Wales, and 432 for sleeping out under the 1824 Act. In 1904 the figures had risen to 739 and 651 respectively as a consequence of the post-Boer War depression. Blinkered magistrates refused to distinguish between genuine young work-seekers on tramp and the more wayward vagabonds. Grimsby justices were notoriously severe before 1914; Lincolnshire was a draw for seasonal potato-pickers, and the port itself a hang-out for tramping sailors and boy absconders from fishing vessels, as we saw in Chapter 4.[21] By 1906, however, the police in Manchester at least were showing more enlightenment by referring young vagrants to local voluntary workers to find them work and lodgings, instead of prosecuting them.

The industrial schools legislation provided for the removal of vagrant, begging, orphaned and morally endangered children (such as those frequenting the company of thieves or residing in brothels) to the schools. This was not properly enforced as the youngsters would then become a charge on the local authority of the district where they were sentenced. Magistrates often preferred to impose a short jail term under the Vagrancy Act rather than a long, expensive sojourn in an industrial school. A justices' let-out was to charge the costs of the stay to the body that had brought the case, and this proved a deterrent to the NSPCC and other philanthropic organizations wishing to 'rescue' youngsters by having them sent to an industrial school.

The 1876 Education Act obliged local authorities to take proceedings for the committal of habitually wandering children to the schools, but this was disregarded in the case of caravan children – transients 'passing through' – for whom the authorities felt no responsibility. Though the 1870 Education Act empowered local authorities to set up their own industrial schools (the pioneer ones were voluntary establishments which received Treasury subsidies), by 1908 most still had not done so.[22] Even if a youngster was committed by a court, this was subject to a school's willingness to take him; the 1908 Children's Act did, however, make it obligatory for a local authority to arrange for the child's placement.[23]

The London workhouse casual wards during 1871 counted children as just over 6 per cent of their intake.[24] As the century drew on, children became increasingly rare in casual wards, as already noted. On 1 July 1893 there were 411 children among about 7,100 adults in the English and Welsh wards, and five years later 251 out of just over 5,000 adults. We have noted the arrangements between the Poor Law and the NSPCC from 1899 and the further drop in numbers in the new century. Tramping families avoided bringing their children to the casual wards if they could; often the mothers and children would go to a common lodging-house, leaving the father to seek admission. Children shared the same wards with the adults, and were kept locked up in them until their parents had completed their work-tasks, such as stone-breaking or sawing firewood, before being discharged on a meal of gruel or bread and cocoa. The experience, deliberately degrading as it was for adults, was demoralizing for the children, and the 1906 Departmental Committee on Vagrancy recommended that children be kept in the resident wards for the night, rather than mix with other adult down-and-outs.[25]

A distinct problem for the Poor Law was the 'ins-and-outs'; these were *local* tramps, beggars and shirkers within the Poor Law unions who had a legal 'settlement', that is, a residential qualification for poor relief. Such people used the workhouse as a convenience, and their own degradation made its forbidding regime no deterrent to them. They came and went at will, and though their numbers were not large they were a parasitic and disruptive administrative burden. Under Acts of 1871 and 1899 the Poor Law acquired limited rights of detention over 'ins-and-outs', up to 7 days for the worst cases.

In the urban workhouses the children of 'ins-and-outs' were removed to separate wards or the district schools (that is, residential workhouse schools situated away from the main workhouse block), but had to leave when their parents decided to go. Any schooling the children received was fragmentary. They were also considered a pernicious influence on the long-term workhouse children, because of their bad language and precocity.[26] In 1905–9 the Royal Commission on the Poor Laws was much exercised by this problem. It cited the case of a man called Marshall, a nuisance to the Alton Board of Governors. He had entered the workhouse with his family, but had been allowed out to look for work. This he found, but refused to support his family and preferred to return to the workhouse. He then took his discharge, with his family, forcing the guardians to ferry his children back from the district school. He promptly returned with them again, and brazenly told the guardians that unless they took his family in but left him free, he would continue to repeat this rigmarole. In 1906 Leif Jones MP raised the case of a pauper called Tasker.[27] He and his wife had already been jailed for child cruelty; five of their infants, whose lives had been insured, had died, and he was in and out of the Malton workhouse at will with his three surviving children. The workhouse was loath to adopt the children, as this would play into Tasker's hands; yet they were faced with the alternative prospect of seeing the children grow up to a life of vagrancy.

Some 'ins-and-outs' were not wilful parasites but feeble-minded drifters; they were not so mentally deficient as to be detainable under the Lunacy Acts, but their freedom to leave – especially in the case of feeble-minded girls – made them liable to reproduce defective stock who would be future burdens on the Poor Law.

The Royal Commission was struck by the 'terribly neglected and backward' state of the children of 'ins-and-outs' and recommended that the guardians should have power to detain them, and where necessary institute the transfer of their parents to some kind of labour colony, a concept much canvassed at that time.

Acts of 1889 and 1899 had given the Poor Law authorities powers to 'adopt' maintained children if they were orphans, had been deserted, or were victims of offences for which their parents had been jailed, or if the parents were otherwise physically or mentally incapable, alcoholic, or of 'vicious habits or mode of life'.[28] If the children had instead been removed to an industrial school or orphanage they would be outside Poor Law jurisdiction and would not qualify for adoption. However, once adoption proceedings had been completed, the Poor Law could *then* arrange for the child's transfer to, say, a private institution for the deaf or blind, or have it fostered out. Adoption meant that the child was under the Poor Law aegis till 18. The parents' permission was not needed for adoption, though they had the right of appeal to magistrates. This 'adoption' did not connote the lifelong acquisiton of a quasi-blood tie; the Poor Law could revoke the adoption and transfer the child back to the parent if it saw fit. Voluntary agencies could not adopt; until an Act of 1891 they had no rights against a parent who wished to reclaim a child; thereafter children's institutions could appeal to the courts for the power to continue fostering. The Adoption Acts applied only to England and Wales. Scotland's more limited Poor Law technically excluded the able-bodied and their children, but in practice parents in extremities would desert their children, forcing the Poor Law to take them over.[29]

There was legal uncertainty as to whether casual ward children were legally 'maintained' so as to be eligible for adoption. In practice there was very little adoption of vagrant children, as the guardians did not want to be charged with a 'foreign' child until it was 18. A practical problem in any case was the delay before the next meeting of the guardians to consider the adoption; the parent would have ample opportunity to decamp from the casual ward with the child in the meantime as there was no power of interim detention.[30]

Another turn-of-the-century proposal to rescue tramp children was to make wandering with children punishable for adults *per se* without proof of cruelty or neglect, and give magistrates full discretion to dispose of the child — to an industrial school, a workhouse, or a voluntary home. A succession of bills along these lines was introduced between 1899 and 1906, and they also proposed that Poor Law vagrant adoptees should be supported out of the county rate (as opposed to the local Poor Law union rate) to spread the financial burden and so encourage such adoptions. The 1906 Departmental Committee on Vagrancy came out against this proposed new offence as an infringement of individual liberty. The NSPCC, as we have seen, was not keen on criminalizing tramp-parents without proof of cruelty. In the event the 1908 Children's Act contained a diluted provision. Vagrants who 'wandered from place to place' and thereby deprived their children of an education could be fined (though where was the money to come from?) and their children could be sent only to an industrial school.[31] Even this measure was not easy to enforce, as the prosecution had to show that the vagrant 'wandered from place to place', and there might be no record of his or her prior movements.

11

THE BLIND-ALLEY
JOB PROBLEM

Much concern was being expressed at the turn of the century about the worrying numbers of school-leavers who, it seemed, were ending up in blind-alley jobs. Modern technology had outdated many traditional craft skills, which had been reduced to a series of repetitive processes on the production line. Prolonged training was seen to be on the decline and, as Spencer J. Gibb put it in 1911, young lads were becoming '"loom-boys", "doffers" or "shifters" in weaving factories; rivet-boys in boiler shops; oven-boys in bakeries; drawers-off in saw mills; packers in soap works; machine minders in furniture factories; labelling bottles in mineral water factories; turning the wheel for rope spinners, and the like'.[1] Robert Roberts, who was born in 1905, recalled his first job in a Salford engineering works where his so-called 'apprenticeship' amounted to a process he was taught in 3 minutes; and this he did for the next 2 years for $8\frac{1}{2}$ hours a day.[2]

The fears were for Britain's future industrial competitiveness, and the prospect of a society made bottom-heavy with a great sump of dead-enders and delinquents. Several causes were blamed for this. Schools were blamed for being cut off from the world of work and making children learn by rote to achieve their 'Standards' (grades); this turned youngsters off any desire to further their education after leaving at 13 or 14. J. H. Whitehouse observed: 'In the two years between 14 and 16 a boy forgets most of what he has learned at school.'[3] Arnold Freeman in 1914 praised schools as character-builders, civilizing youngsters' behaviour – but there was too abrupt a break between school and the world of work, and school-leavers were left to drift on their own.

The habits of moonlighting were said to carry over into adolescence, and school-leavers were reportedly glad to snatch any casual or unskilled job going which paid initially high wages. In 1908 the average wage in London for a 14-year-old was 7s a week whereas a lad in an unskilled trade could average nearly 16s 6d a week at 18, a youth still learning a trade at that age was averaging nearly 2s a week less, though his long-term prospects were far better.[4] Really the image of the adolescent drifter, stumbling towards a dead-end adulthood, was nothing new; in 1883 James Greenwood identified the 'hobbledehoy', 'neither man nor boy', who could survive on a wage of 10s a week, but at 17, when he needed an adult rate of pay, was sacked and left to sink in the residuum or turn to crime.[5]

The doom and gloom here were somewhat alarmist, for it was not uncommon for youngsters, even those who had left school with high Standards, to drift around for a few years before settling down to a proper trade; and there was usually a gap between the school-leaving age and the minimum age of entry to an apprenticeship.[6] The 1905–9 Royal Commission on the Poor Laws found that 70–80 per cent of boy school-leavers entered unskilled trades, as, say, van and shop boys, though some did later later go on to apprenticeships. A few years later R. H. Tawney found that in Glasgow only 12 per cent of a sample of school-leavers went directly into apprenticeships. However, another survey he made of 100 boys showed that while only 23 of them became apprentices or learners on leaving school, by the age of 16 there were 87 training for a trade.[7]

Trade unions were accused of selfishness for restricting entry into trades to the sons of existing members. Employers were accused of unscrupulousness: taking on lads with the promise of training, using them as cheap labour till late adolescence, and summarily sacking them when they needed an adult wage.[8] One gets a variable picture of the utility of cheap boy labour; some factory owners claimed that protective legislation made it uneconomic to recruit youngsters, so they were thrown on to the casual labour market (we saw this trend in Chapter 2); others, the smaller employers, were said to find boys so cheap that it discouraged technological innovation – for example, in continuing to use boy messengers instead of installing telephones.[9]

The cost of apprenticeship could also be prohibitive, with premiums of £20 to £40 a year demanded,[10] but there were charity apprenticeships. However, apprenticeship in London had declined so seriously by 1911 that of the £24,000 a year available in such charities only about a third was being taken up.[11] Among poorer families it was the oldest son, however bright, who was most likely to end up in a dead-end job, as his earnings were needed to help support younger siblings.

The Poor Law, industrial schools and reformatories were also criticized for lack of training of their charges. The Poor Law traditionally had looked on pauper children as fodder for the lower grades of work; it pushed them into farm work, the army, the navy and domestic service to get them off its hands, short-sightedly failing to appreciate the lack of skills was more likely to lead them to return later as adult paupers.[12] Poor Law 'apprenticeships' prior to 1844 had been what Oliver Twist experienced – unsupervised consignment to any tradesman needing unpaid labour; the 1844 Poor Law Act had tightened up the conditions on which employers took on pauper apprentices, but after mid-century such apprenticeships were declining anyway.[13] By the early 1900s the Poor Law was showing a more enlightened concern to give its indoor-relief children a better start, but was still neglecting the larger numbers of children on outdoor relief with their families (such as the children of widows). Around 1911, of the 1 million or so school-leavers a year 15,000 were on outdoor relief, which ended at 14, forcing them to take the first job going.[14]

For boys van, errand and shop work were the most common 'blind-alley' trades on leaving school. A parliamentary return in 1899 showed that 40 per cent became van and errand boys and 14 per cent shop boys,[15] and Tawney's later survey in Glasgow indicated that 53.6 per cent of leavers became milk or lorry boys. At least lads working for shopkeepers were, nominally at any rate, protected by the Shop Acts, but there was no protective legislation for van and warehouse boys, who became the subject of an official inquiry in 1913.[16] Van boys or 'nippers', who were supposed to guard against theft, were said to come from the lowest class of lad, because of the opportunities for pilferage. Hours could reach 70 to 90 a week, and entailed working late into the night; this had an unsettling effect on personal habits and led to insalubrious association with riff-raff and prostitutes who hung about the all-night coffee stalls. Yet the free-ranging character of the work made it attractive to the more restless kind of lad. Railway goods van boys were rather better off, but even then a 14-year-old would work 60–72 hours a week, with night work on shifts; but at least there was the prospect of transfer to other railway work once they became too old. Most 'nippers' were 13–16 years old, and a few were girls. Wages in 1913 started at 7s a week, rising annually to a maximum of 14s. Warehouse boys, though working similar hours, were better off than 'nippers' as their firms might graduate them to adult jobs.

Bakery boys were vulnerable to exploitation, because much of their work was at night when the factory inspectors often could not reach them, and bakers were said to like to take on ex-warehouse boys for this reason.[17]

The army was considered the last resort for boys who had 'failed' at 17 or 18 and would otherwise face a life as casual labourers and street loafers.[18] The Royal and Merchant navies relied on an inflow of boys from the workhouses; in the early 1900s these would join at 14 having served on the Poor Law training-ship, the *Exmouth*. Despite the opportunities to see the world, it was not an attractive life, as I described in Chapter 4.[19]

'Blind-alley' employment for girls was then not an issue, as work was considered just a prelude to marriage. Apart from domestic service, sweatshop work, and factory work in the north of England, shop work was becoming more available by 1900. At 15 or 16 some became waitresses and barmaids but in the 1890s wages were only about 10s a week, and they had to rely on tips. The work was frowned on as holding moral dangers for girls in the bibulous atmosphere of a pub.[20]

Practical moves were afoot in the Edwardian period to fit school-leavers into training schemes. This is examined in detail in Chapter 20 in the context of the education system, but an outline is appropriate here. Much faith was placed in the idea of 'continuation schools'; that is, part-time schooling up to 18 after leaving elementary school, not so much to acquire a vocational skill (this was the job of the local technical colleges) but to keep up – compulsorily if necessary – the learning habit, so fostering the right attitude of mind towards long-term job training.[21] Another transition between school and work was evolved through after-care committees (ACCs), which were offshoots of school care committees (welfare bodies for each school) set up since the 1906 Education Act. The ACCs established links with local employers and acted as youth employment counsellors for their schools. The labour exchanges set up under an Act of 1909 were designed to cater for the over-16s, but juvenile advisory committees could be set up. In Edinburgh and Birmingham the Labour Exchange set up juvenile bureaux, and in London the Hornsey and Finchley education authorities established a formal link with the local labour exchanges.[22] Some headmasters had turned themselves into unofficial job-brokers.[23] In 1910 the Education (Choice of Employment) Act empowered education authorities to set up careers advisory services on their own account. The ACCs also steered school-leavers towards wholesome clubs and youth organizations, some of which were providing unofficial careers guidance, and even laying on trade classes, such as carpentry. However, the boys' clubs, by the very nature of the type of lad they attracted in the first place, tended to serve the 'good', steady types, and the potential lounger and dead-ender was left out of account.[24] The Jewish community was a model of organization. Since the 1860s the Jewish Board of Guardians had had an industrial committee to help arrange the apprenticeship of Jewish children,[25] and Jewish youth clubs were pioneers in careers guidance.[26] The Charity Organization Society and other voluntary organizations were setting up apprenticeship and skilled employment committees from the late 1890s on the Jewish model.[27] The Charity Organization Society scheme had originally been confined to girls, and in fact opportunities for more skilled work in offices and some factories were now opening for girls; by 1904 Reuters Telegraph Agency was employing girls as well as boys. However, their chances to rise were very slender or non-existent.

Some employers with a social conscience were beginning to give assistance to lads who were approaching the end of their employability in blind-alley jobs. Around 1909 there were some 14,000 boy golf caddies in England and Wales, and the Sunningdale Golf Club in Surrey allowed a continuation school to operate on its premises and ran a job agency for the lads.[28] The Post Office, which used to lay off boy messengers at 16, from 1908–9 began a scheme to absorb them into adult grades, so that whereas in that year it laid off 4,322 boys, by 1913 this was down to 38.[29]

The efforts being made to steer boys into skilled lifetime trades were dislocated by the First World War. The shortage of manpower in factories created golden opportunities for boys who were given accelerated promotion to do 'men's jobs', while girls now filled the gap in the more menial grades. Wages for under-18s could reach £1 to £2 a week (£2 was the wage of a skilled worker in 1914). However, this bonanza went to their heads. The Ministry of Reconstruction Committee on Juvenile Employment later recorded:[30]

> In feverish excitement the boys spent their time wandering from shop to shop, from works to works, making short stays, frequently of only one or two weeks, in search of the new El Dorado. Indentures were thrown to the winds; places where useful trades could be learned were left behind .... The persistence with which the boys took up the trail to the great machine shops . . . or to any other place where the processes were repetitive and the contracts ran into millions can be compared almost to the rush of the Klondyke.

With the end of the war, the golden trail came to an abrupt end. The return of demobilized men to their jobs presented the prospect of a wholesale 'shake-out' of boy labour, and the Reconstruction Committee recommended schemes to cushion the blow, such as comprehensive nationwide retraining schemes and an across-the-board school-leaving age of 14. The Fisher Education Act of 1918 did implement the latter, but its other plans for continuation schooling fell by the wayside as the post-war economic depression struck. Boys got whatever jobs they could, and girls were forced back into domestic service.

12

EMPLOYERS, EDUCATION AND THE PART-TIME SYSTEM

Although popular prejudice might assume that the need for child labour militated against any official sanction for education, in fact it was through the early factory laws that the first provision for compulsory education was made. The 1833 Factory Act contained the rudiments of the 'half-time' system. Children of 8 to 13 could not work more than 48 hours in a textile mill, and had to attend school for a minimum period each week – either voluntary schools, like the 'British' and 'National' schools, or a school on the factory premises provided by the employer, for which he could make a deduction from the child's wages. Of course, very many employers hated this restriction and subverted the law by operating complex 'on-off' shift systems for their child employees, which compelled them to hang around the premises till the next shift started; so enabling employers to keep them productively occupied. The 1844 Factory Act, again confined to textile mills, dealt with this by requiring the statutory working day to be performed in one continuous stint; a definite 3-hour period of schooling, Monday to Friday, was prescribed. Not all employers were hostile to education. Apart from the genuinely philanthropic ones, others saw it as an instrument for taming and training a young workforce into habits of obedience and regularity. It was certainly not intended to give the working classes ideas above their station. The *Edinburgh Review* opined in 1831 that through basic literacy and religious instruction

> the poor ought to be made acquainted with those circumstances which principally determine their condition of life. They ought, above all, to be instructed in the plain elementary doctrines respecting population and wages; in the

advantages derived from the institution of private property and the introduction and improvement of machinery; and in the causes which give rise to that gradation of ranks and inequality of fortunes that are as natural to society as heat to fire and cold to ice.[1]

School was also a useful place to corral youngsters and keep them out of mischief in their non-working time. A Derby employer told the 1833 Children's Employment Commission:

All the boys that leave work on Saturdays at four o'clock we compel to attend school for about a couple of hours, not only for their improvement, but to prevent the mischief which . . . they were apt to get into from mere wantonness . . . . All the young persons under twenty are expected to attend Sunday schools.[2]

The half-time system was progressively extended to other types of factory; and in 1860 was applied to a limited degree of boys working underground in mines between 10 and 12 years old. The 1867 Factories and Workshops Acts now made it general in large and small premises alike, but evasion was easier in workshops because of the more flexible shift arrangements permitted. Schooling was thus being more and more comprehensively linked with the right to work. Infants of 5, 6 and 7, too young to start work, were excluded, as were youngsters in street trades, though farm children were brought within its rubric from 1873. The half-time laws, plus technological change, were beginning to prompt a shedding of child labour by the 1860s, with the notable exception of textiles, so by 1870 education was also being seen as a sponge to soak up unoccupied children.[3] But doubts about the comparative quality of British technology as shown up at the 1867 International Exhibition in Paris,[4] followed by the victory for German *matériel* in the Franco-Prussian War of 1870–1, provided another incentive. As a government schools inspector put it in 1902: 'The almost feverish solicitude [for education] that was apparent all over the industrialized world about the year 1870 was not due to any religious revival, but to competition among nations for wealth and power.'[5] It was not a deferential workforce employers were beginning to need so much as a trained and skilled body of workers. Yet did the state system, begun in 1870, meet that need? And were employers doing what they should to train up their youngsters, building on the three Rs learned at school? In regard to the first question, much opinion expressed was subjective. Cyril Jackson's Report on Boy Labour, for the Royal Commission on the Poor Laws (1905–9), commented:

> Everyone sees occasionally in the papers a furious letter from an employer . . . stating that he gave a boy fresh from school a simple sum and that he could not work it. Many employers grumble that education has deteriorated their boys just as mistresses say that servants are not what they used to be. The same complaint of servants was made in the eighteenth century. Few employers nowadays can have experience of employing boys before the Act of 1870.

Jackson's own judgement was that the better-educated and more intelligent lads would pick up skills faster, but that also contained a subjective element, for it says little or nothing about the value of the education *per se*, much of which was then mechanical rote-learning; once the rudiments of literacy were learned native intelligence alone would have probably enabled the bright lad to learn faster on the job.

In regard to the second question, the concern about blind-alley employment and declining apprenticeships discussed in the last chapter would indicate that employers as well as educationalists were remiss in steering board-school products into skilled trades, until the spur of the German challenge started waking them up.

The part-time system was to persist within a framework of state schooling from 1870 to the Education Act of 1918. Overwhelmingly it was the Lancashire and secondarily the Yorkshire textile industries that continued to sustain it. In 1893, 80 per cent of the school part-timers in England and Wales worked in those counties.[6] Part-time law was to become very intricate and must have been a headache for parents trying to understand it, and for headmasters trying to explain it to querulous parents wanting their youngsters out of school and 'into t' mill'. For a start it was not made clear until the 1880 Education Act that in any discrepancies over minimum ages of employment between the education and factory laws, the former would prevail.[7] The 1870 Education Act gave school boards permissive powers to make education compulsory to any age up to 13 in their districts, but they could allow part-time or full-time exemptions from the age of 10 where the local learning age was set above 10. The 1876 Education Act made education almost compulsory by forbidding child employment below 10 and requiring a proof of educational attainment before any employer could employ a child full-time until the age of 13. These proofs were either a 'certificate of proficiency' that the child had reached a nationally prescribed minimum Standard, or a certificate of attendance, that the child had put in a minimum number of annual attendances over the previous 5 years. Thus a bright child who passed that Standard (known as the 'Labour Examination') at the age of 10 could start work full-time. A child who was less bright but had made the required number of attendances, could likewise leave under what became popularly known as the 'Dunce's Pass'. The 1880 Education Act now expressly made full-time education compulsory to a minimum age of 10 and allowed school authorities to frame their own regulations for full- or part-time schooling or total exemption to 13. The minimum school-leaving age was progressively raised and by 1899 was 12. In rural districts children could start part-time work in agriculture at 11, providing they continued in part-time schooling up to 13. However, by 1909, it seems, very few country children were leaving at 11.[8] The effects of the local full exemption rules might be as follows: a child at 12 might qualify by the Labour Examination or the Dunce's Pass for full-time exemption. If a boy wished to work, say, in a cotton mill, he would find that the Factory Acts prevented full-time employment until he was 13, for the Factory Act of 1878 prescribed part-time schooling till that age; he would thus have to continue at school part-time. If he wanted to work full-time between 12 and 13 he would have to find some casual trade, such as van and messenger work, not governed by protective legislation. In 1900 the latest school-leaving age was raised to 14, and a higher minimum Standard was prescribed for full-time exemption from 12. (Scotland had had its own separate laws since the 1870s, the effect of which until the Scottish Education Act of 1901 was that whilst the minimum school-leaving age was only 10, Scottish education authorities could expressly forbid full-time work up to 14.[9])

The Education Acts gave school boards total latitude about the tests for part-time exemption; in 1893 the large majority were setting very low Standards, and some none at all.[10] It was not difficult for a child to leave part-time as soon as he or she reached the local minimum leaving age, and where the child wished to start in a factory that was the mainstay of the local economy, or the parents could plead family hardship, the education authority might prove amenable to waiving the requirements for part-time exemption. In 1918, however, the whole complex mesh of statutes and local regulations about full and part-time exemption was abolished, and schooling was made universally compulsory to 14.

How did youngsters fare mentally and physically under the part-time system? A Victorian lad starting at 10 years old in a textile mill might do the following hours on alternate weeks: 6 a.m. to 12.30 p.m. work, followed by school from 2 to 4.30 p.m.; and school from 9 a.m. to noon, followed by work from 1.30 to 6 p.m.[11] The future trade union leader J. R. Clynes as a boy in the 1870s had to run 2 miles home from the mills for dinner, and then set off for school; while George Tomlinson, later to become Education Minister in the 1945 Labour government, recalled having to sleep off his fatigue in the fields between factory and home.[12] Other part-time arrangements could be made, setting aside part of the week for school and the other for work, or in the case of farm children setting aside part of the year for work.

Fatigue and working contact with adults made continued schooling irksome for youngsters who felt they could be earning in the real world outside. However, it was also claimed that they were learning as much as those in full-time schooling. Before compulsory state schooling, since the right to work depended on a teacher's certificate of attendance, part-timers were said to be more regular school attenders.[13] Edwin Chadwick, the public health reformer, maintained that children in half-time schools performed better than full-time board school pupils, reaching Standard 4 a little earlier on average.[14] Over-cramming of full-timers was being attacked as counterproductive. Dr Clement Dukes, a leading medical protagonist in this 'overpressure' argument, in 1899 cited an experiment by Charles Paget MP, in the village school on his estate. When a regime of part-time schooling and part-time garden work was introduced, the children were claimed to improve both academically and in behaviour. In the poorer board schools, where the children had less mental capacity, a full day's academic work was indigestible, and the pupils should receive a half-day's trade training instead.[15] Even in 1909, when 'Payment by Results' for schoolteachers and the consequent pressure on them to cram their pupils to pass their Standards had long disappeared, it was still being maintained that half-timers did better. E. H. Carlile MP, the former manager of a half-time school in a textile district (and therefore not an unbiased observer), claimed that his school's results were better than those of full-timers in the same district, and that the children were 'healthy and rosy-cheeked'.[16] The practical experience of work stood them in good stead later, it was argued, and their earnings raised their families' living standards and general health; one must distinguish the 'moonlighters' of the same period who did casual work outside *full-time* school hours. Robert Sherard in 1905 cited his visit to Dundee, where the jute industry was a stronghold of part-time schooling. A headmaster there had told him of some ex-pupils who had benefited and risen: one was a sanitary officer, another managed a spinning company and another was a newspaper sub-editor.

However, there was much evidence to condemn the system. Before universal public schooling, any private so-called school could offer certificates of attendance to employers to qualify the children for part-time labour, and a seedy industry of 'private adventure' schools was thereby created, run by unqualified and unfit characters, to meet the law; some were owned directly by the employers, with factory classes set in some odd corner of the works and lessons conducted amid the clatter and clash of machinery. In Edinburgh in the 1870s one 'sham school' of 150 children was uncovered, run by an Irish labourer who had lost an arm in an accident. A school inspector found not one textbook there; 130 of the children could not read words of more than three letters and the labourer eked out a living by selling bogus attendance certificates at 6*d* each.[17] A factory inspector in Birmingham at this period reckoned that 10,000 children in the city were schooled as part-timers under similar conditions; one schoolroom with 35 children was 12 feet by 15. Little real teaching went on and the only equipment was a few slates. For this 3*d* a week was charged.[18]

The advent of state education in 1870 had strengthened the voice of critics; early opponents had no absolute proof of the harmful physical effects of combining work with schooling, but emphasized its dulling effect in the classroom.[19] The Royal Commission on Education in 1887 was satisfied of its dulling effects, but as strong vested interests had defended the system, most notably in Lancashire, it contented itself merely with recommending a rise in the minimum school-leaving age from 10 to 11 (and this was not done until 1893). Teachers found that part-timers disrupted school organization. They fell behind their full-time classmates and sat sleepily at their desks; compassionate teachers would turn a blind eye if they dozed off. Margaret Leonora Eyles who became a pupil-teacher (an apprentice schoolteacher) at 14 around the turn of the century recalled the strain *she* was under having to attend her training centre in the morning and teach classes of 60 in the afternoon, apart from coaching small groups who wanted to take their Labour Examination: 'once the Head Mistress came into the little room and found us all, teacher and children, asleep with our heads on the desk. She was very cross.'

As young earners they liked to act 'grown up' in school, cheeking the teachers and bringing in bad habits like smoking and swearing. When teachers were labouring under the shadow of the 'Payment by Results' code prior to 1890, part-timers were a financial liability. Not surprisingly, the National Union of Teachers were early opponents of the system. Some authorities set up separate half-time schools, but their curricula seem to have been more limited, and they presented travelling problems for the children.[20] Miss Mary Anderson, headmistress of a Paisley half-time school, staunchly defended it before the Royal Commission on Physical Training (Scotland) in 1903, holding that the curriculum in full-time schools was overcrowded, and that her pupils were on the whole 'well fed'.

However, the claims of strain and physical damage were becoming more insistent at this time. Robert Sherard wrote of the anaemic condition of young factory girls: 'They cannot bear the air. Windows must be kept closed for them. They are chilly and bloodless. It affects their sight. You will notice how many young girls wear spectacles. This is caused by strain on the eyes occasioned by picking up fine threads. Clementina Black in 1907 likewise wrote of the 'peculiar mixture of pallor and eagerness' on the faces of the little half-timers when she visited a weaving shed.

The Departmental Committee on Physical Deterioration was told of the ill-health in 1904, though one certifying factory surgeon was apt to blame it partly on the cramming at school.[21] With the advent of the school medical service in 1907 more statistics became available. Lancashire studies in 1910–12, for example, revealed that 15.1 per cent of full-time scholars were 'physically defective' compared with 40 per cent of the half-timers. And the Oldham School Medical Officer reported in 1909 that half-timers were duller, less well nourished and more susceptible to TB, deformity, heart disease and defective vision than full-timers.[22]

The Departmental Committee on Partial Exemption from School

Attendance, appointed in 1909 in the context of Edwardian eugenic and 'blind-alley job' concerns, was fed with opinions, facts and figures purporting to damn half-time labour. Thus a survey in Halifax of twenty 12–13-year-old boys in full-time education between March and October 1908 showed an aggregate increase of 93.5 pounds in weight and 15.3 inches in chest measurement. For a group of half-timers of the same number and age the figures over the same period were only 12 pounds and 3.8 inches.[23] However, the committee was not convinced; contrasted sample groups might not be of comparable social background, and much of the ill-health described could be due to home and other environmental conditions, not just factory labour. The 'doffing' and 'piecing' done by half-timers was said to be light, and delicate children would in any case be screened out by the certifying factory surgeon (though, as we saw in Chapter 2, employers of half-timers sometimes bypassed these medical checks). None the less the committee did come out in favour of abolishing half-time exemptions and raising the minimum leaving age universally to 13 for those who passed their Labour Examination and had 'beneficial employment' to go to.

In fact there had already been a long-term decline in half-time labour; in 1899 there was less than half the number so employed as in 1876, and a further 13 per cent fall followed between 1899 and 1907.[24] Technological change had reduced the demand for 'little piecers', while the raising of the minimum school-leaving age and the abolition of half-time exemptions except in proven cases of poverty in some districts had had a marked effect. Thus in Huddersfield half-timers had reduced from 1,762 to 94 between 1879 and 1901.

The half-time principle had from the 1880s been actively opposed by early socialist groups. It is no coincidence that Bradford, the cradle of the Independent Labour Party, which had taken an early line against part-time labour, was also the centre from which the socialist child welfare campaigner Margaret McMillan pursued her campaign in the 1890s as a member of the school board. A Joint Committee for the Abolition of Half-Time Labour was formed. The Trades Union Congress (TUC) became officially anti-part-time, but within the TUC the textile workers unions put up a strong resistance to its abolition, and even where other unions officially backed the TUC line, many individual trade unionists privately supported part-time labour for the extra money it brought into the family.[25] Ballots among textile union members showed at least 80 per cent support for half-time labour.[26] Textile unions argued that as it was on the decline it should be allowed to die a natural death; abolition would be an interference with a youngster's right to work to gain beneficial experience, and would cause hardship to poor families and widows; while raising the school-leaving age would serve to put 'money only in the pockets of schoolmasters'.

Half-time work was rooted in strong local tradition in the textile counties. The Departmental Committee found that the children themselves did not feel forced into it by their parents:

> The children themselves like going to the mills. At first, at any rate, they enjoy the sense of being grown up and independent, and of having money to spend. We were not surprised to hear of a case where out of 300 children questioned only 7 replied that they would have preferred not to have gone into the mill.

However, they suffered later from the dead-end they had got themselves into. The Report commented: 'The feeling that it is worth making almost any sacrifice to prolong the education of the child is spreading only slowly through society.' The hard-luck stories it found specious: mill workers earned relatively good wages, and the half-timers' contributions – at most only about 4s a week – did not make that much difference. And a teachers' survey in Lancashire and Yorkshire among 13,169 cases showed only 1,296 were the children of widows. Half-time labour increased when the mills were booming and the parents were in funds; it declined in lean times, so there was no definite correlation between such child labour and family poverty.[27] The 'blind-alley' consideration was probably stronger than the alleged physical harm in persuading the committee of the desirability of abolition.

In 1911 the Liberal government introduced a bill abolishing half-time, but this was squeezed out by other parliamentary business. Another bill in 1914, likewise abolishing half-time and raising the minimum total exemption age generally to 13, was hotly and successfuly opposed by the cotton interests in Parliament.[28] Even when the Fisher Act did abolish it in 1918, it was a few years more before the Act's effects fully worked their way through.[29]

13

SCHOOL CURRICULUM CODES AND THE 'STANDARDS' 1862–1918

For the working classes around 1860 there was a variety of private educational provision offering frequently just a token education for a few pennies a week. (I am omitting any detail regarding institutional children, such as those in orphanages, workhouses and industrial schools, as they lie outside the scope of this book.) There were the factory schools for 'part-timers', and the seedy 'private adventure' schools also catering to this market and the needs of working parents for a place to deposit their infants during the day; they were found by the Royal Commission on Education of 1858–61 to be run variously by cripples, discharged servants, barmaids, outdoor paupers, consumptives and decrepits; the traditional dame schools fitted into this category. The schoolrooms were improvisations, like cellars, bedrooms, or kitchens, where disorder reigned in the stuffy and insanitary atmosphere. Sunday Schools and ragged schools offered a smattering of instruction by well-meaning volunteers for the intermittent attenders. Local clergy might run a parish class to supplement their income, but the most highly organized denominational networks were the 'National' and 'British' schools, run respectively by Church of England and Nonconformist foundations;[1] these, too, took factory half-timers.

What proportion of children were receiving any kind of instruction? In 1857 Prince Albert cited the following figures before an educational meeting:[2] of the 5 million 3–15-year-olds in England and Wales only two-fifths attended school at all, and only about 600,000 of these were over 9 years old.[3] Three-quarters of all pupils stayed only up to 2 years at school. Only 4 per cent attended for 5 years. The 1861 census gave more favourable figures; over two-thirds of 5–9-year-olds, and about 50 per cent of 10–14-year-olds were classed as 'scholars'.[4] William Farr, the government statistician, reckoned that a seventh of the child population was middle- or upper-class and as we can assume virtually all these would have been 'scholars', this suggests just over 40 per cent as scholars among the lower classes between 10 and 14. But did the term 'scholar' include the factory half-timers and little girls in the so-called 'lace schools'? Did it include intermittent attenders? In 1861 in Oxfordshire, for example, only 60 per cent of these children attended school even for as much as 100 days a year.[5]

There seems little doubt that the half-time system did much to promote schooling; around 1861 it was estimated that two-thirds of those starting at such schools, when they could begin factory work at 8, had received no prior schooling.[6] The Sunday Schools, too, played an educative role; whilst less than 14 per cent of working-class children attended them in 1801, over 75 per cent did so in 1851.[7]

It would be appropriate here to examine the contribution of the ragged schools to working-class education. They were intended for the benighted street-Arab population of the early Victorian period to serve as a rudimentary civilizing agency and as an antidote to delinquency. The instruction was free, and they set no rules regarding regularity of attendance or dress, in contrast to the church schools. The teachers, as idealistic volunteers, were probably less than acute to the exploitation of the schools, with the shelter and free meal they might offer, by the craftier urchins. Henry Mayhew wrote a series of highly controversial debunking articles on the schools in the *Morning Chronicle* in 1850.[8] He asserted that the schools had failed to offset delinquency, for figures showed that juvenile crime had been increasing; the more innocuous characters who went there rubbed shoulders with the more depraved types; the equation of civic decency with literacy was a myth, for criminals were just becoming more literate; and the 'literary' type of education there was unsuited to the needs of the youngsters, who really needed to learn a trade. The Royal Commission on Education in 1858–61 echoed Mayhew's scepticism. There were then about 21,000 ragged school pupils in England and Wales, a tiny percentage of the working-class child population. An investigator sent to report on the schools at Plymouth and Bristol found that they did not always cater to the waifs they were originally intended for; opportunistic working-class parents were sending their children to them rather than pay the fees at the church schools. He, too, found that delinquency had increased in Bristol since the schools' inception. One complaint from a church school, admittedly biased, was that discipline there had suffered because parents threatened to transfer their children to the ragged school if they were unacceptably chastised.

The investigator dismissed the social and educational value of the desultory attendances:

> to suppose that boys and girls are to receive any real benefit by being taught for a few hours during the week, whilst they pass the larger portion of their time in the streets, or amid scenes of the greatest profligacy, seems a little extravagant. There may, perhaps, be one or two cases in which under unpromising circumstances, a boy or girl has derived benefit from a ragged school, though I admit that I have been unable to discover any . . . . Unless the parent co-operates with the schoolmaster, it is impossible to make children attend school . . . and unless they attend school with moderate regularity, it is impossible that they can receive any benefit.[9]

The welfare role undertaken through the ragged schools, such as the job brigades, starting, as we have seen, with the shoeblack brigades at the time of the Great Exhibition, and the emigration schemes, are a separate consideration. The brigades were a recognition that pedagogy alone was not the way to rescue urchins from the streets; however, they could only be an improvisation as the lads were learning no skilled trade for the future, but they were defended as a social training in discipline and sober enterprise.[10] The National Refuges for Destitute Children were an outgrowth of the ragged school movement, and Dr Barnardo's first contact with homeless youngsters arose out of his experience as a ragged school teacher. The day schools progressively outlived their usefulness once board schools came in in 1870, but the latter remained fee-paying for many years, and there remained a declining residue of the poor parents who continued to send their children to the free ragged schools; between 1870 and 1885 the day schools run by the Ragged School Union (RSU) dwindled from 132 to 24, and attendances fell by some 86 per cent.[11] However, the RSU remained active in the field of community welfare – arranging free meals and outings for cripples, distributing clothing, running 'ragged Sunday Schools' and so forth.

National and British schools had qualified for government grants since 1833, and were subject to inspection. The teaching there was done on the cheap; teachers with a hall full of pupils would relay the lesson via monitors (older pupils) to their respective groups, and inevitably the tuition had to be reduced to rote-learning, and parroting out in chorus, through which the teacher would know that the lesson had been learned. From 1862, the Education Secretary Robert Lowe introduced more stringent criteria for subsidy as an economy measure to ensure 'value for money'. This was the Revised Code, known to teachers as 'Payment by Results', which was to bedevil the education system for the next thirty years. Individual schools' subsidies (upon which teachers' salary levels partly depended) were to be assessed for the year, upon the school inspectors' visits, according to pupils' performances in the three Rs alone; subjects like history and geography were left out of account and so suffered in the school timetable. Children were ranked in six 'Standards', according to age alone, from Standard 1 at age 7 to Standard 6 at age 12.[12] Pupils had to satisfy the inspector in his annual examination of competence in the three Rs at the Standard for their age, regardless (at least in the earlier codes) of the children's individual ability.[13] Attendance levels were also taken into account in the grant assessment. Schools became high-pressure examination factories; all teaching was geared to the annual descent from Olympus by the awesome inspector. From 1870 'Payment by Results' spread its blight into the new local authority board schools, and was to be at the heart of the 'overpressure' controversy from the 1880s. Periodically new codes were issued, and in the long run they did allow for a broadening of the curriculum and a modification of the obtuse rigidity of equating Standards solely with age. From 1867 other 'specific subjects', like history and geography, were introduced into the code, and from 1875 inspectors could also assess grants on the basis of 'class' tests, that is, on the tone and response of the class as a whole, apart from individual performances.[14] Some easing for board school (but not the National school) teachers came in 1883 when they were guaranteed a minimum income out of the rates;[15] school attendances were no longer to be crucial, either. From 1889 children could be entered for examinations at different Standards in different subjects according to actual attainment; individual ability was now being taken more fully into account. By 1890 'Payment by Results' was on its way out; the government's schools' grant now depended only marginally on examination performances, and by 1897 it was officially dead.

The system at its worst put nightmarish pressures on teachers, which they in turn inflicted on their pupils. Various stratagems were employed to improve attendance figures. Attendance registers were falsified; teachers sent pupils round to the homes of absentees to snoop on them; school attendance officers allegedly 'bullied' parents to get their children to school, regardless of the hardship to a poor family when a child's earnings were lost; and incentive prizes and medals were awarded to regular attenders.

All-out efforts were made to get children to school on examination day. Children sick with whooping cough and other infections were ferried in. Henry Jones, the son of a Denbigh shoemaker, born in 1852, recalled how his older brother was brought in a blanket to their Church of England school, though sick with measles and scarlet fever, as he was the school's best scholar – and he carried off the prizes! The codes prescribed that once a child passed a Standard he or she must be progressed to the next Standard; repeated entry at the same Standard to boost the pass rate was thus barred.[16] But the child must stick to the same Standard year after year until he or she passed it.

The elementary schools could not win either way, it seems, under the liberalization of the codes. Lord Norton[17] in 1883 claimed that the apparently enlightened addition of more specific subjects like algebra, chemistry, botany, French and domestic economy, was only a piece of window-dressing, a feeble attempt to imitate middle-class education; children were presented in only two of these for examination from Standard 5, and he maintained that working-class children were being introduced to these pretentious extras when they were still wanting in the more basic skills.

Teachers could request an inspector to excuse a child from the examination for sickness (so the pass rates could not be prejudiced), but the final decision lay with the inspector; and as he was a stranger to the children in his annual visitations, many a blind refusal must have been made; however, the Department of Education maintained that teachers were applying for withdrawals for 'fictitious and frivolous reasons'.[18] A grey area was a teacher's right to manage the pace of a child's progress up the Standards. There appears to have been suspicion of deliberate holding-back of children to improve pass rates, and school inspectors evidently had the power to override teachers and insist on the Standard which on paper was appropriate to their ages.[19] The result could be the situation found by George Sims in a board school in 1889 where he found a child who was 'but one remove from an idiot' sitting next to a very intelligent child, both expected to achieve the same Standard for their age. However, in the 1880s some latitude for low achievers seems to have been accepted,[20] and in 1890 inspectors were officially instructed to take the disadvantages for half-timers into account.[21]

Brighter children could from the early 1880s be accelerated and take their Standards early; from 1882 an advanced Standard 7 was introduced for them and others staying beyond the minimum leaving age. From this, 'higher elementary' and 'higher grade' schools were to develop for 10–15-year-olds; they prepared pupils for commercial, technical and academic examinations (City and Guilds, for instance) and were the beginnings of the local authority secondary 'grammar' schools as they became after 1902.[22]

The 'overpressure' controversy prompted the Department of Education to commission a report by James Crichton-Browne, a medical authority on the subject, in 1884. His report, as we shall see, was damning, but was challenged by the department's chief inspector, J. G. Fitch, who claimed that the codes were sufficiently flexible and humane in allowing for sickness, delicacy and differences of ability.[23] Both experts had their obvious biases, so in 1885 the London School Board conducted its own inquiry;[24] London was a progressive authority, and wanted even more power to differentiate by ability, but it intriguingly came down in favour of Fitch's view and against Crichton-Browne.

There must have been tricky organizational problems for schools trying to take ability as well as age into account in banding pupils. Should the failures be kept back with a younger age group? If so, would there be enough room in the class for these super-numeraries? Should they instead be moved up with their peers to retake the former Standard while their classmates prepared for the next one? How, in that case, would teachers faced with classes of 60 or more pupils cope with teaching different groups within the same class simultaneously? Could the slow learners, while being moved up a year, be taught in a separate class? The answers to such questions would explain the indispensability of monitors and pupil-teachers as teaching auxiliaries. Pupil-management was in part dictated by school architecture. Before 1870 school buildings were not divided into separate classrooms, but had one large hall where children were coached in groups under monitors, and later

121

pupil-teachers. Even when the new board schools were being constructed on the classroom design, the less well-endowed national schools had to continue making do with antiquated conditions; and in village schools the one teacher still had to teach the different age groups simultaneously. Flora Thompson describes how one village schoolmistress grouped the children by age and employed a monitor who gave dictations and heard tables and spellings repeated. The 'babies' were taught to chant the alphabet, and they were left chanting on their own while she went round the other groups. The rector came in as the Scripture specialist.

In urban schools there is evidence that slow learners were being kept back with younger children in the 1880s. Thus in 1885 it is recorded that at Gloucester Grove Board School in London one R. Batts, aged 9, said to be 'hopelessly dull', spent 3 years in Standard 1;[25] this policy seems to have been fully approved by the London School Board.[26] Children who were moved up a year automatically, pass or fail, could present behaviour and truancy problems when they could not keep up with their classmates. On the other hand, the policy of keeping them back was doomed when there was just no room for them to stay with the year-group following, or else the stigma of being kept back itself created behaviour problems. Thus a Tower Hamlets school inspector told the 1898 Departmental Committee on Defective and Epileptic Children of a girl 'with no brains' who through being kept back year after year 'became gradually dirty and untidy and even spiteful'. Finally she was moved up to her age-peers, and though she could not cope with the work, she was better adjusted and more co-operative.[27] Where there were enough poor achievers in a school a way out was to create a special residual class; this was called 'Standard 0', and lumped together the dullards, the partially sighted and delicate children, under the charge of a pupil-teacher.[28] From 1892 Leicester, followed by London, pioneered special schools for slow learners, where the pace was gentle and no work above Standard 2 was given; but these were still in short supply in the early 1900s.[29]

School inspectors were characteristically pompous, self-important figures, whose coming sent fear and trepidation through the teaching staff, which they in turn communicated to the children. Flora Thompson recalls the dreaded visitation to her school by an elderly clergyman 'with an immense paunch and tiny grey eyes like gimlets' who 'looked at the rows of children as if he hated them and at the mistress as if he despised her'. Until 1889 London teachers were themselves assessed annually for their 'parchment' upon which their prospects depended, and this must have added to the pressures on the children.[30] A school song children were made to sing to keep their spirits up had a verse which ran:

> Would you like to know the reason
> Why we all look bright and gay
> As we hasten to our places?
> This is our Inspection Day!
> Fie! What is that you say,
> You hate Inspection Day?

Once the inspector had gone, however, the relief might bring a spate of retaliatory canings against children who had let the teachers down.[31]

The examinations were based on the readers and other texts used during the year (sometimes these had been prescribed by the inspectors themselves). Children were questioned on comprehension, spelling and grammar ('parsing'), individually and collectively in class. They were tested for fluency and modulation in their reading and their capacity to take dictation. Teachers crammed and drilled the children in their texts *ad nauseam* during the year to try to make them word perfect. James Runciman in 1887 recalled one teacher who turned Scripture into a monotonous, miserable grind.

> [He] listened to dreary chapters repeated by rote: he talked about David until the boys wished that Goliath had cut short the career of that eminent monarch; he chopped up the Sermon on the Mount until the Master would certainly have failed to recognize his own sweet words, for even the Apostle Matthew would have made but a poor show in a School Board examination on his own Gospel.

His lessons went thus:

> 'Take page 130. Now begin at "Immediately" and go down to the tenth line. Write out all the hard words four times . . . .' After an interval the word was given, 'Clean slates.' Then the master dictated about six words; then the scholars exchanged slates and corrected each other's errors . . . then the farce began again.

The brighter pupils were held back, till the slower ones (hopefully) caught up, for they all had to attain the same Standard.[32]

Charles Kingsley's *The Water Babies* (1863) contains a famous satire on the effects of Robert Lowe's Revised Code and the fear of the examiner. On the Isle of Tomtoddies the children, reduced to 'turnips with little but water inside' from all the brain-cramming, wail and lament as the examination draws near, and Kingsley parodies the obscure facts and figures the examiner expects them to have at recall: 'What is the latitude and longitude of Snooksville, in Noman's County, Oregon, U.S.?' and 'What was the name of Mutius Scaevola's thirteenth cousin's grandmother's maid's cat?' and 'How long would it take a school inspector of average ability to tumble head over heels from London to York?' This was only a little more far-fetched than the absurdities inflicted by the worst kind of inspectors, who seemed to enjoy catching the children out. One inspector in the 1880s dictated to infants a passage beginning 'While Hugh was culling yew, his ewes ...', while another considered Byron's *The Prophecy of Dante* a suitable text for Finsbury children at Standard 6 (age 12); this contains in the third canto the lines:

> And language, eloquently false, evince
> The harlotry of genius, which, like beauty,
> Too often forgets its own self-reverence,
> And looks on prostitution as a duty.

Another later Victorian inspector for the Greenwich district, the Rev. D. J. Stewart, used to give 6-year-olds the following dictation: 'If you twist that stick so long, you will make your wrist ache, and the knob is so near my dwarf fiddle that I am in a fright. I shall put it in my baize bag with the strap and buckle.'[33] An anecdote is told of a bullying inspector who liked asking trick questions and rounded on the teachers if the children got them wrong.[34] In a text on parts of speech,

> he put his hand on the Bible and asked, 'What is this?' The class held up their hands, and six girls one after another announced, 'A noun.'
> 'You are wrong,' said the examiner, 'This is not scientific teaching, Jane (to the teacher). How can a Bible be a name? Did you never think of that?'

This inspector was also a self-styled expert on needlework. He criticized the quality of the hemming and the uncleanness of the work in the lower classes of another young teacher, Caroline. She tried to excuse this by explaining that some of the children came from poor dirty homes:

> 'Ah! You are good at explanations, Caroline: a useful accomplishment. Well now, next year I shall expect your third standard to do what your fifth standard are doing now in needlework.'
>
> 'I fear it cannot be done, Sir.'
>
> 'But I shall expect it, and I shall expect the quality of your Swiss darning to be much improved. Oh, I've no doubt we shall learn each other's ways, shall we not? Good morning.'

The end result of this kind of treatment was that the teacher was forced to keep pupils back for extra practice till after 5 p.m., draining their energies, and herself ending in an early grave.

What skills did the Standards demand at different ages? Modifications were made under different codes, but if we take arithmetic under the 1903 Code, for example, Standard 1 (age 7) required the 'four simple rules' and division and multiplication not exceeding 6; these were increased up to 12 at Standard 2 and up to 99 at Standard 3. From Standard 2 children were introduced to money questions, and from Standard 4 to weights and measures. Fractions came in at Standard 5 (age 11) and at Standard 6 decimals, square and cube roots.[35] The official assumption was that girls were genetically less capable at arithmetic and the code states: 'The work of girls will be judged more leniently than that of boys, and as a rule the sums set will be easier'; at Standard 6, for example, girls would not be tested on decimals.

Reading exercises were likewise graduated; at Standard 6 the children were expected to be able to read a passage from Shakespeare or other standard authors. Textbooks were geared to the examinations and were commonly 'readers' comprising a miscellany of extracts from different sources, so that children would not get a chance to go through a complete Shakespeare play, for example. Attached to the extracts were exercises in parsing, etymology and spelling. The backs of the books might contain a few pages of potted history and geography – dry data listing the names and dates of kings, wars and battles, the names of countries, their sizes, populations, main cities, capes, bays, rivers and products.

With the ending of every vestige of 'Payment by Results' in 1897, the examinations became just a test for the Labour Certificate and early half-time or full-time exemption, but the Victorian format of readers, such as those published by Nelson, was to survive the ending of early exemption under the 1918 Education Act. To end this chapter I have taken samples from different Victorian textbooks to show what educationalists believed children could learn at different ages. In subsequent chapters we shall see what the children actually did take in.

Henry Major was a prolific compiler of school textbooks. His 'New Code Readers' of 1875 contain passages of varying intelligibility. Book 3 (for 9-year-olds), has a passage on ferns containing this interminable sentence:

> At this sweet season of the year, when the sap is rising in the gnarled knotted oak, when out of the heavy, dull clod of earth, the pure lily and purple violet and creamy primrose draw their beautiful tints, it seems as if the hands which had restrained all the forces of nature during the long, hard winter, were suddenly withdrawn, and life and joy were having a grand birthday again, and what a chorus the birds ring out.

Children aged 9 were being taught to parse in the following fashion:

> Sentence: 'A strong brave man went in great haste to the raging fire and with immense labour he put out the roaring flames.'
> A = Demonstrative adjective, qualifying the noun 'man'.
> Strong = Adjective of quality, positive degree, qualifying noun 'man'.
> Brave = Adjective of quality, positive degree, qualifying the noun 'man'.
> Man = Common noun, singular, masculine, nominative case to action 'went'.
> Great = Adjective of quality, positive degree, qualifying 'haste'.
> Haste = Noun abstract, singular, neuter, objective case after the preposition 'in'.

and so on, word by word through the sentence. Such exercises, when based on the extracts, must have rapidly killed off any burgeoning interest a child might have in good literature.

A typical historical fragment from Book 4 (for 10-year-olds) covering the history of Britain from 55 BC to AD 1066 relates the reign of Ethelred the Unready thus:

Reign – He succeeded his step-brother and reigned from 978 to 1016; thirty-eight years.

Wars 980–993. A Danish invasion took place on the south coast of East Anglia: the English under Brithnot were defeated at Maldon.

993 – First payment of £10,000 to the Danes to induce them to leave England.

994 – Attack on the east cost of Sweyn and Olave, King of Sweden – Second payment of £16,000 to Olave.

1001 – Third payment of £24,000.

1001 – Alliance of England and Normandy . . .

Major's *Daily Spelling Books in Six Standards* (1875) included as appropriate for 7-year-olds worlds like 'prejudice', 'servitude', 'yacht', 'awl', 'wreck', 'destruction', and 'enclosure', and at 9 they were expected to catch the distinctions in pairs of dictated words like 'ingenuous' and 'ingenious', 'eligible' and 'illegible', 'guerrilla', and 'gorilla', 'rabbit' and 'rabbet' (a carpentry term).

The arithmetic could match the parsing for ponderous pointlessness. In the 1870s and 1880s 9-year-olds at Standard 3 were posed such problems as: 'What number divided by 154 brings the quotient 154 and the remainder 54?'; Multiply £26-12s-11$\frac{1}{4}d$ by 16'; '£7,214-8s-6$\frac{1}{4}d$ divided by 9'. At Standard 4 the following bill had to be worked out: '29 fine Cambridge geese at 8s-10$\frac{1}{2}d$'; 26 couples of fat ducks at 2s-10$\frac{3}{4}d$ each; 18$\frac{1}{3}d$ bladders of lard, each 10$\frac{1}{5}$lbs at 8$\frac{3}{4}d$ per lb; 59 pairs of pigeons at 6$\frac{1}{2}d$ each; 114 couples of chickens at 5s 7$\frac{3}{4}d$ per couple.'[36] Eleven-year-olds were required to try one improbable piece of accounting: 'A number of men and boys earn £12-17s-6d a day; how much will it amount to in a solar year (365 days 5 hours 48 minutes)?' and 12-year-olds were confronted by such problems as: 'If 6 men and 8 women can do a piece of work in 14 days, working 8$\frac{1}{2}$ hours per day, in what time will 4 men and 10 women do a piece of work 4 times as large, working 9 hours per day, each man doing double of a woman?'[37]

Victorian textbooks were replete with problems about the time taken for taps to fill unplugged baths and lists of tables of ale and beer measures, dry measures, troy and apothecaries' weights, cloth measures and so on. We cannot be surprised that in 1880 only 47 per cent of schoolchildren reached the norm of Standard 4 at age 10, and around 1904 up to three-quarters of pupils in some slum schools left without ever attaining Standard 4.[38]

14

TEACHING METHODS
1860–1918

The classroom regime was governed by four factors: the imperatives of the codes and examinations, the size of classes, prevailing attitudes about the status of children, and philosophies about what education should be preparing children for in adult life.

The codes and 'Payment by Results' were not entirely responsible for the interminable rote-learning, for the monitorial system in the British and National schools had long necessitated this method as a way of teaching large numbers on the cheap. The Royal Commission on Education of 1858–61, which had been set up to review the effectiveness of the government grants to those schools, itself revealed the ludicrous effects of brute memorizing. One inspector, Mr Foster, reported, for example, how in one school a 13-year-old girl recited the boundaries of several countries:

I asked, 'What is a boundary?'
'It's a year's wages.'
My question had suggested to her mind the terms on which the pitmen are in some collieries *bound* for a year to their employment. Doubtless she did not dream of its connection with the lesson she had just repeated.[1]

Another inspector, Mr Fraser, told of a 14-year-old girl who recited St Luke, chapter 4, verse 14, thus: 'And there went out a flame of him through all the religion round about', instead of 'a fame of him through all the region round about', with no idea of the gibberish she was uttering. When he asked a class in another school 'What is a region?', a boy replied 'A roundabout', which Fraser attributed to the uncomprehending association with the word in the aforementioned verse.[2]

Despite this futility, the Revised Code which followed the

commission's Report reinforced the same methods, and after all they were no different from the methods employed in private middle-class schools to instil 'proper' knowledge, and coach pupils for the developing range of middle-class examinations. Winifred Peck recalled the Scripture and history she was taught in a private girls' school in late Victorian Birmingham, which she attended till the age of 10:

> More than half the lesson was occupied by our recital of an extraordinary rhyme which was designed to teach us the order of the books of the Bible. We would chant . . .
> 'In Genesis the world was made by God's creative hand:
> In Exodus the Hebrews marched to gain the promised land:
> Deuteronomy records the law, holy, just and good:
> Numbers recalls the tribes enrolled, all sons of Israel's
> blood . . . '

A similar doggerel mnemonic was employed in history, ending:

> Till the four Georges and William all past
> God gave us Victoria, the loved and the last.

When she transferred to a Ladies' College at Eastbourne, the methods were the same: wearisome recitations of the order of the Kings of Israel and Judah, for example, but no insight or explanations offered, with the result that 'In short, I suppose I knew more, and understood less, of the Bible than any child to-day.'

History likewise remained for her a lifeless calendar of dynastic doings: 'Of the story of the English people as a whole I had no ideas at all; they were just "the mob" who died of the Black Death, rioted under Jack Cade or stood by at burnings and executions and coronations.

The rote-learning frequently entailed repeating vocabularies and concepts far beyond a child's grasp. Alison Uttley[3] remembered how in her village school at the same period children learned the Scriptures through alphabetical mottoes they could not have understood:

A – Ask and it shall be given unto you.
B – Blessed are the peacemakers.
C – Consider the lilies of the field . . .

and so on. As with recitation, so with calligraphy. Youngsters spent much time practising their copperplate by transcribing words like 'Zumiologist' and 'Xenodochium' or phrases like 'Study universal rectitude' in the 1860s,[4] and in the 1890s the merest infants still had to copy uncomprehended mottoes like 'Flee Evil Companions' and 'Procrastination is the Thief of Time'.[5] It is noteworthy, however, that the autobiographers do recall the mnemonics and chants they had to learn half a century before; and not all found it a chore. They admit to deriving some perverse satisfaction from being able to reel off lists 'just for the fun of the thing'.[6] However, the true cultural and intellectual value of memorization was dubious, to say the least. In the early 1860s Henry Mayhew and John Binny commented how boys in the Tothill Fields Prison were taught to 'chatter catechisms and creeds they cannot understand';[7] Flora Thompson recalled how in her country school boys who had an intelligent interest in farm life and nature outside were completely switched off by the monotonous recitals from the readers.

Critics complained that the emphasis on grammar and parsing dried up pupils' interest, stifled their imaginations and was totally irrelevant to character development.[8] Winifred Peck remembered only too vividly 'the awful morass of adverbial and adjectival clauses and indirect extension of the predicate in which we waded forlornly'. And another young man recalled in 1902 his education in an elementary school in the late 1880s where they were taught parsing 'but we could not for the life of us understand what the good of it all was'. Pupils became dispirited and dazed: 'I can truly say that reading at school gave me no inclination whatever to read any kind of literature when I was at home.' He left school at 11 and only began to read again at 15 – even then his reading was confined to trashy novels and penny dreadfuls, and he only took up serious literature at 17.[9]

Concern about the sterile cramming of useless data was expressed by the Royal Commission on Education in 1887. The ethos of schools was felt to be 'too bookish and insufficiently practical'.[10] The new code of 1890 took these structures to heart and substantially abandoned 'Payment by Results' to enable schools to reduce the time spent on the three Rs, which formerly had 'paid', and to develop practical subjects and manual skills, as in woodwork and domestic science. However, good intentions were one thing; decent facilities were another. The sheer size of elementary school classes necessitated regimentation in class.

Classes could reach 80 in the 1880s, but even at the turn of the century, whilst the average had fallen to nearly 42, some teachers faced classes of over 60 and they had to stay authoritarian and must have relied on memorization and chanting to preserve discipline.[11] Diversification of the curriculum depended on the availability of suitably qualified teachers, equipment, textbooks and space. Teachers, by definition almost, were bookishly inclined and perpetuated the old methods long after the pressures that necessitated them had eased. Up to the First World War criticisms were still being levelled at cramming and memorization.[12] George Orwell fictionally depicted his experience of teaching by these methods between the wars in a seedy girls' private school in his novel *A Clergyman's Daughter* (1935):[13]

> There were only two girls in the class who knew whether the Earth went round the Sun or the Sun went round the Earth, and not a single one of them could tell ... who was the last king before George V, or who wrote *Hamlet*, or what was meant by a vulgar fraction, or which ocean you crossed to get to America.

Their knowledge consisted of a hotch-potch of unconnected fragments – odd stanzas from pieces of poetry and fragmentary French phrases, for instance.

The textbooks were gravely defective. The drawbacks of the readers, geared to the Standards, were alluded to in the last chapter. But textbooks for middle-class schools were just as bad. Molly Hughes, who was taught at home by her mother in the 1870s up to the age of 11, remembered the opening sentence of her geography book: 'The Earth is an oblate spheroid.' Her science book, Dr Brewster's *Guide to Science*, presented its dubious information in catechismal question and answer form:

Q: What is heat?
A: That which produces the sensation of warmth.
Q: What is light?
A: The unknown cause of visibility ....
Q: What should a fearful person do to be secure in a storm?
A: Draw his bedstead into the middle of his room, commit himself to the care of God, and go to bed.'

Where geography texts were not just a catalogue of data, their human information was inane and stereotypic, with characterizations like 'The Irish are a merry people and fond of pigs' or 'Italians are a dark revengeful race where the stiletto is in frequent use',[14] while of the Levantines children learned: 'The Greeks are an enterprising commercial people, restless and impatient to control, while the Turks, though a brave race, are naturally indolent, careless of intercourse with foreign nations, and averse to progress.'[15] Richmal Mangnall's *Historical and Miscellaneous Questions*, a favourite in middle-class seminaries throughout the nineteenth century, embodies all the defects of Victorian schooling, as a catechismal, formula-style hotch-potch, evidently lending itself to memorization, with fragments ranging from classical history and mythology through British history and the British constitution to astronomy. For example:

Who was the Queen of Henry VI?
Answer: Margaret of Anjou, a woman of keen penetration, undaunted spirit and exquisite beauty. She fought twelve pitched battles in her husband's cause, but ambition, not affection, guided her actions; and, wanting principle, she may engage our pity, but has no title to our esteem and reverence.

It is some measure of pedagogic stagnation that while the fifth edition of Mangnall was published in 1806, a revised edition did not come out till 1869. Orwell found a reader of 1863 still in use in the girls' school, its 'Nature Notes' containing this gem:

The Elephant is a sagacious beast. He rejoices in the shade of the palm trees, and though stronger than six horses, he will allow a little child to lead him. His food is Bananas.[16]

A history book in the same school was dated 1888.

Even when efforts were made to diversify the curriculum with subjects like domestic economy, biology and botany, the learning was reduced to theoretical definitions. Lord Norton in 1883 sardonically criticized those elementary schools which were over-ambitiously applying new subjects to working-class children who could barely cope with the three Rs, and reducing those subjects to meaningless lists of scientific jargon:[17]

By 'Animal Physiology' is meant a study of anatomical

diagrams so far as to get by heart the Latin names of every feature, enabling a child to call the back of his head 'hocciput' and his shoulder 'umerus'. Botany . . . is presented to many children in a form of stiffest nomenclature, classifying flowers as monocotyleda or dicotyleda and trees as gymnospermous, confiers or cycads.

Contemporary views of the proper duties of children towards adults also shaped teaching methods. While 'children were to be seen and not heard' and due reference and subordination were expected, sanctioned by a liberal resort to corporal punishment, teaching was inevitably authoritarian and the learning process regimented; it is significant that the earliest form of physical instruction was termed 'drill'. Children were not only taught their place as children, but were also taught their future proper place as adults. Elementary schoolchildren were intended to be operatives or clerks. This attitude was particularly strong in country schools, where the social hierarchy was strictly defined, and the squirearchy (and their lackeys, the clergy) were the bigwigs on local councils and school committees. They wanted to turn out docile farm labourers and domestics respectful of their betters, not social aspirers. Flora Thompson recalled how in greeting their starchy schoolmarm each morning the boys pulled their forelocks and the girls curtsied. When the rector had given them their Scripture lesson he delivered a lecture on morals and behaviour: 'The children must not lie or steal or be discontented or envious. God had placed them just where they were in the social order and given them their own especial work to do; to envy others or to try and change their own lot in life was a sin of which he hoped they would never be guilty.' Kate Taylor, who was born in Suffolk in 1891, remembered how school was used as an agency for enforcing social subordination outside. Kate had a rebellious streak, and one day when she was scrubbing a doorstep, she refused to stop, curtsy and make way for the local lady of the manor, Lady Thornhill. This was reported to her headmaster and next day Kate received six strokes of the cane in front of the whole school.[18]

However, while children might be outwardly cowed into conformity and deference there is evidence that they put on an act for their own ends. Thus a self-seeking motive for attending Sunday School was the prospect of charitable gifts at Christmas and an annual outing, their only chance of a holiday.[19] Just prior to the

First World War, after more than a generation of compulsory schooling, complaints were current that modern youth was less than compliant; the façade of submission at school was doubtless thrown over once they could leave; young men, it was said, preferred sport to duty and girls were only too keen to turn their backs on domestic service for a freer and better-paid life in a factory.[20]

To early and mid-Victorians if education was to be justified at all it must inculcate habits of industry as a preparation for the child's duties in life.[21] The Royal Commission on Education went as far in 1861 in stating: 'Independence is more important than education, and if the wages of a child's labour are necessary [to ease family poverty] it is far better that it should go to work at the earliest age at which it can bear the physical exertion than it should remain at school.'[22]

Approved library texts for Sunday and day schools reinforced the message; the Society for Promoting Christian Knowledge and the Religious Tract Society churned out pietistic fiction for children, in which the 'good' people were religious, forbearing and respectful to their superiors.[23]

Social and academic regimentation were also harnessed to the jingoistic and imperialist mood that waxed in the last two decades of the nineteenth century. Teaching became propagandist in promoting the ideas of Britain's destiny to rule over the 'savage' races. History lessons extolled feats of British pluck and daring. Geography lessons rejoiced in maps showing the expanses of red, the empire 'on which the sun never sets'. Empire Day became a red-letter day in the school calendar. Schools were decked out with Union Jacks, the children sang monarchist and patriotic songs like 'Here's a Health unto his Majesty' and 'Three Cheers for the Red, White and Blue',[24] and they assembled to hear patriotic speeches by visiting dignitaries. One would have thought that this right-wing ethos would have militated against educational liberalism, yet it was precisely at this period that educational philosophies were becoming more reflective. The overpressure controversy was to prompt questions about the value of any kind of schooling for half-starved children; a sense of responsibility for nutrition and health was gradually to seep through into official policy; and there was the unease that schools were failing to turn out youngsters with the right technical and manual skills necessary for Britain's economic future;[25] children should be stimulated; more spontaneity should be introduced into lessons and children encouraged to manipulate objects. Such ideas were associated with the German educationalist Friedrich Froebel and were to filter in from the 1870s but only at the pre-Standards ages below 7. Such a thawing at the philosophic level went hand in hand with the abandonment of 'Payment by Results'. In 1896 the Departmental Committee on Reformatories and Industrial Schools (which were almost military in their regimention) opined:

> If in the early or the middle part of the present century, the idea of education was for mental instruction to impart knowledge, and for morals ... to discipline the child into habits of rectitude and industry, it has come more and more to be felt that while these methods should not cease to be duly exercised, the aim ... should rather be on the one hand to cultivate intelligence, and on the other, by kindness, to develop the affections as mainsprings of good conduct. It is also now better recognized that a child's physical health, its liberty, amusements and happiness, are as inseparable from the formation of its mind, feelings and character as these are from each other.[26]

Fine-sounding sentiments, but against them were ranged the fears of many that liberalization in the classroom would encourage youngsters to get ideas above their station,[27] and the industrial schools themselves remained just as regimented, up to the start of the First World War.[28]

What practical liberalizations were achieved, then, by 1914? Froebel had opened his first 'kindergarten' in 1837 to cultivate infants by 'hand and eye' training; there was much emphasis on modelling, art work, music and games. An early kindergarten-style crèche was set up for women employees by the Salford engineering firm William Mather in 1873 and the Kindergarten Association was formed in Britain in 1874. Froebel had developed his methods in ideal settings, but their application to huge classes of slum children in state schools was another matter.[29] Since 1870 school boards had been empowered to let parents send their children to 'babies' classes' at the local elementary school from 3 years old to 5. Infants' classes started at 5, and remained free from the straitjacket of Standards for another two years. Working mothers found the babies' classes a boon, but the little tots in classes of 60 or even 80 were often made to sit rigidly in serried ranks on over-high backless benches (from which they sometimes had bruising falls) and subjected to a rudimentary version of the regime in the Standards. The Departmental Committee on Physical Deterioration in 1904 indeed recommended their closure, and the Board of Education temporarily complied in 1905, but after protests from employers and teachers (who wanted the extra jobs) they were re-allowed in 1906.[30] The teachers, who were trained for formal teaching, were not necessarily the right sort for the babies, and the male school inspectors applied the wrong criteria for their 'success'; one is said to have reported: 'The mental arithmetic of the baby class leaves much to be desired'![31] Froebelian ideas were beginning to filter into the babies' and infants' classes from around 1883,[32] though initial ideals sometimes tended to ossify again into formalized teaching. Charles Booth reported favourably on London's babies' classes in 1890, saying that the tots had 'little benches comfortably fitted', the 'teachers in them were keen' and they were 'busy contented places';[33] but this is at variance with a public report on babies' classes by women inspectors (appointed in the light of controversy about the classes' unsuitability) which in 1906 criticized London classes as too formal.[34]

The Education Codes had by the turn of the century been prescribing Froebelian methods for the 3- to 7-year-olds: games, drawing, threading beads, matching colours, basic counting with shells and word-building, progressing to measuring and elementary handicraft.[35] The 1906 reports on babies' classes by women inspectors presented a variable picture of their regimes. In the worst classes there was too much sitting still and too little free play; space was wanting, and children had to sleep on the benches or on the floor; this coupled with the over-size benches was condemned as bad for posture. Needlework was frowned on in the reports as cramping little fingers and straining eyesight. Teaching and discipline were too formal and repressive: 'Babies who don't look three', said one report, 'were made to stand for thirty minutes without stirring, for singing and recitation. When standing, the toes of each foot had to be parallel to those of the other.'[36] The classes in South Wales, by contrast, were highly praised for their freedom and informality. Ruth Johnson, who was born in Lancashire in 1912, says there was a long tradition in northern mill towns for mothers to send their infants to school at 3, and her own memories of the babies' class from 1915 show that it was run on proper Foebelian lines:

Under Mrs Griffith's kindly and all-seeing eye we played with sand on big trays; we played with coloured paper and cardboard boxes; we played with everything we could think of. The greatest magic of all, however, was a swing attached by long ropes to the beams of the ceiling.

They learned songs like 'Here We Come Looby-Loo' and 'Poor Mary Sits A-Weeping' and the room was brightly decorated with pictures.[37]

Sometimes the babies' and infants' classes were placed under the least experienced teachers. Margaret Leonora Eyles found herself charged in this way when merely a pupil-teacher at 14 around the turn of the century. Inevitably the classes were informal to the point of disorder. Children were in danger of cutting themselves on the sharp edges of the counting shells, or stuffing them into facial orifices; sand trays got tipped over, and there were the inevitable toilet 'accidents', when a child made a 'wet mess' on the floor, and the 'best' child had the privilege of carrying over a bucket of sawdust and pouring it over the wet, which Margaret then swept up. She recalled one amusing episode when an 8-year-old girl who happened to be niece to a 4-year-old boy asked her, 'Please miss, can I take me uncle Jim to leave the room because he has had brimstone and treacle?'

Higher up the school, in the Standards, liberalization was taking the form of a widening of the curriculum, as the codes were relaxed. However, as we have observed, not everybody viewed the trends favourably. The introduction of sciences, domestic economy and French, for example, was attacked as 'window-dressing', of no practical value to working-class youngsters on leaving school; 'culture' could be acquired later on at evening classes, but its emphasis at school was said to encourage a contempt for manual labour.[38] Some of the critics were motivated by class prejudice; education should not encourage working-class children in ideas above their station. Others may have been just attacking the desiccated, theoretical methods of imparting these new subjects. In domestic economy in the early 1880s it was complained that 'future kitchen maids' were being taught without kitchen facilities, and their 'training' comprised theoretical classifications:

[They] are taught to distinguish warmth-giving from flesh-forming foods respectively as carbonaceous and nitrogeneous. They can enumerate the ingredients of starch, fat, and sugar in the former as farinaceous, oleaginous and saccharine matter; and white of egg, fibre, curds &c in the latter as 'halbumen', fibrine, casein, gluten &c.[39]

Other critics believed in emphasizing vocational subjects at the expense of the academic for pragmatic, not 'class' reasons; most youngsters could absorb only a limited amount of academic learning each day. J. G. Legge, the Chief Inspector for Reformatories and Industrial Schools (where this principle was practised), said in 1902 that the school day should be equally divided between the academic and the vocational and those who opposed this could not 'grasp the idea that in teaching a particular trade you give a general training of value'.[40] Sir John Gorst, a former Conservative Education Minister, was not opposed to a measure of vocational training; he was sceptical about the value of formalizing the new subjects into examinable disciplines, the result of an overwhelming poedagogic compulsion to give teaching an 'aim' in class; and he believed that the curriculum should be derived more from the children's environment to stimulate their curiosity.[41]

Some efforts were being made towards more stimulation in class in the late nineteenth century. The Art for Schools Association was formed, numbering the book illustrator, Walter Crane, among its founders, to promote the decoration of the otherwise bare school board classrooms with bright pictures.[42] The Royal Commission on Education in 1887 recommended a Froebelian approach in the Standards with demonstrations and experiments, elementary draughtsmanship (for boys), cookery for girls and 'Slojd' (Swedish educational woodwork).[43] By 1904 the magic lantern was being used in London schools for geography lessons.[44] From the 1890s 'object lessons' had come into vogue. Children were shown objects – plants, mineral samples, products like tea and sugar and so forth – which were treated as the nucleus of different areas of instruction radiating from them.

By the 1890s drawing was compulsory for boys, and needlework for girls.[45] Cookery and laundry work were becoming increasingly available for girls, but I shall be dealing with the girls' curriculum more fully later. By 1904 a typical London board school was offering, in addition to the three Rs, drawing, needlework, class singing, geography, history, elementary science and some form of 'drill' or physical education. Some boasted optional subjects such as

French, book-keeping, shorthand, algebra, hygiene and more specialized sciences like physics and botany.[46]

Manual subjects were still only available to the minority; in 1909 of boys in England and Wales only 36 per cent did handicraft and 5 per cent gardening; of girls only 34 per cent did cookery and 8.5 per cent laundrywork, and criticisms were still being voiced that elementary education was reflecting the values of schoolteachers, turning out future white-collar workers and insufficient trainees for industry.[47]

The evolution of physical education (PE) reflects the liberalization process. The 1870 Code allowed only for 'drill', in imitation of the well-drilled Prussian army, a set of mechanical movements performed to order. As many early board schools lacked playgrounds, drill was suited to the classroom; it was intended more to promote obedience than give healthy exercise to the body:

> One! and you stood at your desk. Two! and you put your left leg over the seat. Three! and the right one joined in. Four! and you faced the lane between the class. Five! you marched on the spot. Six! you stepped forward and the pupil teacher chanted 'Left, right, left, right.[48]

So long as it was not a 'paying' subject under the codes schools neglected it, and many offered no drill at all in the 1870s.[49] The Royal Commission on Education in 1887 called for much more attention to be paid to sport and games, and the 1890 Code allowed for wider forms of physical education. Swedish drill, entailing the use of staves and clubs, had appeared in some elementary schools in the 1880s, and gymnastics by 1900. Working-class schools just began to introduce team games like football in the 1880s, but lagged far behind the public schools, where seasonal games had become an integral part of their culture since the mid-nineteenth century.[50] The late Victorian and Edwardian boys' club movement was to help fill the gap for working-class youth with the formation of club teams. Physical education remained a low status subject in state schools even when it ceased to be a 'non-paying' subject, and in 1903 some schools devoted as little as 15 minutes a week to it. Parents were not keen on it where it interfered with their children's studies for the Labour Certificate and early exemption.[51]

After 1900 there was stronger official interest in PE as part of the contemporary concern about the 'strength of the race'. Both the

Royal Commission on Physical Training (Scotland) (1903) and the Departmental Committee on Physical Deterioration (1904) recommended more emphasis on physical education. The irony was that the poorest areas which had most need also had the worst facilities; though it was also pointed out to the Scottish Commission that PE was not necessarily beneficial to malnourished children. Medical authorities were setting up a National League for Physical Education and Improvement, and in 1909 the Board of Education made PE a grant-earning subject in recognized continuation schools. Thus in the period 1870 to 1909 physical education had changed in intent from another form of regimentation to a means of promoting the health and vitality of schoolchildren, akin to the school feeding and medical inspection programmes. But in facilities elementary schools were still lagging behind the later-appointed workhouse district schools, with their own swimming-pools and gymnasiums, and the industrial schools, which had their own football and cricket leagues.[52]

The Victorians had very rigid ideas about sex roles and were hidebound with myths about supposed psychological and emotional susceptibilities of the female, and this was reflected in the education system. Women internalized many prejudices against their own sex. Ellen Barlee in 1863 called for a differentiation between boys' and girls' curricula.[53] Girls needed a 'different training of mind':

> Care should, I think, be taken not to instil too much independence of action into a being whose sphere in life is defined as one of subjection, obedience and ductility and whose position from the cradle to the grave, as daughter, wife or servant, subjects her to the will of another .... A forced cultivation of intellect gives them a taste and yearning for books and mental pleasure, which invariably engenders a distaste for work, the practical handwork, I mean, that falls to a servant's lot.

Girls should be learning washing, cooking, nursing and needle-work, not the smattering of history, geography and grammar alongside the boys, and she defended the old dame schools whose teachers, though unqualified, provided precisely such rudimentary instruction for girls. 'Payment by Results' in the British and National schools now meant cramming for the same paying subjects by boys and girls alike; even the needlework time offered girls was too short and broken to develop skills. Interestingly, though, while Barlee condemned any academicization of the girls' curriculum in working-class schools, there were the beginnings of a move in that very direction in middle-class education; the Misses Buss and Beale had opened respectively the North London Collegiate School (1850) and Cheltenham College (1853), reacting from the footling 'accomplishments' offered in run-of-the-mill seminaries, in a conscious effort to emulate the curriculum for boys. None the less, strong prejudices persisted into the 1920s that an over-emphasis on cerebral training would de-sex girls, upsetting their biological development, and turning them into dried-up, blue-stocking spinsters. As late as 1919 a Board of Education circular suggested that the girls' curriculum should be tailored to their 'different' requirements and 'capacities'. In 1917 Catherine Whetham's *The Upbringing of Daughters* deplored career-mindedness in modern girls. A professional life would divert them from their naturally ordained role as wives and mothers and was 'unnatural'; a working-class girl doing menial jobs at home was at least obeying her true feminine instincts.

The elementary school codes steered girls towards sewing and domestic science on the timetable, at the expense of academic subjects. As we have seen, the codes prescribed greater leniency towards girls in arithmetic, as they were deemed innately less capable than boys. Chemistry and physics were 'boys'' subjects, and only botany was properly a 'girls'' subject, too. The science lessons were differentiated, so girls might learn, for example, about ventilation, thermometers, the seasonal appropriateness of cotton and woollen fabrics, convected water currents in boilers, and the best atmospheric conditions for drying clothes.[54]

The codes made needlework a compulsory subject for girls, and it was commonly done in the afternoon while the boys did extra maths. The girls were coached for the (male) examiner with 'thimble drill' or 'knitting pin drill', and there were to be complaints about the effect of so much needlework on the girls' eyesight, and indeed its over-emphasis in the age of the sewing machine.[55] The widening of the codes into the 1890s brought in laundrywork and cookery. In laundry girls learned starching and stiffening, the properties of hard and soft water, the uses of alkalis in water and different kinds of soap; the Board of Education was to provide grants for laundry facilities.[56] Early cookery courses left much to be desired, for, as the schools lacked kitchens, lessons took the form of demonstrations, and semi-academic theory. Molly Hughes's experiences at Miss Buss's academy in the 1880s matched the early practices in the elementary schools. In 'domestic economy' pupils learned the theory of nutrition, carbohydrates, 'hydrogenous foodstuffs', and so forth, but the school had no kitchen or laundry (presumably because they were 'infra dig' for young ladies), and Molly 'darkly suspected that our teachers had never entered such places'. Laundrywork and cookery improved as education authorities began setting up purpose-designed centres. In 1874 only 844 girls in board schools were studying domestic economy; in 1882 this was nearly 60,000 and by 1896 nearly 135,000. Between 1891 and 1896 the numbers attending laundry classes increased from 632 to 11,720. By 1900 the London School Board had 168 cookery centres. However, the conditions at the cookery centres were too ideal. The gas stove at the centre was a far cry from the coal range at home, and the sophisticated recipies and delicacies girls learned there were non-starters among harassed and crowded families lacking kitchen scales, time and inclination, and conditioned to a diet of kippers, bloaters, pickles and chips.[57] The prime objective of domestic science was to turn out good home-makers, not to prepare girls for domestic service,[58] but this was not good enough for the (female-run) National Association for the Promotion of Housewifery, which in the 1870s and 1880s campaigned for girls to be specifically steered towards a career in domestic service; it alleged a shortage of good servants, and rationalized its self-interest by maintaining that the experience of service would make them better home managers when they did marry.[59] However, this view did not become official policy of the Board of Education.

The Departmental Committee on Physical Deterioration in 1904 saw the quality of domestic training for future home-makers as fundamental to the 'health of the race'. It criticized the over-ambitious approach in the cookery centres when compared with working-class girls' home conditions, and recommended that domestic economy should be concentrated in the final years at school. The Code of 1906 tried to meet these criticisms by prescribing more basic cookery with simpler equipment at the cookery centres.

How successful was domestic science training at school? Surprisingly, its influence appears to have been limited. Widening opportunities in factories and offices in the early 1900s were possibly disinclining young girls to the homely skills. During the

First World War a Coventry girl guide, Joan Denny, formed a company for young munitions workers, and commented later:

> It was amazing how ignorant these girls were of home duties, such as laying a fire, making a bed, turning out a room. 'Oh well,' they would say, 'when I left school I went into a factory, and when I got home the work was done'; or 'Mum says it's less trouble to do the job herself.'[60]

In the Second World War, the appalling standards of inner-city children billeted out as evacuees brought to light the inadequacies of their mothers, products of the inter-war elementary schools. A survey of 1943 revealed that

> some of the children had been unused to sit down to a meal or to use cutlery; they were accustomed to have a 'piece' in the hand, always of white bread and generally spread with margarine and cheap jam, and to eat it on the doorstep or in the street, or to buy fish and chips which they ate from newspaper wrappings . . . . Some children said they had never seen their mothers cook and that they had no hot meals at home.[61]

It was not simply a matter of poverty and slum surroundings obliterating all the good training at school, for some mothers 'combined substantial incomes with a low social standard' and were wasteful of food at home and tended to indulge their children with unwholesome sweets and biscuits. Whatever had been learned of domestic science at school would seem to have been forgotten in the adult world outside.

HEALTH AND SCHOOLING

It was an irony in the last quarter of the nineteenth century that schools, which were proclaimed as vehicles of child advancement, were also standing accused of mental and physical oppression.

'Overpressure' was the in-word of the period in attacking the effects of the codes and 'Payment by Results' in the elementary schools, and the examination rat race in middle- and upper-class schools. Following studies of the causes of headaches and 'brain exhaustion' among Prussian pupils in the 1870s, British medical journals were beginning to publish articles and correspondence on the subject, and as the country moved towards compulsory education in 1880, so the issue came increasingly to the fore.[1] Edwin Chadwick, the public health reformer, had implicitly criticized the indigestibility of full-time learning when he maintained that half-timers could learn at almost the same pace, and he recommended that lesson times for 5–7-year-olds should not exceed 15 minutes, rising to a maximum of 30 minutes from 12 years old.[2] Dr Pridgin Teale's *Effects of Compulsory Education and Competitive Examination on the Mental and Physical Health of the Community* criticized the hot-house atmosphere of competitive examinations in the public schools and the Damocles sword of 'superannuation' (dismissal) which hung over those who failed, compelling parents to send their sons to crammers. Dr Clement Dukes, physician to Rugby School, was a leading voice against 'overpressure' and in the 1890s criticized the excessive length of the school day. Children under 13, he reckoned, ideally needed at least $10\frac{1}{2}$ hours' sleep a night, and he condemned the stresses placed on 3-year-olds in the babies' classes and the neglect of physical education in the elementary schools. In middle-class education he claimed that youngsters might work up to 14 hours a day, including homework time; teachers and parents regarded the youngsters as 'brains without physique'.[3] In elementary schools children were found who could not concentrate more than 5 minutes at a time; 'moonlighters', as we have seen, were under particularly heavy stress.[4] Unlike the situation in the public schools, the overpressure controversy in board schools was linked to malnutrition and general ill-health. Some doctors blamed the environment rather than the codes for the children's stresses.[5] Others blamed overpressure for all manner of syndromes including hydrocephalus, squinting, high pulse rates, constipation, irritability, broken sleep and delirium.[6]

The Education Secretary, A. J. Mundella, was sensitive to the issue, and in 1882 he urged school inspectors to watch out for signs of strain and to use their discretion freely in exempting vulnerable children from the examinations. However, while 'Payments by Results' persisted, teachers were bound to put pressure on pupils, but the Education Department stayed conveniently blinkered, blaming the teachers not the codes for the cramming, and refused to regard the general health and stamina of schoolchildren as any part of its sphere of responsibility. Mundella appointed Dr James Crichton-Browne, a leading medical authority on the subject, to conduct an inquiry. His report on overpressure, which was published in 1884,[7] was a graphic and highly emotive indictment. Children, he claimed, were being kept back for long periods beyond their school day, for extra coaching by teachers for the inspectors' examinations. (However, one wonders how far parents would really have allowed this, especially where the children were needed for tasks at home.) Homework was hard labour when done under unsuitable home conditions, straining eyes, rounding backs and depriving youngsters of sleep. It was the dull and the delicate who were put under severest pressure to pass the Standards at school, for, as we have seen, he claimed the Standards made no allowance for differences of ability. The prospective arrival of the inspector struck terror in the children:

> The supernatural terrors of the past have given place to the dread of the School Board. The infantile lip that would curl up with contempt at any reference to a witch or a ghost, quivers with anxiety at the name of a Government Inspector, and the examination day has appropriated to itself much of

the foreboding which used to be reserved for the day of judgement.

Much dullness at school was due to hunger, he found. At a Clerkenwell board school up to 40 per cent of pupils might come without breakfast. At another school poverty-stricken mothers, such as charwomen and flower-sellers, would turn up on the premises during school hours, bringing morsels they had been able to buy with their meagre earnings that day. He found poignancy in the sight of forlorn and half-starved children in class.

> toiling at their allotted tasks, wondering no doubt sometimes what it all means, but bearing their burdens patiently. Very pathetic it is to hear them sing in thin quavering voices . . . . 'Happy little sunbeams, Happy are we.' Sunbeams! one feels inclined to exclaim motes in sunbeams! germs of disease!
>
> These children want blood, and we offer them a little brain polish; they ask for bread and receive a problem; for milk the tonic-sol-fa system is introduced to them.

A sample survey of London schoolchildren, he claimed, revealed that 46 per cent of them professed to suffer from headaches; and he attributed to 'School Board Brain' variously chorea, neuralgia, toothache, short-sightedness and insanity! More soberly he attacked the rigidity of the Standards and their failure to make allowances for the socially disadvantaged, and he called for systematic studies of the physical development of schoolchildren to be undertaken, so that variations between social groups could be identified and flexibility then built into the examinations. Indeed, independent anthropometric studies were beginning at this time to provide such information. We saw in Chapter 13 the defence of the reasonableness of the Standards examination by the school inspector J. G. Fitch, and broad confirmation of Fitch's view against Crichton-Browne by the London School Board. The latter put the blame for schoolchildren's ills on environmental handicaps rather than the Standards (the Report of the Royal Commission on Housing had just been published), and it saw the encouragement of cheap feeding schemes as a relief. However, it did recommend more exercise and games, less needlework for girls (the requirement for which under the code was regarded as bad for their eyesight), and a modification of 'Payment by Results' that would enable teachers to classify children by ability rather than age in presentation for the Standards.[8]

The overpressure issue was to grumble on into the twentieth century despite the progressive abandonment of 'Payment by Results' after 1890. Children still crammed for the Labour Certificate and early exemption, and those with aspirations in the burgeoning field of secondary education crammed for the scholarship and subsequently the leaving qualifications; and there was the perennial issue of the supposed stresses on girls during adolescence. The eugenic movement of the early 1900s, including luminaries like Sir Douglas Dalton, echoed the views of Dr G. Stanley Hall, whose pioneering study of adolescence affirmed that girls needed a more relaxed academic regime to develop their biological attributes unimpaired.[9]

It was not just the learning pressures that could be harmful to the children's health but also the physical surroundings of the school. The elementary schools of the 1860s were generally bleak and undecorated. Separate classroom design was only just coming in; generally the whole school was taught in one large hall, and children had to spend much of their time standing in groups to be coached or heard. Sanitary arrangements could be very primitive. One man who attended a Wrexham school in the 1860s recalled having to use a communal iron bucket for ablutions, filled up once a day by a monitor from a nearby stream: there was no soap and he could not recollect a towel being supplied.[10] The advent of board schools from 1870 was to inspire fresh thinking on school architecture. Early schools in more deprived urban areas lacked playgrounds,[11] a reflection both of the shortage of space and the disregard for physical education and children's need to run and play; the space problem in turn-of-the-century London board schools was met in part by flat rooftop playgrounds. Flush toilets, when introduced, were early on of a crude institutional utility type, such as the trough latrine. This was an elongated metal bath part-filled with water and with a series of seat-holes running along the top. Perhaps once a day it would be flushed and refilled; apart from being malodorous and insanitary, it also gave scope for childish mischief – lighted paper boats could be floated along towards an unsuspecting user! Toilets might be inconveniently located, and as they were often not cleaned out properly, odours would waft through the windows of classrooms.[12] At Robert Roberts's Salford school in the early 1900s washbowls in the lavatories were not laid

on; they were installed later, and provided cold water only.[13]
Church of England schools were worse off financially than board
schools and their conditions were even more unsatisfactory. This
was a serious matter as in 1900 roughly half the country's
elementary schoolchildren were attending the National schools;[14]
the Educational Act of 1902 was intended to bring them up to
board school standards with subsidies out of the rates. Flora
Thompson's rural National school in the 1890s only had an earth
closet, with washbasins filled from a bucket. Urban drinking water
was becoming 'safer' by this time but remained doubtful in rural
districts. In one Fenland school in the 1890s the water came from a
pump only a few feet from the cesspool of the school privies.[15]
Scandals were also exposed about Poor Law schools at this period.
In one such school no drinking water was laid on, and the children
were found drinking from puddles in the playground; other schools
relied on rainwater tanks, but these were liable to pollution.[16]

Country children often had to walk long distances to and from
school in all weathers, and sit in damp clothes in class if the
education authority was too parsimonious to provide enough coal
for the classroom fire. Coal fires themselves caused problems,
vitiating the air in already crowded classrooms, or creating
draughts. Accidents sometimes happened from inadequately
guarded fires. Children hung around in the yard in wet or frosty
weather, waiting for school to open. In Robert Roberts's
playground the rain shed stood over a covered hole, down which
the school refuse was periodically shot, and children would climb
down it to scavenge.

The cold and damp could bring on rheumatic aches (then often
ascribed to 'growing pains'); rheumatism and spinal curvature were
aggravated by the uncomfortable, backless forms children had to sit
on before the advent of desks from around the turn of the century.
The forms were of uniform height and infants' feet could not reach
the ground.[17]

Class sizes might reach 60 or more, as we have seen, and in an
effort to reduce crowding a government regulation in 1899
specified the minimum cubic capacity per child, but this had to be
withdrawn in 1900 as the church schools did not have the funds to
create the extra space.[18] Infections spread easily under these
conditions, and 'respectable' parents were apprehensive about what
their children might pick up from less sanitary classmates.
Ophthalmia, head lice, ringworm, scabies ('the itch'), chicken-pox,

149

scarlet fever, diphtheria, even TB were part of the occupational hazards of school life, for schools concentrated what was picked up in the neighbourhood. In the earlier days of the board schools some female teachers wore sulphur bags stitched to the hems of their dresses for 'protection', and in the worst schools, where among girls 'the lice simply dropped from their hair on to the desks',[19] teachers changed their clothes on returning home for fear of infestation.[20] Epidemics, notably of diphtheria in the 1890s, could shut down whole schools, though it was a debatable point whether the consequent dispersal of schoolchildren during the day would spread the outbreak more extensively. Absence or death through disease was part of the routine of school life. An E (for Epidemic) in the attendance register was the regulation mark to indicate a child's absence under quarantine in an infectious house.[21] Joseph Stamper told of his South Lancashire school in the 1890s, where his teacher, Miss Landslow, was almost blasé about being notified of a pupil's death:

> she would take her ruler and draw an ink line through the child's name in the register. She would then write a capital 'D' at the end of the ink line. That was all. Then forget about it. Not because she was callous; children did die, some of them, it was the Law of Nature.

The schoolchildren became directly involved in the obsequies. At W. H. Barrett's school in the same decade:

> Sometimes we were asked to bring pennies to school which would be expended on the purchase of an artificial wreath under a glass dome. This would be placed on show so that we could all read the card: 'In tribute from the teachers and scholars of Southery Board School,' but it never mentioned that the dead child was a victim of scarlet fever or diphtheria.

Despite all the deficiencies of schools, they did serve as invaluable social prisms, focusing all the manifestations of child deprivation in a way that the authorities could not ignore if education was to have any benefit for the child. The 'overpressure' controversy was to focus attention on malnutrition among schoolchildren. Whilst the Department of Education refused to regard school-feeding programmes as any part of its responsibility, A. J. Mundella personally took a more enlightened view in the early 1880s. He viewed the pioneering cheap dinner scheme at

Rousden in Devonshire as an admirable model, and became president of the Central Council for Promoting Self-Supporting Penny Dinners to encourage similar schemes.[22] The school boards themselves had no power to provide dinners; the initiative came from charities which offered cheap meals, or free meals to the neediest. The earliest initiative was associated with the ragged schools; the Destitute Children's Dinner Society gave dinners from 1864.[23] Scattered penny dinner schemes were founded in the 1870s,[24] but the influential Charity Organization Society (COS), a co-ordinating agency that screened applicants for different kinds of charities, disapproved of this development. Its philosophy was to dispense charity through family case work; to look at the cause of family poverty – say, drink or parental sickness – and to help the family to help itself. Child malnutrition was a symptom of family failure, and by indiscriminate schemes of cheap feeding 'do-gooders' were only cushioning feckless or cadging parents.[25] None the less, the immediate pathos of the situation carried more weight with philanthropic enthusiasts than this detached rationalism. Indeed the COS could be rebutted. S. D. Fuller's article on 'Penny dinners' in the *Contemporary Review* in 1885 vindicated the schemes on the grounds that children of the poorest parents in London were bringing their pennies; the poor still had their pride against accepting charity. And even if some worthless parents did slip through the net, what, he asked, was the alternative? To continue letting the children suffer? His answer was to make parents legally liable to feed their children, or ideally remove the children from unworthy parents altogether.

Dr T. J. Macnamara, who was a Bristol board school teacher betwen 1884 and 1892, and later to become a Liberal MP and junior education minister, saw famished boys hanging around the playground during lunchtimes because they had no meals to go home to. He once saw two brothers eating a turnip for a midday meal in winter, and others eating crusts and raw onions. Boys, he recalled, vomited in the morning through lack of food.[26] Among schoolchildren a lack of compassion for their hungrier classmates is suggested by the use of 'bread horses' in play. These were malnourished youngsters who allowed themselves to be ridden pick-a-back by their more fortunate companions in return for their lunchtime left-overs.[27]

Charles Booth's monumental survey of London life took in the plight of hungry schoolchildren; he confirmed the COS opinion that many were not the victims of 'pure' poverty but of parental drunkenness and neglect, but he expressed more direct sympathy with the children.

> The practised eye can readily distinguish children of this class by their shrinking and furtive look, their unwholesomeness of aspect, their sickly squalor ... their indescribable pathos, their little shoulders bowed so helplessly beneath the burden of the parents' vice.

The other tell-tale signs of malnutrition were on the one hand a nervous excitability coupled with rapid exhaustion, and on the other a profound inertia. One Liverpool doctor illustrated in the case of the latter the mindless mechanical reactions of starved children,

> if I told one of these children to open its mouth, it would take no notice until the request became a command, which sometimes had to be accompanied by a slight shake to draw the child's attention. The mouth would be slowly opened widely, but no effort would be made to close it again until the child was told to do so.

Whilst some teachers were compassionate and turned a blind eye if some ever-hungry moonlighter dozed off in their lessons, others could be unfeeling martinets. Bill Harding, who attended a Bristol school notorious for its harsh discipline, recalled falling asleep in class through malnutrition; the teacher summoned him to the front, and when he could not correctly place an apostrophe in a word on the board, punched him so severely on the ear that his eardrum burst and left him permanently deaf that side.[28] Against this, one must give all credit to teachers for their prominent role in initiating feeding charities. In 1874 Mrs E. M. Burgwin, headmistress of Orange Street Elementary School in Southwark, a very deprived area, started a feeding scheme there. The eminent journalist G. R. Sims, editor of the *Referee*, visited the school in 1880 and was inspired to use his newspaper as a fund-raising vehicle for cheap dinners. By 1906 the *Referee* scheme was by far the largest such operation in London, raising £4,000 a year, followed by the London Schools Dinner Association (founded 1889) which then raised £2,000 a year.[29] Another interesting scheme, the East Lambeth Teachers' Association, had been formed in 1892 by the headmaster of Victory Place Board School, Lambeth, when he saw two brothers very weak and listless. They said they were hungry, and he tested them with the stalest pieces of bread he could find, which they wolfed down. With the help of other local teachers he built up a feeding operation which by the winter of 1902–3 was to provide nearly 93,000 dinners in 38 London schools.[30] By 1904 there were 150 feeding schemes in London and 200 in the rest of England and Wales.[31] In Bradford Margaret McMillan, the socialist education reformer and member of the Bradford School Board, began in 1894 a campaign for medical inspection and school feeding, and she worked with 'Cinderella Clubs' to provide supplementary meals. (Bradford was later to be in the forefront of public feeding of schoolchildren after the School Meals Act of 1906.)[32] Other notable provincial schemes included the Children's Help Society, Bristol, the School Children's Benevolent Fund, Newcastle, and the Food and Betterment Association, Liverpool. Country children were far less well served, as charitable feeding was more difficult in scattered rural districts; hunger was compounded by the long travelling distances between home and school, and the youngsters were tempted to scrump turnips, carrots and fruit *en route*.[33]

An accumulation of evidence about the link between malnutrition and under-performance at school from the 1880s was progressively to shift attitudes about the need for official intervention, though the civil servants of the Education Department remained more die-hard. A survey conducted by the Anthropometric Committee of the British Association in 1881–3 showed, for example, an average difference of about 6 inches between the heights of professional-class and urban slum children at the age of 12. At the age of 16 a sample of boys of the former class averaged nearly 130 pounds in weight, compared with nearly 94 pounds among a sample of boys from the latter. Dr Francis Warner's further anthropometric surveys from 1889, underlining the same contrast, the exposure by the Boer War of the poor physical shape of recruits, and the sociological studies by Charles Booth and Seebohm Rowntree into poverty, all contributed towards a climate of opinion which favoured more state intervention. In 1906 Sir John Gorst, a former Conservative education minister, could brand the attitude of the Board of Education that state involvement would undermine parental responsibility, and that it was therefore preferable to leave the child to its fate, as 'repugnant to the most elementary principles of public duty and interest'.[34] It is interesting to note that the Home Office seemed more aware of the damaging effects of 'moonlighting' on children's performance at school than did the Board of Education about the effects of hunger at the turn of the century.

The largest educational authority in the country, the School Board for London, had likewise ignored the importance of nutrition, but began changing its attitude from the mid-1880s when, as we saw in its report on overpressure Surveys in 1885, it was indicated that in the poorest districts a quarter of the children came to school without breakfasts;[35] this corresponds roughly to Dr Macnamara's impression that a fifth of the boys at his Bristol school were undernourished.[36] A London school hunger survey of 1889 showed that overall nearly 13 per cent of pupils were underfed, whilst charities could reach only half of them.[37] However, in 1904 Dr Alfred Eichholz, a school inspector, estimated London's figure at 16 per cent, while the Manchester school medical officer at this time gave a very comparable estimate of 15 per cent for his city.[38] Eichholz believed that the London School Board's figures were an underestimate; figures were based on known numbers receiving assisted dinners, but there were centres that the board did not know of; Eichholz's own information indicated that 122,000 of London's 760,000 schoolchildren were being fed by charities.[39]

Figures fluctuated according to the season and trade conditions. Some charities operated only in the winter months, when the need for a hot meal was greatest and vulnerable sections of the poorer working population, like dockers and building workers, could be 'frozen out' of work.[40] It was the 1889 survey that had led to the formation of the London School Dinner Association. The school board, while having no power to feed children itself, played an active role in co-ordinating the voluntary efforts and avoiding duplication of relief through the Joint Committee on Underfed Children.

One school became a particular focus of interest as typifying the whole problem of deprivation in relation to educational performance. The Johanna Street Board School in Lambeth, just 7 minutes' walk from the Houses of Parliament, was cited by Dr Eichholz in his evidence before the 1904 Departmental Committee on Physical Deterioration.[41] The parents were costers, cab-runners and other casual workers; parental drunkenness was rife, and often the mothers were too drunk to make the children's breakfasts. Their poor diet – largely comprising cheap and poor-quality fries from the fish and chip shops, bread and margarine, and rotten fruit scavenged from underneath costers' carts – made them dull at school. Ninety per cent of the boys there were anaemic, and the older children were on average 3 inches shorter than their counterparts at a more middle-class elementary school. Eichholz added, 'A good many children suffer from blight in the eyes and sore eyelids. The hair is badly nourished and wispy, the skin is rough, dry, pale and shrivelled, giving a very old look very early in life.'

A third of the children required free feeding for 6 months in the year. The academic performance was poor – only 8 per cent reached Standard 5 – and the boys were too weak to sustain a full-length game of football.[42]

In March 1905 the school received a visit from Dr Macnamara, John Gorst and the Countess of Warwick, to see for themselves the state of hunger there. They used their good offices to secure from the local board of guardians a promise of help in feeding some of the neediest cases. The Local Government Board subsequently produced the 1905 Relief (Schoolchildren) Order, an attempt to encourage the Poor Law to step in directly to relieve children, without branding the full mark of pauperism on the parents.[43] Poor Law guardians had had the discretionary power to award outdoor relief (that is, assistance outside the workhouse) where there was no able-bodied father. If there was an able-bodied father, the father himself and possibly some or all of his dependents, would have to go into the workhouse as a condition of relief; alternatively the father might have to do 'Test Labour' – some kind of heavy labour such as stone-breaking – while remaining an outdoor pauper. For many destitute families the stigma of pauper status was too distasteful, and so the children suffered. Since 1868 the boards of guardians had had the power to prosecute (non-pauper) parents who wilfully failed to feed their children, but the guardians had never really bothered, and this power was in any case superseded by the 1889 Prevention of Cruelty to Children Act. A high proportion of hungry pupils were the children of widows, who in principle could be eligible for outdoor relief but were slipping through the net, perhaps because their mothers did not want to be classified as paupers. The 1905 Order provided that able-bodied fathers could obtain relief specifically to feed their children in the form of a 'loan' from the local Poor Law, without having to go into the workhouse or do Test Labour; the only mark of pauperism they incurred was disqualification from the right to vote. It was a well-intentioned attempt to evoke more appeals for relief on behalf of suffering offspring, but the Order was a failure. Fathers were either still too proud to have any dealings with the Poor Law, or where they did accept 'loans', were failing to pay them back once they were in funds again; at Bradford, where the Poor Law (in contrast to the education authority) was strict, this led to a spate of prosecutions. Some boards of guardians, actuated by meanness, were perversely interpreting the Order (which happened to refer to able-bodied fathers only) to mean that they had no further responsibility for outdoor relief to families without fathers, so widows and their children were left cut off. Their plight was made more dire by the decision of some feeding charities, which mistakenly believed that the Order had made their work redundant, to switch to other forms of relief.

This sorry bungle had to be cleared by the passage of the School Meals Act of 1906.[44] The flinty-hearted Poor Law guardians were now bypassed, and local education authorities were given discretionary power to provide school meals and to charge parents as they saw fit for them. Schools set up care committees, composed of school managers, teachers and other co-opted members, which among other welfare activities approved cases for free meals, while being empowered to recover the costs where appropriate from defaulting parents under pain of prosecution for neglect.[45] Many education authorities were reluctant to exercise their new powers and for some years still relied on voluntary feeding agencies.[46] The inspiration of the Act was 'eugenic', to prevent deterioration of the 'race', but it faced hostility from the Charity Organization Society and also, interestingly, from Robert Parr, director of the NSPCC, on the grounds that it undermined parents' prime responsibility to feed their own children.[47] Parr believed that the judicious threat of prosecution under the Cruelty Acts would of itself be sufficient to force delinquent parents to do right by their children, and he believed that the whole 'underfed children' cry was alarmist and 'much exaggerated'. This was a surprisingly blinkered attitude when in March 1908 the LCC's own Sub-Committee on Underfed Children found that 79 per cent of the children fed by the LCC were below the defined poverty line.[48] In 1911, the LCC was providing free meals to a maximum of 50,000 in winter, down to 26,000 in summer, out of the capitals 780,000 schoolchildren.[49] H. D. C. Pepler, the LCC's first organizer of care committees, had by 1912 become sceptical about the value of local authority feeding; he had swung to the COS view that the underlying family causes of poverty should be investigated and dealt with; free meals were just a poultice on the sore and, in his view, were aggravating that sore by inducing families to put up with lower wages. School meals were by 1912 costing the LCC £80,000 a year, and the service did not even reach the most helpless cases – children too ill to attend school, and those whose parents were too proud, obstinate, or secretive, and would not allow welfare investigators from the care committees into their homes.[50]

The early school-feeding arrangements were appallingly primitive. As schools had no kitchens or dining-halls, the soup, prepared in a central depot, might be brought to the schools in milk churns; or the children would go to some makeshift centre. At Bootle before 1914 breakfasts were served in cloakrooms, classrooms and even cellars with whitewashed walls and sawdust on the floor.[51] The Minority Report of the 1905–9 Poor Laws Inquiry stated that

> in some centres absolutely no plates or mugs or knives or forks were provided, the children, as it was said, being 'fed like hounds' and eating the food out of their hands. In other centres no sufficient provision was made for washing the plates etc., and several children had to use the same article without any attempt being made to cleanse it. Only rarely did the children sit down at a table provided with a table-cloth, to a meal served with decent amenity.[52]

A 1911 Report on the working of the 1906 Act presented a similar picture.[53] Children were forced to eat with their fingers; seats were too high for the younger children, who ended up spilling soup over themselves. Pandemonium reigned in some centres where up to 500 children were supervised by only 7 or 8 staff; at one centre 'there was a certain amount of actual disorderly conduct, throwing bits of food at each other and so forth. Grace was sung in a repulsively loud shout by any children.' A lack of discrimination over ages and appetites led to wastage of food in some places; however, the Report acknowledged that other centres were better organized and more civilized.

Early feeding arrangements also suffered from a lack of consistency among education authorities as to eligibility for free meals. Some applied a strict poverty test, while others decided according to the physical needs of the child, regardless of the failure of the parents' potential capability to support the child.[54] Some malnutrition was due to dietary ignorance among parents who were not desperately poor, and whose idea, for example, of a midday meal for their children was a piece of cake or tart to take to school.[55] In 1913–14 about 10 per cent of England and Wales's 6 million schoolchildren were being publicly fed, but in many cases the feeding was too intermittent to do lasting good.[56] The 1906 Act did not allow for feeding at weekends or in school holidays, though this omission was remedied by another Act in 1914 after the outbreak of war.

Despite all the general deficiencies, there was evidence of benefit, too. In 1913 the decline in rickets and improvements in the weight of schoolchildren were discernible in some places like Bradford and Manchester, and by 1914 Bradford claimed to have eliminated fainting from hunger at school.[57] To take a case history: Jean Rennie, born in Scotland in 1906, was a weak child who suffered from a drunken father. Her anaemia handicapped her school progress but during the First World War she was fed on an enriched diet of Stranraer creamery butter and in 1919 was able to go on to secondary school.[58] In fact during the war the numbers of children being publicly fed declined, for though many fathers were under arms, their families were enjoying high wages and there was less child poverty.[59]

The wider problem of child health in relation to schooling had prompted some educational authorities to appoint school medical officers from the 1880s; London's first dated from 1890.[60] Their early duties were confined to examining school buildings for sanitary defects, and examining children suspected of having infectious diseases with a view to sending them home. Dr James Kerr's name stands out prominently in this field; as Bradford's first school medical officer he was vigorously backed by Margaret McMillan in the 1890s. He found during his pioneering inspections that 'Apart from crippled and diseased bodies, many children were so dirty and verminous that they had to stand on large sheets of paper while they were being undressed. Dirty clothes had to be burnt by the school caretaker, when, as sometimes happened, clean ones were provided.'[61] Such revelations enabled Miss McMillan to get school baths built in the city. Sheffield School Board did have a rudimentary grasp of the role of poor eyesight in school underperformance in the 1880s, and supplied teachers with boxes of spectacles which were lent to children to try out in class.[62] Early medical officers had no legal power to treat children; they could only advise the authorities and the parents. Germany forged ahead in the field of school medical care prior to 1907. By that year Wiesbaden had 7 school doctors for 9–10,000 schoolchildren, while London had only some 21 part-timers for over half a million.[63] However, some authorities were making the maximum use of existing public health powers. Since 1902 the school boards had been absorbed into the general local authorities and schools could now be served by the public health departments; thus children from infectious households could be removed to the isolation hospitals run by those departments. School medical officers were used to check up on children kept away from school as allegedly 'ill', and advise parents in their own homes on treatment; the NSPCC and the prospect of prosecution under the child cruelty legislation could be held over the heads of recalcitrant parents. Even before 1907 the education authorities had the power to prosecute parents who failed to have their chldren's verminous heads cleansed, though this was rarely exercised. Teachers were harnessed as paramedics; in some areas they were trained to recognize symptoms and from 1901 were even expected to conduct eyesight tests on test-type charts, so that parents could be advised of remedial treatment. 'Visiting committees', semi-official precursors of the care committees, also used to advise parents on the need for treatment and arrange for charitable assistance. Ranged against any proposals to empower the education authorities to treat sick children were the COS (sensitive as ever to the undermining of parental responsibility when the poor had charitable dispensaries and the Poor Law as last resorts) and doctors with practices in the slums, who feared a loss of custom.[64] However, the post-Boer War eugenic alarms led to the appointment of a Departmental Committee on Medical Inspection and Feeding of Schoolchildren in 1906. The subsequent Education Act[65] imposed a duty on education authorities to inspect children, but there was still no power to treat them until the 1909 Act permitted this with the parents' consent, and empowered the education authority to recover the costs from the parents where they could afford to pay.[66] From this legislation was to emerge a network of school clinics with Bradford again in the lead,[67] and the familiar visits by the 'nitty Noras' to inspect children's heads. Robert Roberts remembered how in his Salford school the issue of a 'green card' signified to parents that their children must be kept away as verminous, and school attendances noticeably fell following the school nurse's visit.[68]

16

SCHOOLING AND THE
UPPER CLASSES

The Taunton Commission of 1864–8 which enquired into the structure and quality of middle-class education revealed a whole miscellany of private schools – the public schools, the endowed grammar schools, the 'private academies' and proprietary schools; the last were run as joint-stock companies and offered a more commercially orientated curriculum to the sons of businessmen. The commission sought to rank the schools in a hierarchy, and such status was determined partly by the predominance of classics on the timetable, according to the values of the time, and partly by the lateness of the pupils' leaving-ages, up to 18.[1] Around 1860, of nearly 2,600,000 children estimated to be attending schools, just over 14 per cent were of the upper and middle classes in various forms of private establishment.[2]

It had been traditional for the upper middle classes to send their sons away to boarding-school at 7 or 8 to learn to 'rough it'.[3] At 13 or 14 the boys might proceed to the public schools like Eton and Rugby, ranked by the Taunton Commission as the first grade. Though such schools had firmly established their social exclusiveness and superiority by the 1860s[4] their quality left much to be desired. The commission found Eton lacking in laboratories and gymnasiums. The much-vaunted classics were so badly taught there that Oxford dons found that they had to go over the same ground again with Old Etonian undergraduates and the majority of Eton youths had to go to 'grinders' (crammers) to bring them up to scratch before going on to university. The school calendar was riddled with holidays for ridiculous reasons, such as the birth of a child in a Fellow's family, a promotion of an Old Etonian to a judgeship or bishopric, a saint's day, or a visit by some notability, so that 'there is scarcely one regular week's work done in the whole

161

school term'.[5] Cribbing in classics lessons had become an ingrained custom and truanting, or 'shirking absence', was winked at by the staff under the decadent and lax regime; by school custom a master did not 'see' a boy in a place where the pupil should not be, provided the latter just hid his *face*![6]

The Christianizing influence that is supposed to have permeated the public school ethos since Dr Arnold's model regime at Rugby in the 1830s appears to have been illusory. Undercurrents of rowdyism remained: in 1870 a mob of Eton boys threw an unpopular master from a bridge in the High Street into a pool, and, as we shall see later, beatings and bullying were long to remain a hallmark of public school life. The tradition of supplying beer at supper persisted in some public schools into the early 1900s. It was banned at Rugby in 1905; Dr Clement Dukes, one-time physician to the school, condemned it partly on temperance grounds, and partly because it encouraged sexual improprieties in the dormitories.[7] At Eton in the late 1860s drinking was rife. The *British Quarterly Review* commented in 1868: 'It appears that at least a hundred boys may go to the "Tap" and the "Christopher" every ordinary day and stay there "for hours" and that the number of boys and the time spent in these places, are greatly increased on Sunday afternoons after four o'clock.' The headmaster turned a blind eye to the initiation ceremony among the 'swell set' known as the Cellar of downing the contents of a glass 12 to 15 inches deep in one go.

The fact was that the so-called 'first grade' schools were often dumps for the less than bright sons of the wealthy, preparatory to their fathers finding a commission for them in the army, or some place for them in the colonies.[8] It was the 'second grade' schools, like the endowed grammar schools, which by the 1890s were showing more progressiveness and increasing the science content of the curriculum, encouraged by the grants available from the Science and Art Department and county councils under the 1889 Technical Education Act.[9] Some idea of the total stranglehold of classics in the public school curriculum can be gained from the memoir of Molly Hughes whose brother Tom attended Shrewsbury in the 1870s:

> What Tom learnt at Shrewsbury was clear enough – Latin and Greek, with the ancient history and geography

pertaining to them. The only English literature that reached him were lines to be put into Latin verse, while Milton was used for punishment. There is a pencil note in his copy of *Paradise Lost*: 'Had to write 500 lines of this for being caught reading *King Lear* in class.' The only modern geography that he knew was the map of Scotland, because this too was chosen as a punishment.

Religion was taken very seriously in late Victorian public schools and many of the teachers were in holy orders. Outward displays of religious conformity were rigidly insisted upon;[10] at Harrow in the early 1900s boys had to be at chapel by 7.15 a.m. after a cold bath, and breakfasted afterwards. Evening prayers were said at 9 p.m., and up to that time special Sunday clothes of tail-coat and topper had to be worn.[11]

Boarding-school regimes could be very spartan – unheated dormitories, cold baths and earth closets – but the atmosphere varied from school to school. Winston Churchill's experience of the Rev. Herbert William Sneyd-Kinnersley's preparatory school at Ascot which he attended at the age of 7 in 1881 was most unhappy – by his account a regime of floggings, religious hypocrisy and a forced diet of classics. In 1883 his parents transferred him to a more modest school at Brighton run by two ladies; here he found more kindness, and less emphasis on the classics, with activities like riding and swimming much more to his taste.[12] Maurice Baring, who attended Sneyd-Kinnersley's school just after Churchill, recalled it as stuffy, though cricket and rugby were offered; he was transferred to a new school at Eastbourne where the regime was more refreshing – soccer, swimming, drill, horse-riding and sailing, and the boys put on plays. The academic side was played down: 'Altogether it was an ideal school life.'[13] A multiplicity of private academies 'for the Sons of Gentlemen', both day and boarding, catered to the pockets of middle- and lower-middle-class parents. Often they were just converted private houses run by teachers with doubtful qualifications, perhaps spinsters whose inherited family house was their one asset. Whatever their quality they offered a patina of gentility, for though the new board schools were tending towards social stratification in the 1880s and charging differential fees according to neighbourhood, there was still widespread middle-class contempt for them. H. C. Barnard recalled how in the 1880s and 1890s 'it would have been considered an unspeakable disgrace if one of us had to be transferred to an "elementary" school'. For all that, the facilities in private schools could remain surprisingly behind the times. At Eton in the late nineteenth century L. E. Jones found conditions so antiquated that no education authority would have tolerated it – inadequately lit classrooms, unheated in winter and unventilated in summer, with desks too narrow to write on. H. C. Barnard went to a private school with about thirty pupils staffed by a headmistress and two women assistants. There was no physical education or organized games and for recreation they only had an asphalted yard, though they did receive dancing and piano lessons as gestures towards the 'accomplishments'; Latin was timetabled as a similar claim to gentility, and Barnard remembers having to translate sentences like 'The queen gives an eagle to the husbandman', though 'I had no idea what a husbandman was, and it never occurred to me to ask'. In other respects the teaching methods were similar to what would have been found in the board schools; an emphasis on memorizing, with snippets of literature gleaned from readers. They practised copperplate writing; sums were done on slates; and history, geography and Scripture were learned by a set-form question-and-answer 'catechism' method, as I have already illustrated in Chapter 14.

Such schools could be seedy to a degree. Some idea of the doubtful levels of expertise required of staff can be gauged from an advertisement in 1891 for a private schoolteacher capable of offering 'English, Mathematics, Natural Sciences, Latin, French, Drawing, Freehand, Model Perspective, Geometry, Book-keeping, Drill', with preference given to applicants with a musical accomplishment![14] Miss Beale told the Taunton Commission that the standards of many girls' private academies were so low that for the entrance examination for her school (Cheltenham) only 4 out of 52 candidates could correctly write out the tenses of the French verbs set, and 10 even failed on *avoir* and *être*.[15]

It was from around the mid-nineteenth century that girls' 'academies' began to multiply for the pretensions of the growing industrial middle classes.[16] It had not been unknown for girls to be sent away to boarding-schools in the early nineteenth century; but there were health dangers in concentrating them in schools when sanitation was still primitive. The Rev. Patrick Brontë sent his five daughters to a Lancashire boarding-school, which in 1825 was swept by fever.[17] However, middle-class girls were far more likely to be taught by governesses (or occasionally an educated mother) in their own home, and two or more households might by arrangement share a tutor between them, all meeting at one house.[18] Governesses as a breed were not highly qualified; they were of 'genteel' background and commonly had been forced into earning their own living through a failure in family fortunes. Around 1912 a governess might earn £30 to £60 a year, compared with a cook's £60 or more;[19] their enthusiasm was not high and household turnover could be high. Ethel, Lady Thomson, who was raised in York in the 1880s, and Gwen Raverat, daughter of a Cambridge don, both had pitying recollections of their sad, drab governesses, and both experienced a whole succession of them, each new one covering the same ground as her predecessor. Governesses taught in schoolrooms at the top of the house, and were expected to offer the whole range of subjects from arithmetic, history and needlework through Scripture and drawing to the rudiments of French, and perhaps piano. Older girls might learn alongside younger brothers, before the latter went on to boarding school. Eleanor Acland recalled how lessons became duller after her brother left; Latin and algebra were dropped as the governess did not consider them 'girls' subjects'. Even if science was taught it was confined to botany, for chemistry and physics were regarded as 'masculine'. The education methods were standard: memorizing tables, dates and passages from literature and the Bible, and practising copperplate. Above all, parents expected the governesses to teach their daughters to be ladylike, and the governesses, whose neurotic unhappiness was compounded by fear for their jobs, could sometimes be viciously strict with their more wilful charges, even whipping them and tying their hands.[20] All the time the girls were enjoined to avoid colloquial speech, to be demure and modest, and to deport themselves properly; backboards were employed to enforce the last. Strenuous activity was considered unladylike and damaging to the development of an adolescent girl; exercise consisted of chaperoned walks with the governess, or lessons at a dancing academy; however, there were private commercial gymnasiums for children, and in the late nineteenth century some households preferred to send their very young children to Froebelian kindergartens.[21]

The 'private academies' for girls offered the same curriculum and often the same lack of real teaching commitment. Jane Brough, headmistress of an 'academy' in 1856, wrote a precept on the proper objectives in educating girls: they should be spiritual, moral, physical and (last of all) intellectual.[22] The school must be permeated with religion, and in her school the Bible was the only book the girls were allowed to bring in with them. All gifts, parcels and visitors were carefully vetted; self-indulgence was discouraged and girlish gossip and tittle-tattle were firmly suppressed. At 'Miss Pinkerton's Academy', a popular school with several branches in the early Victorian period, apart from the usual accomplishments, physical education consisted of formal 'drill' with poles and dumb-bells, but otherwise they were only allowed out for dreary walks while reciting French verbs. Seminary girls walking out 'in crocodile', the girls lined up in order of height, was a common sight in the smarter parts of town. At Miss Pinkerton's 'penalties were inflicted for not having finished lessons or piano practice by bedtime, for stooping, for having shoestrings untied, for being impertinent and for telling lies'.[23] Other establishments offered restrained physical outlets such as calisthenics, archery, croquet and gentle ball games. Later in the century, the more progressive schools, as pioneered by the Misses Buss and Beale, offered more vigorous games like hockey, netball and tennis in a conscious imitation of the boys' schools.[24] Even then there was a reluctance to recognize that young ladies actually perspired and no concession was made to games attire that would compromise their modesty. Gwen Raverat recalled the hockey dress at her school:

> We played in white blouses and blue skirts, which had to clear the ground by six inches; and our waist-belts were very neat and trim over our tight stays. And when we came in from a game ... all covered in mud and steaming hot, we had to go straight into school, without having time to change, or wash, or comb our hair, at all.

Prudery, prissiness and in the more devout schools, religiosity, were carried to absurdly repressive extremes. Girls bathed behind screens, no private conversations were allowed in dressing-rooms or cloakrooms, or on staircases, and sexual matters were absolutely taboo. Contact with boys was forbidden; at some schools all letters had to be read by staff to ensure that the girls would not be 'so wicked as to write to boys'.[25] One anecdote tells of an Oxford girl who was admonished at school for speaking to a boy in the street; she protested that he was her brother, to which the reply was 'But everyone does not know it was your brother.'[26]

Molly Hughes found that Miss Buss's North London Collegiate School in the 1880s, for all its semi-emancipation, was just as riddled with pettiness as any old-fashioned seminary: it was, for example, forbidden to get wet on the way to school, to walk more than three abreast, hang a boot-bag by only one loop, drop a pencil-box or run downstairs. Winifred Peck attended Miss Quill's academy at Eastbourne around 1890; it was a generation or more behind the times; the girls were taught in one large room, sitting in groups at different tables, and the teachers were indifferently qualified. The school was infused with a strong Evangelical ethos, and it evidently catered to parents who put fear of God above cultural attainments in the training of their daughters. There was no science, no handicrafts or organized games, and the emphasis was on teaching the girls to be ladylike. The walls were covered with homiletic mottoes. When the girls had to speak up to make themselves heard by one slightly deaf teacher they were put down with a reproachful finger pointing to the motto: 'Her voice was ever soft, gentle, and low, an excellent thing in woman.' They learned deportment by walking around with weights on their heads. Petty rules reminded them of their female modesty. A dormitory rule instructed 'Assume your underwear as modestly as possible under the covering of your nightgown'; and if they were caught lapsing into vulgar colloquialisms like 'awfully', 'jolly', or 'Great Scott' they were fined a halfpenny. Confessional assemblies were held and girls had to bare their souls publicly with admissions like 'I forgot to say my prayers', 'I laughed in Bible reading', and so on. When a girl confessed to having exclaimed 'Damn it', Miss Quill had a seizure and 'lay back gasping in the chair till restored by Mademoiselle's vinaigrette. Then she rose in her trailing majesty; she wept, the mistresses hid their faces in their hands, and the girls sat in stunned silence.'[27]

Such schools were obviously not intended to prepare girls for the realities of life and self-reliance but to enhance them socially for marriage and spiritually for motherhood; they were destined to grow into helpless and dependent ornaments to their husbands. The school was a gilded cage in which girls were trapped and expected to perch and perform prettily. Intellectualism was frowned on as not only unfeminine but also de-sexing, dooming a girl to sterility and spinsterhood. It was in reaction to this intellectual construction that in the 1850s Frances Buss and Dorothea Beale established their new 'progressive' academies: the

North London Collegiate School and Cheltenham College; Roedean was to be established in the same mould. Maths, science and German as well as French were offered, and in Molly Hughes's day the schools aspired to send the girls to university or teacher-training college. One historical view holds that the advance in middle-class girls' education by the end of the century was due to changing demographic and economic patterns; professionals' families were becoming smaller, so 'transforming the position of middle-class women',[28] while middle-class profit margins were falling, so they had to find something useful for their women to do. However, virtually the only acceptable professional outlet for middle-class girls was teaching, and it is claimed that by 1900 only a third of such girls were attending these 'reformed' schools;[29] there were still thousands of shabby-genteel finishing-schools where physics and chemistry were excluded as 'masculine' subjects, where there was no social or civic education and newspapers were generally banned.[30] Carol Dyhouse states that even in the progressive schools there was no aim to make the girls ambitious or career-minded, or to compete with men; their ideal product was a girl who was intelligently knowledgeable as a helpmate to a future husband, someone who could combine independence of thought with loyalty, and whose usefulness would revolve around educating her children, managing the servants, and perhaps some charitable work. It was only around 1900 that it started becoming socially acceptable for the aristocracy to send their daughters to boarding-school, for up to then private tutoring at home had been the rule. Gwen Raverat recalled a conversation between a peeress and her mother in which the peeress snobbishly cut the latter off with the remark, 'We do not send our daughters away to school.'[31]

To what extent in reality did the Buss- and Beale-type schools measure up to the progressive ideals? The autobiography of Molly Hughes gives us an excellent impression. She was a child in London in the 1870s, the daughter of a City businessman, and was taught till 11 by her mother. From then till 16 she attended a typical 'Establishment for Young Ladies' as a day pupil (her brothers now being at boarding-school); she did a lot of private studying under her own steam of subjects not provided at the school to pass the Oxford Senior Locals, a rudimentary ancestor of the School Certificate and GCE of the twentieth century. In 1883 at 16 she entered the North London Collegiate School after passing an entrance exam that was in fact easier than the Locals; for example, in one question they were given a blank map of Africa and asked to fill in 'all they knew', and after the academic papers they had to make a buttonhole. Looking back after half a century Molly could write of the school's 'glaring faults and absurdities'; I have already alluded to what she called the 'porcupine' of petty regulations, and she summed up the place as 'an elaborate machine for doing the minimum of useful things with the maximum of fuss'. But she acknowledged that Miss Buss was a pioneer, just feeling her way and with only the curriculum and examinations offered in boys' schools as a model. Molly's memoir does not suggest anything novel or stimulating in teaching methods. In French lessons there was scarcely any French conversation, only translations from dull French texts. In English literature they virtually had to learn off by heart the footnotes explaining obscurities in the text studied. Whereas in her previous school the girls played rounders, at the North Collegiate there were no games, and there was only a small playground. In the gymnasium they could only do Swedish drill – 'bouncing balls or balancing poles – and marching around to music'. Domestic science consisted of the theory of food chemistry but there was no practical cookery, and there was no embroidery or fancy sewing, only plain sewing in Dorcas sessions (making up clothes for charity). One is left with an impression of dabbling and dilettantism; but the curriculum was geared to the requirements of the Oxford and Cambridge Local Examinations, and Molly herself was given encouragement to pursue a seemly career and went on to teacher-training college.[32]

What recognized leaving qualifications were on offer from middle-class schools? The era of public examinations appears to date from the 1850s; competitive exams for entry to the Indian Civil Service began in 1853, the Royal Military Academy from 1855 and the home Civil Service from 1870. The College of Preceptors began school examinations in 1853 and the Society of Arts from 1855 (the last were really geared to the 'non-privileged classes'). In the 1850s first Oxford and then Cambridge University instituted their 'Locals' (junior for the under-15s and senior for the under-18s) for middle-class schools. The College of Preceptors, as a private examining agency, was offering academic subjects like history, classics, French, maths and science. The Society of Arts, also a private foundation, was more practically geared to promote 'arts, manufactures and commerce' and examined the over-15s about to leave school in technical drawing, science, maths and, later on, commercial subjects. This should not be confused with the government's Science and Art Department at South Kensington which set exams and offered grants to elite elementary schools geared heavily to the sciences.

The Oxford and Cambridge Locals (Scotland had from 1888 its own equivalent, the Scottish Leaving Qualification) were stepping-stones to university entrance or teacher-training college, enabling candidates to bypass pupil-teacher apprenticeship.[33] Molly Hughes leaves us with a confusing picture of the relationship between the Locals and university entrance, for though she passed the Cambridge Locals with flying colours at the North London Collegiate, she had to take a separate entrance examination, matriculation, when she contemplated going to Cambridge University.

By the early 1900s there was a whole miscellany of examining bodies offering certificates from schools, technical institutes and evening classes; to those aforementioned we could add, for example, the City and Guilds (technological subjects), London Chamber of Commerce (languages and commercial subjects), and the LCC with its 'Merit' certificate.[34]

The confusing multiplicity of certificates led to a rationalization in 1917 with the establishment of a standardized School Certificate ('Matriculation') examination at 16 and a Higher School Certificate for sixth formers, the latter to be recognized by universities as the actual entrance qualification.

The importance of competitive examinations in middle-class schooling was to create an 'overpressure' controversy parallel to that in the public elementary schools. Examinations were becoming a totem by the later Victorian period and curricula were enslaved to them; 'Examination', said a school inspector, 'is to the student what the target is to the rifleman; there can be no definite aim, no real training without it.'[35] Against this Dr Crichton-Browne was in 1883 to talk of examinations as an 'epidemic' which threatened to 'blight all true education' and to 'make serious inroads into the health of the people'.[36] Over twenty years later the situation had not improved in the eyes of medical pundits; exam-worship was ineradicably entrenched. Dr Clement Dukes complained in 1905 that 'Instead of education fortifying the mind and body for the world's work . . . education, as now conducted, seems rather to be the cramming and forcing into the mind of certain descriptions of knowledge, calculated merely to enable one to "pass" in a competitive examination but of comparatively little use in the business of actual life'.[37] Has much changed since?

17

PUPIL SOCIETY AND SCHOOL DISCIPLINE

Children can be notoriously cruel to each other and for a good many school could be an unhappy medium for intensifying the pain of Victorian social prejudices. Class snobberies could make life miserable for a child who was obviously poorer than his or her classmates. Even within the working class there was a sense of snobbery. Dorothy Ogersby, the daughter of a Yorkshire stone-mason, recalled how around the turn of the century at Sunday School the better-off girls 'flaunted their new clothes, poking fun at those not so fortunate'.[1] 'Emma Smith', the 'cornish waif' described in Chapters 9 and 10, was shunned by other children at school in Penzance for her neglect and ragged appearance, for however poor they were, they were still one up on her. Hungry 'bread horses', as we have noted, were made to work by their better-fed schoolmates in return for a crust. The attitude of teachers could ease or sharpen the sense of inferiority. Kindly and understanding teachers could protect the child: one teacher in the Forest of Dean in the late 1890s would give a boy with no money at home a penny to buy shoeblacking, to save him from chastisement by the headmaster for coming to school with scruffy shoes.[2] Other teachers delighted in making some unfortunate the butt of the class; unkempt children were humiliated by being made to sit at the back of the class and being given less attention, andin the 1920s Mabel Yeo, who wore cast-offs at her Exeter school, was sent back to school from a nature ramble she had been looking forward to, because a button had come off her shoe.[3] Children in poor neighbourhoods who won the scholarship to the new secondary schools after 1902, and whose parents scrimped and saved to send them there, could find themselves cruelly caught between two worlds; their former schoolmates might taunt them in the street as social renegades, while at school snobbish fee-payers sneered at the poorer (but probably brainier) scholarship child, an attitude reinforced by some snobbish teachers.[4]

Worst off, however, were Poor Law and illegitimate children. One Potteries child of the 1840s remembered how on leaving the workhouse and joining a Sunday School he was shunned as a 'workhouse brat' by the other boys, for however poor they were they still felt superior to him.[5] Dorothy Hatcher was born before the First World War, the illegitimate child of a Kent girl farmworker. She spent some time in Tenterden workhouse, and was fostered out, and attended a local school. Although the other girls played with her, they never invited her to their homes. She got friendly with a new girl, and at first her mother was nice to her, but when one day Dorothy called on her to go to school together 'I . . . was told that she was not ready, and I was not to wait for her. Then when I did see her, she said she was not to play with me any more as I was born in disgrace.' She always felt this barrier and stigma at school. She remembered a teacher one day asking each pupil in turn what they intended to do when they left school:'When he got to me he said, "You haven't got a choice. All workhouse children will be put in domestic service"'[6]

Another group who suffered from schoolteachers' insensitivity and ignorance were the 10 per cent or so of the school population who were left-handed. Just what was the source of this almost superstitious prejudice against left-handedness among a supposedly 'educated' group is not easy to fathom. Some teachers presumably saw it as a sign of perversity and deviation. The notion that left-handedness was 'unlucky' or ill-omened goes back to the ancient Greeks and Romans, and the traditional association of sinistrality with shadiness and criminality was given pseudo-scientific credence by the late nineteenth-century criminologist Cesare Lombroso; though contemporary medical men did understand that left-handedness was physiologically perfectly natural. Some teachers took active repressive measures to discourage left-handedness, like making offending pupils wear gloves on their left hand or tying the hand to the desk. George Baldry, who went to school in Norfolk in the 1870s, at first had his knuckles rapped for the offence, and when this did not 'cure' him was severely caned on the left hand to make it unusable in lessons; this 'cured' him for life, though he always felt that writing with the right hand was unnatural. Not all teachers shared this irrational prejudice. One former schoolteacher writing in *Notes and Queries* in 1937 recalled that during his career he 'was warned by many intelligent people never to rebuke my pupils for that habit, for if I compelled them to become right-handed they would certainly begin to stammer'.

Whilst for some school was an unhappy period of stigmatization and discrimination, for a greater number the most abiding memories would have been their misbehaviour, and the capacity of teachers to control them. The half-time schools required by the Factory Acts prior to 1870 were sometimes run by crippled or elderly former factory operatives who were themselves barely literate and could not control their classes. The Royal Commission on Education in 1858–61 revealed how parents would send their children to the cheapest possible half-time schools run by such people. Schools were instanced where the teachers were 70 or older; the children 'seemed all idle, and some evidently laughing at the master'. Teachers' incomes at these private adventure schools depended on the number of pupils, so classes of perhaps 50 or more youngsters of all ages could be crammed into rooms smaller than the through lounge of an average modern terraced house. No doubt the fact that the children were earning wages part-time made them feel more grown-up and assertive against the teacher; on the other hand fatigue might make them lethargic and quiescent.[7] Dame schools varied in quality and at their worst were as bad as any factory half-time school. Adam Rushton who was born in Cheshire in 1821 recalled attending a dame school run by infirm and elderly Nanny Clarke. On his first day he 'found the room full of children, some at play, some at mischief and some repeating lessons in the broadest and roughest dialect'. Nanny Clarke tried to keep control with periodic swishes of her birch rod but Adam really began to learn to read and write only when he started at Sunday School.[8] In another dame school surviving in 1870 a poor widow held a class in a room 10 feet by $8\frac{1}{2}$; she could not really teach as she had no roof to her mouth, and the children had no desks, slates, or reading books.[9] Dame schools were branded by one factory inspector as run by utter incapables, devoid of basic equipment, with 'the larger proportion of the children doing absolutely nothing for nine-tenths of the time they are under confinement'.[10] Church-run schools were found on the whole to have the best discipline. The British National schools of the early 1800s for Nonconformist and Church of England children respectively relied on the carrot-and-stick approach; good pupils were rewarded with money, toys, books and medals; bad children were humiliated, for example, by wearing a fool's cap or being suspended in a basket, or subjected to more dire punishments like confinement in a closet, or being locked in handcuffs or a pillory![11]

At the lowest end of the social scale a special flair was needed to handle the ragged school children. The schools were purely voluntary but many young urchins who attended came there for shelter, the chance of a free meal, and the opportunity for a bit of devilment. Quintin Hogg established a ragged school in London's West End in the 1860s for younger boys. His female assistant then took on older boys in an evening class in 1864 with disastrous results. The new arrivals were like wild animals and the police had to be called in. On Hogg's arrival he found 'the whole school in uproar, the gas fittings had been wrenched off and used as batons by the boys for striking the police, while the rest of the boys were pelting them with slates'.[12] He relates that he was able to quell them, and in time he developed a highly successful school out of this very rough and raw material. Doubtless Hogg had a special rapport with the lads, for conventional sanctions of the cane or birch would not have worked.

The lower working-class children in the board schools after 1870 were not far removed from the ragged school types and in the early days there was a grudge against compulsory education; faced with classes of 60 or more, teachers had a hard time. 'School board laryngitis' from having to shout all the time was a recognized occupational complaint. Early board schools could be chaotic at times. One teacher recalled how he had 'unwisely' had all the inkpots in the desks filled: 'before the end of the morning all the boys had emptied their inkwells, most of them down the neck of other boys', and his most vivid memory was of a boy who used to take off his wooden leg to belabour his fellows.[13] A poor disciplinarian would be mercilessly baited; Flora Thompson related how in her village school a new teacher was led a dance – water was poured into the inkpots, frogs were placed in her desk, her cane was hidden, fights would break out in class, and the children would cough in chorus when she spoke to them.

Children could protest at schooling by absenteeism rather than misbehaviour. Indeed the high rate of absenteeism in early 'slum' schools – up to 25 per cent on any day – must have eased the teachers' physical stress; and many children were too malnourished or too fatigued from 'moonlighting' or half-time labour to misbehave in class.

Once compulsory schooling became more accepted by the end of the century, schools became more orderly. In 1890 Charles Booth was satisfied that given the right teachers and a firm but kindly discipline, even the most scampish slum children would be won over. He recorded how on visiting such a school.

> The first thing that strikes a stranger is the wonderful order that everywhere prevails. There is nothing to indicate harsh control. On the contrary, children and teachers seem as a rule to be on quite amicable terms. There is even in some schools what approaches to cameraderie between them. But the discipline is perfect .... The turbulence of the streets is subdued into industrious calm. Ragged little gamins run quietly in harness, obedient to a look, a gesture of the teacher in command. No matter what door we open we find the school work going smoothly and steadily along.[14]

This is almost too idyllic to be true. Perhaps the children were made aware that a special visitor was coming and were on their best behaviour when Booth arrived. How 'smooth' the relationships could be without threat of the cane must be open to doubt given the enormous class sizes. Admittedly by no means all teachers were harsh disciplinarians. Many had compassion and understanding of their pupils' predicaments, and as evidence of this I have only to recall the leading role played by some teachers in promoting cheap feeding schemes. But whilst children may well respond positively to humanity, they are also inclined to play up at any sign of leniency; moreover it is doubtful if they saw much point in a curriculum comprising so much parsing and memorizing of unusable facts. Booth himself confirmed this when he visited one school class where the children were 'dazed and beaten, their faces worried and vacant' by the exercise in parsing. They were not unruly or disobedient, just uncomprehending and apathetic. Yet, said Booth,

> the same boys, when questioned presently on things that came home to them, penny bank-books, spending and saving, medals, prizes and punctuality, Band of Hope, earning a living &c, showed no lack of shrewdness and commonsense. Their faces changed. The slum look fell off. Their

individuality came out. They all looked eager, bright, responsive.

It is likely therefore that apathy rather than indiscipline was more typical of a late Victorian slum school.

At the opposite social extreme, public schoolboy society of the early and mid-Victorian period could be more barbaric than any street-Arab gang; their well-nourished vitality and class arrogance made their peer-group cruelties the more exquisite. Rebelliousness, brutality and bullying had been endemic in the unreformed public schools. The old adage that 'the Battle of Waterloo was won on the playing fields of Eton', was not a compliment to any noble *élan* or *esprit de corps* cultivated by the school, but the toughening effect of its rough-house atmosphere. Dr Thomas Arnold, the famous headmaster of Rugby in the 1830s, is celebrated for having introduced a new civilizing Christian influence, an upright 'play up and play the game' ethos which is supposed to have permeated the public school system thereafter. He has been immortalized since the publication of *Tom Brown's Schooldays* in 1851,[15] but his true influence is open to doubt. His approach was to entrust the discipline and moral guidance of the younger boys to prefects with the right Christian character, but it was notorious that the prefect system could degenerate into legitimized exploitation and covert sexual fancying of younger boys. The boys probably played up to Arnold while the fires of rebelliousness still smouldered. In 1833 he could not get his sixth form elite to reveal who had thrown a keeper into the river; evidently loyalty to the group overcame any Christian regard for the truth, and Arnold was forced to expel six boys, thereby nearly provoking a riot.[16] Even around 1870 rowdyism against authority was not dead in the public schools. At Eton window-smashing was common, and the ducking of an unpopular master in a pool by a mob has been alluded to. Maurice Baring, who attended Eton in the later 1880s, recalled the ragging of some masters. One maths teacher had his lessons disrupted by a boy practising the national anthem on the violin under his window, prompting the class to stand to attention. Another master, Mr Bouchier, had such poor discipline that he had to leave, but later became a distinguished *Times* correspondent in the Balkans. Baring commented: 'He was a man who could do what he liked with the Bulgars but could not manage a division of Eton boys.'

Barbarianism was equally directed against the younger and weaker ones within their own fraternity, perpetrated under the guise of time-honoured custom and protected by the schoolboy code of honour not to complain to authority. Augustus Hare, a delicate boy who went to Harrow in 1847, recalled initiation ordeals inflicted on new boys: forcing them to drink liquor mixed with tallow, and tossing them to the ceiling on a counterpane. Young boys who were not quick enough carrying out orders as 'fags' could expect a 'licking'. The youngsters were caught between the devil and the deep blue sea, for if they failed to carry out an illicit order to smuggle in drink the sixth formers 'wapped' them, but if caught they would be flogged by the headmaster. Some sixth formers got sadistic pleasure out of making boys box each other for their amusement, and if they failed to 'keep up' at football they were made to cut large thorn sticks out of the hedges and were flogged with them till bloody'[17] Winchester could match Eton in viciousness; a fag who let a prefect's fire go out would have his hand and wrist burned with a brand as a warning for the future; and other rituals included being swung from the gas brackets and being jabbed with pen nibs.[18]

How far had the situation improved by the turn of the century? Dr Clement Dukes acknowledged in 1905 that while gross bullying had diminished (this he ascribed to a challenging of energies into school games), it still persisted; prefects were still abusing their power and only a few years before a boy had died after blows to the back.[19] At Edwardian Winchester things do not seem to have changed much; a memoir of time there recalls: 'I saw a lot of bullying. I remember a boy who was roasted in front of the fire. And there was endless beating by the boys with ash sticks. But I only ever beat two boys. They were throwing bottles and they insulted the poor old matron – they were terrible bullies.'[20] In 1918 when young Henry Green went up to public school newcomers who failed a 'knowledge' test of the school – its topography, house colours and so forth – were beaten by the prefects. Public schoolboy sub-culture remained a law unto itself when in the rest of society there was a reduction of beating. Any lessening of cruelty and violence between 1850 and the early 1900s would have been part of a wider amelioration of behaviour in society at large rather than any supposed long-term permeation of Dr Arnold's influences.

Casual schoolteacher sanctions like ear-pulling, hair-tugging and enforced drinking of soap and water for swearing were commonplace and class discipline relied heavily on corporal punishment. Indeed the British predilection for flogging was notorious among Continentals, who, it seems, resorted to it far less.[21] By 1906 Britain was steadfastly retaining it when it had been abolished in the British colonies, France, Germany and the USA.[22] The upper classes, with their public school nostalgia, were its keenest supporters; their attitude was 'We were flogged at school and it never did us any harm', a view burlesqued in a Victorian doggerel:

> 'Spare the rod and spite the child,'
> Solomon said in accents mild.
> 'Be they man or be they maid
> Whip 'em and wallop 'em,' Solomon said.[23]

Flogging put grit into young Britons, claimed the blimps, and made Britain the great nation it was:

> When British boys from shore to shore
> Two priceless boons shall find:
> The Flag that's ever waved before,
> The birch that's waved behind.[24]

Children's periodicals and comics from the late Victorian period to modern times, the *Gem* and *Magnet*, the *Beano* and *Dandy*, have reflected the omnipresence of the cane in the minds of their juvenile readership by delightedly caricaturing teachers as sour-faced swishers.[25] School sub-cultures abounded in supposititious folk preventives against the pain of a beating, such as working resin or lime juice into the hand, rubbing the hand through the hair, or placing a hair across the palm.[26]

Children were sometimes victims not only of hard-pressed teachers' understandable exasperation but also of their prejudices, vindictiveness and even sadism. Sir Henry Jones recalled a cruel Welsh village schoolmaster in the 1860s whose regime was a perpetual cycle of beatings: 'The answer to a sum is wrong, the boot is not exactly on the chalk line, the child has turned his head round, there are more than a certain number of errors, say three, in a dictation – any one of these might be a reason for a whacking' and he showed obvious favouritism towards the better-off children who went to church as against those whose parents were 'chapel', 'and especially those who were poor or slow ... were stung by many a vulgar sarcasm levelled at their "religion". Welsh-speaking was stamped on in the same way; culprits were caned or made to learn Bible verses by heart as punishment. Kate Taylor, self-willed Suffolk schoolgirl at the turn of the century, was the target of a vendetta by her headmaster, who deliberately taught her weakest subject, map-drawing, for an excuse to hit her every time she made a mistake. We see that Victorian and Edwardian girls were beaten as well as boys;[27] while boys might be caned on their backsides, sometimes even with their trousers down, for girls the beatings were usually confined to hands or shoulders. Alternative humiliations could suffice for girls, for example, being made to stand with pinafore or slates held over their heads.

Board school teachers who were not naturally tyrannical were impelled to resort to corporal punishment owing to pressure of class sizes, and the demands of 'Payment by Results'.[28] However, teachers with a good psychological rapport would use it only sparingly. James Runciman, a headmaster-turned-journalist, wrote in 1887 of the different types of pupil who must each be handled in a different way; street urchins could be regular tearaways but 'are capable of a devotion almost canine in intensity when kindly treated'; the cane, he advised, should be confined to the malicious and potentially vicious types.[29] None the less, there was, it seems, a Victorian myth that corporal punishment was actually a beneficial intellectual stimulus, a view refuted by Dr Crichton-Browne in 1884; children might learn facts by rote out of fear of a beating, but, he said, this did nothing for the cultivation of higher reasoning powers, and excessive canings traumatized the nervous system.[30] This was borne out by the experiences of Richard Church who attended elementary school before 1914 and remembered bitterly the repeated canings for his inability to do his maths, experiences which 'paralysed not only my brain but nerves'.[31] His experience was not that exceptional. Indiscriminate and capricious use of corporal punishment persisted in many schools before 1914, despite more emphasis in teacher-training colleges on understanding rather than regimentation of children since 1900, and the spread of Froebelian ideas.[32] Authority still tended to see the teacher as society's professional chastiser; police and magistrates sometimes gave parents the choice of allowing their child to be thrashed by their teacher for some minor misdemeanour committed outside school as an alternative to a trial.[33] A minority of teachers were undoubted brutes. In 1907 the NSPCC prosecuted two teachers: one a west country master at Frampton School who repeatedly punished and caned a weakly 9-year-old girl whenever she got her sums wrong, the other a teacher at Woodstone who savagely caned a 10-year-old boy when he could not recite his tables; he held the boy's head between his knees, beating his back and telling him to 'Beg for mercy'.[34]

Children by no means always took this punishment lying down. Desperation or defiance sometimes provoked a reaction. When Patrick Macgill could take no more mistreatment at the hands of a tyrannical village schoolmaster in Ireland at the end of the last century he struck him on the nose with his pointer and ran out of school, a hero to the other children.[35] Juvenile reprisals sometimes took the form of a guerrilla war, with acts of vandalism like damaging toilets and desks, and smashing lights and windows.[36] In 1894 when a new headmaster at a very rough school at Headington Quarry near Oxford tried to impose strict discipline he was twice assaulted by youngsters in his first year. Two years earlier children had instigated anti-Tory riots at the school, and the excitement spilled over into out-of-school unruliness when they threw stones at female staff.[37] There were other individual instances when long-suffering children rose and attacked their teachers. 'Institutional' schools lie outside the scope of this book, but workhouse and industrial school children were more vulnerable to arbitrary and excessive beatings than those in elementary schools; Charlie Chaplin recalled the Friday morning caning ritual at Lambeth workhouse in 1896 when boys due for punishment were called out in succession, bent over a desk and belaboured so hard with a thick 4-foot cane that they had to lie on their sides for ten minutes till the pain eased somewhat, and boy onlookers were known to faint at the spectacle.[38] But even downtrodden workhouse children had their moment. At the workhouse school of St Asaph's Union in Denbighshire around the middle of the century the desperate children were driven to rebel against their brutal and deranged teacher, an ex-collier. Henry Morton Stanley, later to be the famous discoverer of Livingstone, remembered as a pauper child then how 'our poor heads were cuffed and slapped and pounded until we lay speechless and streaming with blood', and a boy was to die from maltreatment. One day while the teacher was in the middle of flogging a boy, the children rose against him, Stanley himself kicking the schoolmaster and beating him with his own stick.[39]

The outward display of conformity and obedience enforced by the cane occasionally crumbled when children felt caught up in a wider social excitement. The years 1889 and 1911 were marked by industrial unrest, inspiring children to stage their own school strikes.[40] In 1889 school strikes started in Scotland and spread south, and in 1911, starting in Llanelli, they spread to 60 towns and cities over the next fortnight. Pupils marched and picketed, calling for a reduction in school hours, no homework, the abolition of corporal punishment, better heating, free meals and the lowering of the school-leaving age, among other demands. When these short-lived strikes disintegrated, the ringleaders were caned in front of the whole school. The prominence of corporal punishment in the memories of former elementary school pupils should not mislead us into believing that teachers were universally regarded with fear rather than affection, for there were strikes in favour of teachers, too. When in 1914 Herefordshire schoolteachers went on strike for higher pay, the local authority dismissed them and replaced them with unqualified staff. Children then went on strike in support of their teachers (the 'copy-cat' factor again), though it became an occasion for disorder and vandalism. Herefordshire did reinstate the teachers. A more impressive pro-teacher strike started at the village of Burston in East Anglia in 1914. Two compassionate and popular teachers who were socialists and trade unionists, and were uncongenial to the local squirearchy, were dismissed on a fabricated charge of hitting two Barnardo children at the school. Pupils went on strike supported by their parents; the village school was boycotted and a separate 'Strike School' was established, funded by well-wishers, lasting for twenty years.

Legally a teacher was *'in loco parentis'* and the courts would uphold the teacher's right to inflict the same corporal punishment as a parent would be permitted. However, a local authority was empowered to restrict this right, and though parents could not sue a teacher for assault if the chastisement was reasonable, the teacher might still be dismissed from the school for breach of contract.[41] From the early days of the school boards there had been official regulation of the use of the cane. A London School Board regulation of 1871 restricted its use to headteachers, and though teachers were to protest, the board took the 'enlightened' view for the time that youngsters who were on the receiving end of violence were more likely to dish it out themselves when adult.[42] Around the turn of the century, regulations in Leeds and Bradford, for example, proscribed striking on the head or boxing ears; at Bradford the cane was forbidden for failure to do work, and might be used only for 'morally culpable' offences.[43] The London Board was to make a concession to teachers by allowing headmasters to delegate the right to cane to selected staff, and the board issued its own regulation 2-foot cane.

Official attitudes towards corporal punishment appear to have been mellowing from around 1900. Perhaps some contemporary scandals about brutality in industrial schools played a part. In 1900 Parliament rejected a bill which would have extended the courts' powers to inflict judicial floggings on youths. In the same year schools had to start keeping caning registers,[44] and from 1904 the Board of Education disapproved of the use of the cane for infants and girls.[45] However, regulations were widely ignored, and unofficial resort to corporal punishment with hand, slipper, or ruler was commonplace. The National Union of Teachers supported teachers' right to use corporal punishment in principle, and the NSPCC supported it as a social discipline but objected to the extent of its use, as for petty offences.[46] The Humanitarian League, formed as a pressure group against official flogging, also totally opposed corporal punishment in schools.

Working-class parents' attitudes to the physical punishment of their children was very individual. At one extreme there was total passivity or deference to their social betters, the teachers. When the Bristol schoolboy Bill Harding had his eardrum perforated by a blow from the teacher his mother's response was 'Oh, you must have been misbehaving youself.'[47] 'Respectable' working-class parents supported the disciplinary and corrective role of school and would back teachers against their own children.[48] Others might hve justifiable grievances against excessive or unfair beatings and write letters of complaint or come up to the school in varying degrees of temper,[49] or take the teacher to court for assault. Most galling for teachers were the parents who were unwilling or unable to control their own brats at home, yet were keen to start proceedings against teachers.[50] Obnoxious louts who knew something of the state board regulations on corporal punishment, and knew their parents would support them, taunted teachers with comments like 'I know wot's in the papers. My father'll have you afore the bloomin' beak if e'er a one o'you [blank] touches me.'[51] However, magistrates with their middle-class view of the virtues of a beating, generally took the teachers' side, even in cases which shocked the NSPCC itself; as in a case of 1888 where a JP discharged a teacher who had given a boy 25 strokes on the behind, badly bruising him.[52]

Middle- and upper-class schools had an ethos of their own in regard to corporal punishment. Parents who paid directly for their children's education expected their children to be corrected and chastised as part of their social education. The severe spartan conditions in the great public schools were accepted as 'making men' of their sons; and floggings were a hallowed part of their tradition. The higher the class of a girls' private school, it is reckoned, the less likely it was that corporal punishment would be resorted to,[53] but in the cheaper girls' schools it certainly was inflicted. Gillian Avery recalled from direct experience such a school she attended before the Second World War where in handwriting lessons 'Our hands were beaten by the headmistress if we could not make out pot-hooks properly'. In George Orwell's *A Clergyman's Daughter*, already cited in Chapter 14, the headmistress pointed out the daughters of the good payers to the new teacher, Dorothy, with the instruction 'you're not to smack any of that lot, not on any account.' It was all right to smack the daughters of the medium payers if they got saucy 'but don't go and leave a mark that their parents can see. If you take my advice, the best thing with children is to twist their ears.'[54]

Beating was so integral to the boys' public school way of life that schools even had their own vernacular terms for it; at Eton you were 'swished' and at Winchester 'tunded'. Victorian Eton had a traditional birch, like a short besom with a 3-foot handle and a 2-foot 'bush'. Senior boys had the right to 'swish'; the victim was bent over a chair while the prefect ran at him with a cane. A flogging by a master was a public ritual. The culprit was set on a block and two boys deputized as 'holders down', while the master laid in. It was a degrading and brutalizing public spectacle, when the boys would come running to enjoy another's torment. Brinsley Richards remembered the eager rush when he was a pupil there:

> Several dozen fellows clambered upon forms to see Neville corrected and I got a front place, my heart thumping and seeming to make great leaps within me. Next moment, when he knelt on the step of the block and when the Lower Master inflicted upon his person six cuts that sounded like the

splashing of so many buckets of water, I turned almost faint
.... It is true that the eyes and nerves soon get accustomed
to cruel sights. I gradually came to witness the executions in
the Lower School not only with indifference but with amusement.[55]

The schoolboy ethic demanded stoicism under the ordeal. For
sensitive boys like Algernon Charles Swinburne, a ritual 'swishing'
was a memory carried into adult life. His poem 'The flogging
block' brings out the *schadenfreude* of the boys and the victim's
painful effort not to 'blub':

> At each fresh Birchen Stroke they smile afresh
> To see 'the young one' suffer in the Flesh.
> Each time the twigs bend round across my Bum
> Pain bids 'Cry out' but honour bids 'Be dumb'.[56]

There was a certain kudos in having come through a swishing, and
those who had undergone at least three birchings formed
themselves into the select 'Eton Block Club'. Public school Old
Boys had nostalgic memories of the 'good' a beating had done
them, but Dr Crichton-Browne expressed a more objective view of
this public school machismo:

> The notion prevalent that it is conducive to manliness, self-
> reliance and other peculiarly British virtues to cut a boy free
> at an early age from his mother's apron strings and send him
> to rough it amongst boys of his own age, has no good
> physiological foundation. The process of roughing it,
> especially when there is no smooth haven at home to return
> to, is often a very painful one, and some boys are permanently
> damaged by having to pass through it .... Manliness comes
> soon enough, and need not be anticipated by swagger and
> affectation, and perhaps that is the best sort of manliness
> which is founded on a delicate regard for the feelings of
> others, not that which is an expression of blunted
> sensibilities.

He cited Thomas Carlyle's unhappy memories of his schoolfellows
– the 'damage and defilement I got out of these coarse, unguided
tyrannous cubs', forcing him with distaste at last to give as good as
he got.[57]

Boys were reluctant to complain to their parents about

excessive or unauthorized beatings; it was 'not good form' to complain. L. E. Jones, who attended Eton right at the end of the last century, remembered some very rough masters.[58] A classics master once threw a book so violently at a boy that he knocked him off his bench. Another, who suffered from neuritis and was given to fits of anger, once seized a boy he accused of staring at him, dragged him across the classroom and hurled him down the stairs. Only occasionally would such excesses come to light. At Shrewsbury in 1874 the headmaster inflicted 88 strokes on a boy for illicitly bringing alcohol into his study. In 1877[59] at Christ's Hospital a 12-year-old boy, William Gibbs, committed suicide. His life had been made a misery by bullying monitors and he had run away twice; on the second occasion he was locked up in the infirmary, where he hanged himself. In 1894 a master at a public school paid damages out of court when sued by a parent for boxing his son's ear so severely that he damaged his eardrum.[60] And as late as 1906 a housemaster at Manchester Grammar School caused an outcry when he caned a boy on his bare bottom.

At the lower levels of private education, the second-rate boarding-schools also went in for thrashing, but without the style and mystique attaching to the great public schools. At the Hertfordshire boarding-school attended by C. S. Lewis in 1908, 'the only stimulating element in the teaching consisted of a few well-used canes' resting on the chimney-piece of the single schoolroom.[61] The headmaster was a desiccated cleric, a vindictive man who had favourite victims, notably those from less favoured social backgrounds: 'I have known Oldie [the head's nickname] enter the schoolroom after breakfast, cast his eyes round, and remark, "Oh, there you are, Rees, you horrid boy. If I'm not too tired I shall give you a good drubbing this afternoon." He was not angry, nor was he joking.' In contrast to Eton the boys got no pleasure out of watching one of their friends beaten – 'the grey faces of all the other boys, and their deathlike stillness, are among the memories I could willingly dispense with'.

Perhaps the most famous victim of boarding-school sadism was young Winston Churchill who was sent at the age of 7 in 1881 to a highly rated preparatory school at Ascot run by the Rev. Herbert William Sneyd-Kinnersley. The floggings he inflicted there, said Churchill later, 'exceeded in severity anything that would be tolerated in any of the Reformatories under the Home Office'.[62] Periodically he would assemble the whole school in the library, and the predetermined victims would be escorted to an adjoining room and beaten ferociously 'until they bled freely, while the rest sat quaking listening to the screams'. Winston himself was removed by his parents after he received this treatment. The impression he leaves of the sanctimoniously sadistic headmaster was borne out by Roger Fry who was a pupil there just before Churchill. Kinnersley would beat boys' bottoms till they were 'a mass of blood'. On one occasion a boy voided himself with diarrhoea under this onslaught but the 'irate clergyman instead of stopping at once went on with increased fury until the whole ceiling and walls of his study were spattered with filth' (which he cleaned up himself afterwards with the help of a boy 'favourite').[63] However, Maurice Baring, who was born the same year as Churchill, and attended the school from the age of 10, gives a different picture.[64] Winston, it seems, was something of a menace:

> Dreadful legends were told about Winston Churchill, who had been taken away from the school. His naughtiness appeared to have surpassed anything. He had been flogged for taking sugar from the pantry and so far from being penitent had taken the Headmaster's sacred straw hat from where it hung over the door and kicked it to pieces.

He was continually at odds with authority and the other boys had little sympathy for him. Baring himself has pleasant memories of the place (but then in his autobiography written in 1922 he makes no mention of floggings during his time at Eton, either). He gives no impression of wanton cruelty, just the 'normal' disciplines of the period – being kept in to do extra work, silence at meals for a week, losses of privileges and so forth: a curious contrast with the accounts of sadism left by Fry and Churchill.

I have dwelt on the harsher aspects of school discipline at all levels of society. But did school discipline have beneficial effects, too? James Walvin has concluded that it did have an important taming and socializing influence in cultivating habits of punctuality, standards of dress, and the duties of obedience and silence. Edwardian children were better behaved than their mid-Victorian counterparts, and the schools must take much of the credit, he maintains. However, I remain a little sceptical about the permanent 'socializing' effects of a regime of petty rules coupled with teachers' weaknesses for magnifying minor faults out of all proportion; since the alternative to schools would have meant for the majority of children staying out on the streets, schools could not fail to have had a regulatory effect on children *while* children.

18

SCHOOL ATTENDANCE

Even before the 1870 Education Act many working-class parents, as we have seen, were prepared to pay to see their children receive some rudimentary utilitarian instruction. For a good many parents the discipline of school was the prime appeal, rather than its instruction. One son of a farm labourer in the 1860s was allowed to work as a farmhand 'if he was a good boy', but 'if he was naughty he was sent to school'.[1] But generally parents did not like the idea of compulsion to come from the schools themselves. For many, British and and National schools were objectionable for their insistence upon standards of dress and regularity of attendance, so dame schools and other 'private adventure' schools filled the gap, for however inefficient they were they did not impose on their working-class patrons; in 1851 it appears that 30 per cent of the 2 million children at school were taught in such classes, where the regime was more lax and they were not punished for absenteeism.[2]

The 1870 Education Act was intended to supplement the church school network with board school districts where the former were lacking; only school boards could make education up to 13 compulsory in their districts if they wished; this power was only given to the National schools by the 1876 Education Act, which also encouraged school attendance by restricting children's employment rights under 13 unless they made a minimum number of school attendances or had passed Standard 4. It was the Act of 1880 that made attendance mandatory to a minimum of 10 years old. The process of improving enrolment figures among those eligible for education was slow. In 1873 enrolments were just under three-quarters of those eligible, and in 1880 nearly 78 per cent. Compulsion must have helped, for by 1900 the figure was nearly 88 per cent;[3] the shortfall would still have included, for example, the children of canal and fairground folk. The absenteeism rate among those who were enrolled was high in the early period of the Education Acts but was declining to the turn of the century. In the early 1870s on average a third of the class was absent on any one day but by 1900 this was down to under a fifth.[4] (The 1900 figures still meant that only 72 per cent of all children who should have been at school were actually attending.)

Absenteeism may have been partly due to the requirement to pay school fees. The 1891 Education Act empowered school boards to abolish them, though they did linger on. In 1896 750,000 of England's 6 million elementary schoolchildren were still paying fees.[5] Fee-paying was not totally abolished until 1918. However, fees shold not be exaggerated as a deterrent, for children at poorer schools paid less (1*d* or 2*d* a week) than schools in better-class neighbourhoods (up to 6*d* a week in London in the 1890s). School attendance panels could remit fees in hardship cases,[6] and the Poor Law could pay fees as a form of outdoor relief. Absenteeism was determined by other factors. Resentment at compulsory attendance was one; this was more marked among the very poor than the 'respectable' working classes of the artisan type, who wanted to give their children a decent foundation of schooling.[7] For very poor families a child's ability to contribute to the family income was far more important than school where the child was plied with useless facts and useless memorizing.[8] Parental drunkenness and neglect kept many children off school and the mental horizons of destitute parents were narrowed by the daily struggle for survival. In 1907 Mrs Achibald Mackirdy visited a home worker with five children and a drunken husband she supported by making waistcoats; her life was further burdened by insistent visits from the school attendance officer: '"What good", said she to me bitterly, "does this schooling do the kids? I 'ad precious little and they ain't likely to be better off, nor me! Is it better to be 'ungry or to be hignorant?"'[9] Some parents cynically viewed the education system as a money-making operation for educationalists, and in the early days of the London School Board parents were known to walk on to school premises to collect their child at midday, or the end of school hours, saying to the teachers, 'He has been putting money into your pockets, now I want him to put some into mine.'[10] School attendances improved as parents became resigned to the system, and some sanguine observers saw this as a genuine sign of changing working attitudes to education. George Sims's poem 'Polly' (1879) put into the mouth of a coster the fear that schooling would make his son turn up his nose at following in his father's footsetps:

> It's the school board that gives 'em these notions, a-stuffin boys' heads full of pride,
> And makes 'em look down on their fathers – these school boards I ne'er could abide.[11]

Ten years later, however in *How the Poor Live* Sims was saying that it was now easier to get the urchins into school and he felt confident that the cumulative effect of education through the generations would be bound to uplift the 'residuum'. Similarly Henry Reader Williams of the Ragged School Union told the 1887 Royal Commission on Education that the 'great bulk' of working-class parents now saw the value of education, but he was being sanguine. The 1909 Departmental Committee on Partial Exemption from School Attendance commented: 'The feeling that it is worth making any sacrifice to prolong the education of a child is spreading only slowly through society.' Any parental interest in their children's progress up the Standards was spurred only as a talking-point for comparison with neighbours' children,[12] and more importantly as a pointer to how soon the child could gain exemption and start earning.[13] Robert Roberts, growing up in Edwardian Manchester, the son of a shopkeeper, suffered from a philistine father who spurned his son's acquisition of a scholarship to the grammar school for the extended schooling this entailed.[14] The value attached in the family to the intelligence of his older sister Ellie was summed up by their grandmother? 'She'll pass that labour exam – no trouble at all! You'll get her off school for twelve an' into that mill. Not like them boobies so daft they got to stay till they're fourteen.' Ellie's mother had hopes of sending her to commercial college but her father insisted he could not afford it; the mother rashly pointed out that he had plenty to spend on drink: 'Beer is my food!' he roared. And that was it. Ellie sat lost in disappointment.

In some cases poverty was a genuine cause of absenteeism, even when parents were willing to send their children to school.[15] Lack of shoes or winter clothing, sheer hunger and epidemics, all conspired to keep children off. The inspections by the 'nitty Noras' were followed by a fall in attendance as verminous children were sent home. In poorer London districts in 1890 absenteeism could be as high as 30 per cent and at Salford at the turn of the century 25 per cent.[16] However, at the deprived Johanna Street School in Lambeth in 1904 attendances were said to be good because children preferred to be in school rather than in their slum buildings.[17] But apathy was probably the main cause of working-class school absenteeism. Hunger and lack of suitable clothes were often just pretexts as schools were now becoming channels for feeding and clothing charities. Monday and Friday were the commonest days for absence, also pointing to inertia,[18] and the absence of verminous children should not normally have been prolonged as parents were legally obliged to cleanse them and ensure their return to school.

The long-term rise in school attendances has been ascribed not to evidence of a readier embracing of education but to a decline in children's employment opportunities due to technological change.[19] The hoped-for inroads on 'moonlighting' under the 1903 Employment of Children Act were also claimed in 1909 to have improved school attendances, which were then said to stand at 90 per cent. Attendance incentives to acquire the 'Dunce's Pass' for partial exemption to work in the mills could not have been that overriding. The law required 250 (later 300) attendances a year; an 'attendance' was a morning or an afternoon session, and so an attendance rate of only 70–5 per cent was required for partial exemption. Attendances fluctuated seasonally in some areas; thus in rural districts, despite the replacement of children by machinery prior to 1914, children were still being kept off for harvesting,[21] and meetings at Epsom and 'hopping' expeditions in Kent would seasonally strip south London classrooms.[22] Girls had a somewhat higher rate of absenteeism as they were needed to help at home, and the authorities were more lenient about enforcing their attendance; education for girls beyond their home-making role was perhaps taken less seriously than education for boys anyway.[23] Jewish children had a low rate of absenteeism. In Commercial Street School in Whitechapel where there was a high Jewish element, attendances in 1897 stood at 97 per cent, though again it was less good for girls.[24] Robert Sherard in 1905 remarked on the impressive attendance record among Jews, but ascribed this not to any traditional aspect for learning or higher social aspirations than among Gentiles but to parents' desire to get them 'out of the schools as fast as possible so they can start them earning money'. Children of Jews long settled here, it seems, did not go in for street trading, and so this was weaker as a motive to play truant.

Among the lowest grade of urban working class there was a positive anti-school ethos among parents. School attendance officers – 'kid-coppers' and 'hopeful-snatchers' as they were pejoratively nicknamed – ventured at some personal risk into districts like the notorious rough 'Jago' slum of Bethnal Green in the late nineteenth century, where they would be faced with abuse, threats and perhaps dead cats and other missiles ('Coppin' a School Board').[25] They were looked on as snoopers and bullies, and local folklore told highly coloured tales of the hardships they caused poor families by taking them to court, and depriving them of their children's earnings. In Deptford in the 1870s and 1880s attendance officers worked in twos for protection, and the school staff had to be ready to fight off assaults from older relatives of the pupils. In both districts, be it noted, such anti-school manifestations had abated by 1900.[26]

Slum dwellers living hand-to-mouth were constantly on the move from lodging to lodging, 'doing a moonlight flit' to dodge landlords and other creditors or to evade the education authorities where they were keeping their children from school. This problem even acquired a bureaucratic jargon term, 'capricious migration', and turnovers in some schools were so high that in 1878 the London School Board appointed a committee of inquiry.[27] The headmaster of Maidstone Street Board School in Haggerston, explained, for example, that between April and December 1878 of the 289 boys presented for examination 89 had left, and he expected the figure to rise to 118 by the new year. The authorities could not keep track of these migrating children, who were left to roam the streets or hawk during the day. 'Capricious migration' persisted into the Edwardian period. George Haw in 1910 told of one slum family with six children which suddenly disappeared one night when the father had received a summons for his children's non-attendance at school. Unencumbered by any furniture the father relocated his brood forthwith 'in a similar room in a court at the other of the parish where he was as effectively lost to the troublesome school attendance officer as though he had crossed the Atlantic'. Robert Sherard likewise in 1905 told how in mining areas around Wigan miners would move around the lodging-houses to evade the attendance officers as their children were illegally working underground.

News of the 'kid-copper's' arrival spread rapidly on the tenement grapevine, and there was a rush for cover:

legs and bodies may be seen in many houses sticking out from under sinks or behind piles of firewood, where children have vainly tried to hide themselves. They cry bitterly when discovered and dragged into the light. Foolish mothers use the officer as a bogeyman to frighten the babies when naughty.[28]

Seedy doctors in the slums would sell bogus sickness certificates for a few pence, and it was argued in favour of school medical inspections that it would put paid to this fraud.[29] Parents had other dodges. If a child had a verminous head, parents were known to rub sand on the sores to keep them open. One Birmingham woman deliberately 'cultivated a vermin farm on her little daughter's head and body' to keep her at home doing domestic outwork.[30] A children's dodge for exploiting teachers' fears of classroom epidemics was to press a button to the neck, show the teacher the mark and innocently ask if it could be the sign of something ominous.

Rural schoolchildren also had a poor attendance record. The long distances they had to trudge to school, especially in winter, the difficulties their poorly paid parents had in meeting the fees, the paucity of school-based feeding and clothing charities in the countryside, the need for child labour at harvest time – all conspired to keep children off school. The country squirearchy's reactionary sentiments against working-class education, especially when it conflicted with their interests in perpetuating a docile and deferential labour force, ready to supply its children at command, ensured that the school attendance laws would not be properly enforced. There were cases in the 1890s of country children not even starting school till they were 10.[31] Although rural school attendances had improved by the turn of the century (abolition of fees and mechanization of farming were contributory factors), the backwoods mentality among the rural ruling classes persisted before the First World War, and they still did not accept deep down that education should be compulsory, or that the state had any right to stop a parent exploiting a child's labour as he or she saw fit.[32]

Schools had to devise incentives to encourage attendance. The mere fact that they were charity vehicles induced some parents to stay on their good side and send their children to school; as one old denizen of the 'Jago' put it:

My mother, poor old dear, didn't care much if we went to school or not. But she knew it was the law of the land, that she could be punished if we didn't ... and she liked to be well in with the Mission. There was always a few bob to be got from them, provided you behaved yourself.[33]

Schools offered certificates, prizes, medals and even awards of free clothing to regular and punctual attenders. In 1890 Charles Booth wrote that the London School Board had issued over 9,000 medals the year before.[34] Children were allowed to sport their decorations in school as a good example: 'Some of the scholars', said Hugh Philpott in 1904, 'are entitled to wear almost as many decorations as a victorious general; eight, nine, even ten medals are the splendid testimonial both to punctual habits and good health which some of them can show.'

Defaulters' parents would be summoned before the school attendance panels, and the local authority would be faced with the decision whether to prosecute in the most obstinate cases. Court fines were usually low, and the authorities were often deterred by the legal costs. In the rural districts where school attendance officers were likely to be mere part-timers, such as postmen and Poor Law relieving officers, prosecution was pointless when the magistrates were themselves the employers of seasonal child labour.[35]

Apart from the prosecution of parents the authorities might get the chronic absentees committed to a day industrial school or a truant school. Both were created under the 1876 Education Act, the former for those deemed to be victims of their environment and the latter for wilful truants. The day industrial school children attended for up to 3 years, combining elementary schooling with some trade training; children returned home at night, but any non-attendance would be immediately chased up. Truant schools were more penal, in effect short-term reformatories, which children attended residentially for a few months and where they were put through a brisk, strict regime. It was a measure of the improvement in school attendances that in 1911 there were only 9 truant schools in England and Wales which had received 773 children out of a total school population then of about 6 million and the Departmental Committee on Reformatories and Industrial Schools in 1913 could even call for their suppression.[36]

19

THE FORMATIVE RESULTS
OF EDUCATION

The Royal Commission on Employment of Children in 1864 plumbed some astounding depths of ignorance among working children. In the Midlands at one metalworks factory an investigator found that nearly three-quarters of the 80 7–16-year-olds there were completely illiterate.[1] Even where they had received a smattering of schooling, the scraps of knowledge retained by such children were vestigial and muddled. Replies to various interviewers' questions included such answers as 'I've heard that [Christ] but don't know what it is'; 'The devil is a good person; I don't know where he lives'; 'Christ was a wicked man'; 'The Queen has a name; it is "Prince"'; 'Have not heard of France or London' (from a 12-year-old Midlands girl) and 'Have not heard of Scotland' (from a 19-year-old). One limited Leeds survey in 1859 revealed literacy rates of 24 per cent among 13–16-year-olds, and of those who could not read just under a quarter had worked as part-timers between 8 and 13 and therefore had experienced some half-time education.[2] Full-time schooling, as it developed after 1870, was destined to face some initial uphill struggles to raise basic levels of literacy. In the early years of the board schools, despite the pounding in the three Rs, literacy standards remained below Standard 1 for over a quarter of pupils in some schools serving the poorest districts; that is, they could not read simple sentences.[3] At the most rudimentary level – the ability to sign one's name – there were distinct advances through the century even before the era of state schooling. In 1840 66 per cent of males could sign their names; in 1870, just before the board schools were established, 80 per cent could do so, and in 1900 97 per cent.[4] Among juvenile prisoners in 1842–53 nearly 43 per cent were totally illiterate, just over 30 per cent could read and write imperfectly, 24 per cent could read but not write, and only the small residue were fully literate.[5] In 1891 of youths sent to reformatories (presumably of the same social class as the juvenile prisoners of the 1840s) 17 per cent were totally illiterate and 70 per cent could read and write imperfectly,[6] showing a definite advance through schooling. However, the magistrate J. W. Horsley in 1913 reckoned from observing young offenders that the high proportion who were of the reading standards of 8- and 9-year-olds indicated a *regression* in their literacy since leaving school;[7] school, he concluded, had only a temporary effect on mental development. The abysmal spelling of mothers in notes to school explaining their children's absence was to him further evidence of the fading of school influences. For example, absences due to children being sent on an errand were rendered variously to 'To go of anarrand', 'To get some arrants' and 'To go on an arreind'. Other reasons for absence were penned as 'Ceapt by his father', 'Whas kept away becos he was hill', 'Very pooly so I keep him Atomb' and 'He plad the truent'.[8] Such were the jottings by 1913 of people who had certainly experienced full-time education. However, against Horsley's scepticism we can set the recollections of others. Edna Bold who was born in 1904 into a respectable working-class family remembered her starchy, strict schoolteacher armed with chalk and stick: 'Both these instruments of her trade were used to such effect that by the time I left . . . . I could read, write and spell. Everyone could read, write and spell.'[9] Robert Roberts recalled likewise how in the pre-1914 Salford slums children were more literate than their parents and might have to perform chores for them like reading the racing lists in the newspapers and filling in their betting slips. With the advent of silent movies children were taken to the cinemas to serve as 'readers' for illiterate or short-sighted elders: 'When a picture gave place to print on the screen a muddled Greek chorus of children's voices rose from the benches, piping above the piano music. To hear them crash in unison on a polysyllable became for literate elders an entertainment in itself.'[10]

Going beyond literacy to the higher aspirations of education, as a cultural and character-building experience, what 'success' could be claimed here? Even at the mid-nineteenth century Henry Mayhew was cynical about the uses to which youngsters put their literacy. He noted how the street-Arabs fed their minds on the lurid penny dreadfuls,[11] and he and John Binny in 1862 were dismissive about the idealists who believed that education was an intrinsically morally edifying experience which would lift the masses out of their ignorance and reduce juvenile delinquency – 'a fallacy of the most dangerous nature because it is one of the popular notions of the day'. Years before, Mayhew had offended the sensibilities of philanthropists when in a series of articles in the *Morning Post* he had demonstrated that the ragged schools were having no effect on juvenile crime levels, and he concluded that education did not reduce crime but served to create more educated criminals: 'in the words of an intelligent policeman, "we are teaching our thieves to prig the articles marked at the highest figures".'[12] Much later in the century, in 1885, with state schooling firmly established, Samuel Smith MP, a sympathizer of the dead-end plight of the street-Arab, could express similar scepticism of the value of literacy by itself; lurid crime rags like *Police News* were the staple of reading in the slums: 'One sometimes wonders whether this so-called "education" does not in the case of many multiply their power for evil.'[13] His answer was to devote less time to pedagogic subjects like parsing and more to trade training and give youngsters the practical skills they needed to lift themselves out of the slums. This was nothing new; in the 1840s voluntary trade schools run on these lines were set up and began to qualify for Education Department grants on a par with the British and National schools. But they were more expensive to run than the 'bookish' schools, and the Revised Code of 1861 laying down the criteria for future grants under 'Payment by Results', emphasized the 'bookish' attainments, and the trade schools began disappearing.[14]

However, it should not be assumed that 'practical' subjects, so far as they were taught, were either put across meaningfully or indeed had any long-term effect on the former pupil's later life-style. I have already cited Lord Norton's complaint about science teaching in Chapter 14.[15] So low could the state of science teaching sink that in one school in 1890 55 per cent of the children were found not to know that all things of wood came from trees, 69 per cent did not know where wood came from, and 75 per cent did not know what season they were in.[16] The failures of domestic science training for girls have likewise already been discussed in Chapter 14. The Second World War booklet *Our Towns: A Close-Up*, revealing the gross ignorance of evacuee working-class mothers in basic homecraft, made the point in relation to the decline in infant mortality since 1900:

A leading article in the press said the nation had made the

mistake of thinking that the decline of infant mortality was due to our girls' having learnt cleanliness in the elementary schools; that we now realise this to be fallacious, many of them having learnt neither cleanliness nor decency; that the improvement in infant mortality was due to other causes, such as better ventilation, clothing and nutrition ... and that the problem of teaching the principles of decent living to the future mothers of the race remained to be solved.[17]

Samuel Smith also expressed concern about the speed with which the supposed moral influences of school evaporated in the post-school adolescent years and he spoke of the 'critical period' of a child's life from 12 to 16 when 'at that vital stage the child population of the slums are prowling about the streets getting initiated in the arts of vice and crime'. A generation later in 1917, when the term 'adolescent' as a recognized phase of emotional storm and stress had gained wider currency, and the country had passed through a scare about alleged rampant teenage hooliganism, a sociologist, J. W. Slaughter, made similar observations about the failure of education to 'train' the character.

Existing educational devices are ostensibly for the purpose of training the intellect, while character is not even thought to be within their field of operations; it cannot be claimed that the semi-militaristic habits of the school have any learning beyond their immediate purpose. The school is even open to the accusation of giving assistance to the making of criminals through sheer boredom imposed upon adolescents.

This was just another version of a criticism levelled against the school system over the previous fifty years — that mechanical drilling and rote-learning had no long-term beneficial effect and even prompted antisocial reactions when the child left school.[18] Yet there were others who were prepared to affirm the contrary; that schooling had had a marked civilizing effect on youth. Gertrude Tuckwell in 1894[19] claimed it had reduced delinquency and pointed symbolically to the fact that 'a Board School now stands on the site of Clerkenwell gaol', and in 1914 Arnold Freeman, a commentator on the problem of youngsters drifting into 'blind-alley' jobs, was convinced that without 'this great influence' of school 'we should be manufacturing a race of hooligans'.

In the high Victorian period a clear aim in the ethos of schooling was to teach children their proper station in life, and the virtues of industry and obedience. I have already quoted in Chapter 14 Flora Thompson recalling how in her country school the rector used Scripture lessons to reinforce the pupils' place in society, saying that he hoped they would never commit the sin of trying to change their appointed lot in life. Education was intended to be a medium for turning out obedient, tamed hands for the factories, mines and farms. Yet by the Edwardian period this role of underscoring the status quo was to be modified by the evident need to train up children to meet the growing industrial competition from abroad. The education system was groping towards raising children's aspirations above their current station; the 1902 Education Act, with its provision for secondary schools and scholarships, was one indicator of this, and the calls for continuation schools and further education were another.

Did school have more social influence on the middle and upper classes? For them it extended into late adolescence and so covered a longer period of a boy's life. And the mystique and ethos of public school life — notions of 'not letting the side down', 'playing the game', and so forth — echoed nostalgically in the memories of Old Boys as they advanced down the years. Some, however, felt no gratitude to their Alma Mater; the academic regime was less than stimulating. Augustus Hare (1834–1903) bitterly recalled his abiding memory of Harrow in the late 1840s — the subjugation of young boys by older ones, and the pointlessness of the curriculum: 'I may truly say that I never learnt anything useful at Harrow and had little chance of learning anything. Hours and hours were wasted daily on useless Latin verses with sickening monotony. A boy's education at this time, except in the highest forms, was hopelessly inane.' We observed in Chapter 16 how decadent the regime was at Eton in the 1860s: the classics, which dominated the timetable, became a game of avoidance and cribbing.[20] Yet the Taunton Commission Report of 1868, which damned Eton academically and quoted Oxford dons as complaining that Eton youths 'come to us with very unawakened minds and habits of mental indolence and inaccuracy', could also speak glowingly of public schools as character-builders: instilling in boys a 'capacity to govern others and control themselves' and an 'aptitude for combining freedom with order ... public spirit ... vigour and manliness of character'. Certainly the public school ethos fostered a keen sense of imperial pride and patriotism, and their Officers Training Corps brought forth many a young gallant destined to die in the trenches of the Western Front. The social, more than the academic, experience was the chief formative influence of the public schools.

Religion as a medium for 'taming' and socializing children ran through all social levels of schooling. How effective was it as indoctrination? There is strong evidence that it went in one ear and out the other, leaving children with a garbled hotch-potch of impressions, a golden treasury for the collector of howlers and anecdotes. We all have our own memories of the misunderstandings and puzzlement generated by the archaic biblical language: I used to incant 'Forgive those who trespass against us' in school assemblies, dimly associating trespassing with playing on forbidden lawns in the park or scrumping fruit in other people's back gardens. Eleanor Acland had the same trouble with the Lord's Prayer in the 1880s. She and her brother recited: 'We chart in heaven. Hullo'd be thy name.' She knew a chart was a short of map, and when her brother asked what the line meant, she explained: 'It means that we're lost on the map of heaven and we call out to God to come and find us.' Lilian Boys Behrens recalled a children's prayer, 'Pity my simplicity, Suffer me to come to Thee', which the children recited so quickly that its meaning was lost:

It was not surprising the child asked: 'Why do we pray for mice, Mummy?'
'What do you mean, Dora?'
'When we say, Pity mice implicitly.'

Spiritual concepts were lost on very young children, who reduced them to concrete, material wants. The young and highly intelligent Edmund Gosse was subjected to the most austere spiritual exercise by his intense father, a Plymouth Brother. His father told him, 'Whatever you need, tell Him and He will grant it if it is His will.' Edmund, it happened, badly wanted a humming top 'a great deal more than I did the conversion of the heathen or the restitution of Jerusalem to the Jews, two objects of my nightly supplication which left me very cold'. Though his logic was impeccable and his parents had no answer, his father abruptly cut him short on the matter. On another occasion Edmund did win in the end. He wanted to go a children's party but his puritanical father enjoined him to search his conscience and seek guidance directly from the Lord. When he returned from his communing, his father confidently asked him, 'Well, and what is the answer which our Lord vouchsafes?' To which the canny boy rejoined with the divine revelation: 'The Lord says I may go to the Browns.'

Middle-class Victorian social investigators erroneously identified lack of scriptural knowledge among the working classes with their 'low moral state', whereas in fact this was likely to be due to their perception of religious humbug in childhood. Church attendance and Sunday Schools were remembered by many in later life for the hypocrisy and utter tedium. W. H. Barrett did harvesting work in the Fens at the age of 8 around the turn of the century for a pittance. On Sunday he had to attend chapel and 'sit on a hard wooden bench to listen to a discourse on the merits of suffering here below in order to reap a greater reward up above. I noticed the farmer who had bought me body and soul for sixpence a day, nodding his head to show that he approved all the preacher was saying.'

Steve Humphries cites the recollections of Bill Harding who was taught in a Catholic school. He attended a socialist meeting with his father and brother. This was anathema to reactionary Catholics, and Bill was called out by the priest who visited the school and had his face slapped for attending the meeting. His feelings about religion began cooling from that moment.[21] Catholic schools could be instruments for blackmailing children into attending Mass or Sunday School, for the priests would soon be n touch and defaulters were shamed and beaten in front of their classmates.[22] Children were forced to go to Sunday School by their parents as a mark of 'respectability (even when the parents were not churchgoers), or simply to get them out of the way on father's day of rest. Sunday Schools could themselves become markers of snobbery. Very poor children whose dress did not come up to standard were turned away; better-off children deliberately flaunted their Sunday finery in front of less fortunate pupils; and most snobbishly of all, the upper classes turned their noses up at Sunday Schools altogether and had private Bible classes at home. Dorothy Whipple recalled attending such classes after church around 1900, hob-nobbing with rich pampered girls 'smelling of scented soap'.[23] Children saw through the humbug, hated Sunday School but went because they were forced to. As one former pupil recalled:

The 'best' boys played up to their teachers and the parson and most of them were the veriest toadies, sneaks and liars; but they were the ones I was told I must copy. I saw little to admire in them, and tried my best to get turned out of school; but now my Father rented a pew . . . and put sixpence in the plate every Sunday and I couldn't get expelled.[24]

The sheer bordeom of religious instruction is readily appreciated from examples of the dense and turgid language children were subjected to, and the meaningless incantations they had to master. John Mill Chanter's *Help to an Exposition of the Catechism* (1850) catalogues the formula answers to formula questions children had to learn off by heart in this fashion:

Q: How came Christ to contend with and overcome the Devil:

A: He came into the world for this purpose, to conquer for us *our* enemy: 'For this purpose was the Son of God made manifest, that he might destroy the works of the Devil.' (St. John iii, 8) . . .

Q: What does our Lord say of the Devil in the parable of the sower?

A: That 'he taketh away the good seed from our hearts' (St. Luke viii, 12) . . .

Q: What are the works of the flesh which sinful lusts lead to?

A: Adultery, fornication, uncleanness, lasciviousness &c. (Gal. v, 19)

Children also had to learn the collects – short prayers for special occasions. A prescribed prayer for the times of tribulation printed in 1885 expected children to empathize with the following: 'O Lord, pour not out Thine anger upon us, neither chasten us in Thy hot displeasure; but according to Thy mercy show us that Thou are the Physician of souls; heal our souls, guide us to the haven of Thy will' and so on.[25]

We can therefore find understanding of this playground chant of spleen against Scripture: 'I one the Bible, I two the Bible, I three the Bible . . . I *eight* [hate] the Bible.'[26]

For all the shortcomings of Sunday Schools, they did give many poor children a smattering of literacy before the board school era; and positive attractions appealing to children's material self-interest were the fringe benefits of prizes, outings and charitable treats for regular attenders. For the residuum who were too poor and unkempt to be accepted into reputable Sunday Schools there were the non-sectarian ragged Sunday Schools, a perpetuation of the old ragged day schools outdated by the 1870 Education Act. In 1870 there were 250 Sunday ragged schools with a claimed 23,000 attenders;[27] these perhaps came closest to the original principles of Christianity.

It is doubtful, from the evidence I have cited, whether Scripture lessons had any lasting influence on the behaviour of former scholars. Even for those who turned out well in later life, religion might be worn as a cloak of social convenience. But many did not turn out well. In one survey of Leeds jail in the late 1860s out of 230 prisoners 23 had been Sunday School teachers, and 180 Sunday School pupils. This was confirmed in another survey in Salford jail in 1872 where 593 out of 645 prisoners had been to Sunday School; drink was alleged to be the cause of their downfall.[28] The Band of Hope (the juvenile temperance movement) criticized the Sunday Schools in the early 1870s for the inadequacy of their instruction on the evils of drink. Some northern publicans, needing singers for their music-halls, even advertised for Sunday School choristers, till local temperance groups threatened to object to the renewal of their licences.

It is not so surprising that such a large proportion of prisoners should have been former Sunday School pupils when it is surmised that up to 75 per cent of working-class children attended them around the mid-nineteenth century,[29] and in the early 1900s some 5 million children went each week.[30] By this time outward religious observance quickly wore off in adolescence.[31] In 1911 it was reckoned that only a fifth of adolescents went to Sunday Schools and churches, and most of the older youths drifted away from religion altogether.[32] Commenting on the decline in religious practice generally in society in the mid-1930s Eleanor Acland commented: 'The so often deplored disinclination of middle-aged people to attend Church services or to urge attendance upon their children is probably the aftermath of the intolerable boredom that we endured in church when we were children rather than a symptom of callousness towards religion.' There were more fundamental reasons for the decline of religious influence from the turn of the century; scientific developments and new forms of entertainment were both contributory but this takes us beyond the scope of this book.

I am sceptical therefore about the strength of any long-term influence of schooling upon people's behaviour as adults. So much of what children had to learn at school was irrelevant to their lives and ephemeral in their memories. The pettiness of classroom values may well have produced a reaction in many cases once the youngsters had thrown off the yoke of school and had started earning. After all, the 'hooligans' of the turn of the century were products of the elementary schools. And taking religion as an example of a 'fundamental' theme in schooling, I have shown how tenuous its hold was on captive youth.

20

EDUCATION AND ECONOMIC MOBILITY

Among the artisan and petty bourgeois class there was more aspiration for their children to do well out of the education system, and the Department of Education responded by allowing the creation of 'higher grade' elementary schools after 1870 for pupils prepared to stay on till 14 or 15, offering a Standard 7 or 'higher tops' grade. They offered more domestic economy for girls, and literary, commercial and scientific subjects for those destined to become skilled artisans and office workers.[1] Those schools concentrating on science, known as 'organized science schools', received additional funding from outside the mainstream education system. The Science and Art Department of South Kensington, formed after the Great Exhibition of 1851, funded technical courses till it was subsumed within the Department of Education in 1899.[2] Pupils were entered for the Science and Art Department examination. Around the turn of the century there were some 200 organized science schools. Their fees were higher (in the 1880s Manchester was charging 9d a week) and this effectively excluded the lower working classes, though a few free scholarships were available on the basis of a competitive entry examination. (By 1904 he LCC were offering scholarships to pay for university tuition.) In 1899 a court ruling, the 'Cockerton judgment', declared that departmental funding of schools beyond the basics under the Education Acts was unlawful. This prompted the 1902 Education Act expressly providing for the creation of secondary 'grammar' schools to which elementary school children could go on if they paid the fees or passed a scholarship examination for a free place.[3] These new local authority grammar schools aped the syllabuses of the public schools and the old endowed grammar schools with arts and classics, as well as science subjects. From 1911 local education authorities were to start developing intermediate schools, the central and technical high schools concentrating on science and vocational subjects, and halfway between the elementary schools and grammar schools in status. Even before the 1902 Act the endowed grammar schools had been increasingly making free scholarship places available, and one exceptional school, a National school at Kennington, in 1890 achieved 23 such scholarships. From 1907 25 per cent of all places at local authority grammar schools had to be free scholarship offers.

Who benefited from these new opportunities? Charles Booth in 1892 said it was only boys from the artisan class who found their way into secondary education, and 'artisans' were reckoned to form about 15 per cent of the working class (with another 45 per cent as skilled or semi-skilled).[4] Within working-class homes, it has been suggested that the younger children stood the best chance of 'staying on' in schooling, as the older ones were expected to contribute to the family income as early as possible.[5] The chances for a working-class child to get into a grammar school were very slender indeed right up to the end of the period covered by this book. In 1915 there were only 203,000 local authority grammar school pupils compared with 5,636,000 elementary school-children,[6] and about 30 per cent of them were on free scholarships. Children from the unskilled working classes are reckoned to have held a fifth of those free places,[7] forming about 6 per cent of the grammar school population. None the less this was an advance from the 1 per cent in the early years of the schools,[8] and in 1908 the leading Fabian socialist, Sidney Webb, had expressed pleasure in the accelerating progress of secondary education, which he believed now matched the quality of that of Germany and the USA.[9] The idea that education should enlarge children's aspirations and enable them to become 'upwardly mobile' was beginning to supersede the classic Victorian view that it should condition them to their set station in life.[10]

Historically those intelligent working-class youths who hungered for knowledge and self-improvement had found their outlets in further education through the mechanics' institutes and evening classes (originally founded by religious organizations).[11] Exceptional boys became virtually self-taught, seizing whatever spare time they had after work. Will Crooks, later to become a trade union leader and MP, was born in Poplar in 1852, spent part of his youth in the workhouse and was working by 11, but was an avid reader of good literature, like the works of Dickens and Scott.[12] Another future trade union leader, J. R. Clynes, born in Lancashire in 1869, was working full-time in a mill by 12, but spent all his spare money on books to educate himself and was even scornful of the quality of the limited formal schooling he had received.[13] For aspiring youngsters of humble background half a century later the grammar schools seemed like gleaming turrets, but their hopes were crushed by pressing family need to have them earning as soon as possible, often compounded by philistine parental prejudice against 'fancy' education for their young. Robert Roberts, born in a Salford slum in 1905, passed his scholarship and badly wanted to further his education; but it all depended on his father:

> One dinner-time I saw Father, half-drunk and frowning, fingering a slip of paper. 'I see you passed!' he shouted down the kitchen.
> 'Yes', I said boldly, 'I came top!'
> He rose, threatening, from his chair, 'Get out!' he roared. 'Get out and find work!'

This prejudice ran even more strongly against girls. Ruth Johnson, who was born in Lancashire in 1912, was stopped from even entering for the scholarship by her widowed mother: ' Stay at school till you're sixteen! Whatever's Mr Craggs [the headmaster] thinking about? Why, you'd be a young woman before your were earning. Who'd keep you till you were a young woman? Don't be daft.'" Ruth was fated to leave school at 14 and start work in a laundry.[14]

Even if working-class children did make it to the grammar school, they might find themselves caught between worlds. A boy would be marked out as a rarity in his own neighbourhood; the resentful local scruffs might jeer at the social renegade walking down the mean streets in his 'posh' uniform, and at school he might be snubbed by the less bright but socially superior fee-payers because he could not afford their expensive equipment. Some teachers got a snobbish pleasure out of making a poor scholarship child feel inferior,[15] for example, by excluding a girl from some school excursion if her uniform was not up to standard.

One specific avenue of advancement for a poor child offered by the education system was through pupil-teacher apprenticeship. There was a long tradition in the church schools as an economy measure of employing pupils as monitors to serve as teaching ancillaries. Flora Thompson recalls how in her late nineteenth-century village school a pair of 12-year-olds were employed for 1*s* a week to give dictation and hear spellings and tables repeated. 'Pupil-teacher' apprentices, who actually taught lessons, originated in workhouse schools after the 1834 Poor Law Act, and the idea was taken up in the British and National schools. They were recruited from pupils who had reached Standard 6 or 7. Apprenticeship started at 13, and this was revised to 14 in the 1880s. But one lad at least claimed he started at 12, in the 1880s.[16] Pupil-teachers did a 5-year stint at school under the headmaster's supervision. The headmasters were supposed to give the apprentices out-of-hours tuition to help prepare them for the Queen's Scholarship examination for a grant to go on to teacher-training college at 18. However, it seems that in default of this, a young aspirant could continue to teach as an 'uncertified pupil-teacher'. From the later 1870s the headmaster's lot was made easier with the advent of training centres for pupil-teachers. Originally trainees attended before and after school, but from 1884 they went part-time during the school day. But even at the end of the century day-release centres were not universal and the old practice of tuition by the headmaster out of hours still persisted.

Pupil-teachers did menial jobs like lighting fires and filling inkwells, but they were used to coach small groups, teach infants and more backward pupils, supervise needlework, mark books, hear spellings and so forth. For a bright workhouse child a pupil-teacher apprenticeship in a workhouse school was a way out and up. Workhouse teachers were worse paid than school board teachers, and good ones were hard to recruit, so workhouse pupil-teachers filled the gap. They received privileges, such as a partitioned dormitory and a place at the head of the table at mealtimes, and if they got the Queen's Scholarship they were on their way to teacher-training college.[17]

There are several memoirs attesting to the value of pupil-teacher apprenticeships and the Queen's Scholarship as an avenue of opportunity. Henry Jones, born in 1852, the son of a Welsh village shoemaker, took the scholarship to a training college at Bangor and subsequently was to rise to become Professor of Philosophy at Glasgow. Margaret Leonora Eyles, the daughter of a failed businessman, saw in her appointment at 14 around the turn of the century (at a rate of pay of 16*s* 8*d* a month) a chance to gain a quasi-university education without paying fees, and to stand on her own two feet; for teaching was then considered about the only proper career for a middle-class girl. Caroline Louisa Timings, a middle-class girl born in 1874, won a scholarship to a grammar school, but her parents could not afford to send her to Cambridge so after $2\frac{1}{2}$ years at school she took the pupil-teacher examinations and attended special classes for 3 mornings a week.[18]

It was a real baptism of fire for youngsters to cope with classes of children not much younger than themselves. G. A. Christian, who started as a pupil-teacher in 1868, related that 'it was no uncommon thing in the absence of a head teacher for a boy in his teens to take charge of a school of 200 or more pupils'. Only the fittest could survive and some skill as a boxer, he said, 'was of no little value' as a defence against bullies outside school.

Margaret Leonora Eyles was put in charge of an infants' class at 14 and had to cope with infantile tantrums, taking boys as well as girls to the toilet and clearing up 'wet messes' in the classroom. There were some unsuitable types, of course. In the 1860s in Caernarvon a pupil-teacher named Owen was found to bully his charges into submission by chasing and beating them with a stick, and also to take 'bribes' of sweets and apples in return for 'merits'.[19]

Whilst the pupil-teacher system was a useful social ladder, what effect did it have on the health and well-being of the youngsters, and was it good for the children they taught? Dr James Crichton-Browne's report of 1884 on overpressure, described in Chapter 15, also criticized the pressures placed on pupil-teachers, with consequent occupational disorders like neuralgia, headaches and loss of voice, while the constant cramming and tensions over examination results stultified them. Although J. M. Fitch, the Chief Inspector of Schools, challenged Crichton-Browne's findings, they were borne out by the Cross Commission on Education in 1888 and the Departmental Committees on the Pupil-Teacher System in 1896. The latter had been appointed in response to the growing criticisms of the utility of putting inexperienced and immature youngters in charge of classes, and concluded that the practice was 'economically wasteful and educationally unsatis-factory and even dangerous to the teachers and the taught in equal measure'. The pupil-teachers sometimes ended up with anaemia, bad throats, or defective eyesight. Their training was too narrow and geared to examinations when they needed a broader, more liberal education. And they were often exploited as dogsbodies in schools; they were put in front of whole classes to teach when too young, and headmasters did not tailor their training, so a pupil-teacher might have spent an entire apprenticeship taking nothing but dunces' classes or infants.

Some idea of the prevalence of pupil-teachers may be gauged from the fact that in the 1870s they formed about two-thirds of London's board schools' teaching force, and even by 1900 they still formed one-third.[20] Pupil-teachers were predominantly female – the low pay tended to put boys off.[21] The Departmental Committee recommended that the minimum age for pupil-teachers should be raised and the apprenticeship period reduced, and moves were made in this direction in 1900. From 1907, after the advent of the new grammar schools, a new scheme was introduced bypassing the apprenticeships; pupils who had been a few years at the grammar schools could obtain free scholarships to 17 or 18 if they pledged themselves to go on to teacher-training college.[22] This made rapid inroads on pupil-teaching. Whereas in 1906–7 there were 11,000 new pupil-teachers, by 1912–13 there were only 1,500; the system was to survive in rural districts till the early 1920s.[23]

'Further education' in the mid-Victorian period was provided by voluntary foundations: the mechanics' institutes for technical courses, and liberal studies night schools run by religious organizations. The Science and Art Department funded the former, and the Department of Education funded further education courses corresponding to school subjects, until, as noted, the Education Department embraced them all from 1899, and from 1900 extended its funding to non-school subjects like economics. Under the Technical Instruction Act of 1889 local authorities could set up technical colleges, offering a range of technical and commercial subjects, and could gear them to the employment needs of their own localities.[24]

Even in the 1850s unfavourable comparisons were being made between the British provision for schooling and evening classes and that in Germany and Switzerland.[25] Criticisms of the education system were to become more vocal in the later Victorian and Edwardian period, as people sensed the build-up of foreign industrial competition. It was said to be too 'bookish' and (allegedly) to disincline children to manual work; there should be more emphasis on handicraft and, for girls, domestic training; and much of the learning in schools was dissipated in the post-school adolescent years. Once they had left school youngsters were left to drift, and rather than take up low-paid apprenticeships they were said to be drawn to initially high-paid 'blind-alley' jobs (see Chapter 11). The idea of 'continuation schools' was much canvassed as a solution. Working youngsters would be required to attend liberal studies classes for a certain number of hours a week as a 'refresher' and an extension to their school studies. Subjects like history, economics, nature study, gardening, tool work and gymnastics would be offered. They would keep 'loafers' off the streets and would help steer youths in their unsteady post-school years onto the straight and narrow in job selection and life-style. M. E. Sadler's book *Continuation Schools in England and Elsewhere* (1907) was a plea for such schools and more trade training. Similarly, the Royal Commission on Physical Training (Scotland) in 1903, the Departmental Committee on Physical Deterioration in 1904, the Minority Report of the Royal Commission on the Poor Laws (1905–9), and the Departmental Committee on Partial Exemption from School Attendance in 1909, all spoke favourably of the continuation school idea. Between 1897 and 1908 there had been a succession of bills in Parliament whose terms varied but whose overall object was to raise the minimum standards for total exemption from school, or to combine the right to leave with a requirement of compulsory attendance at continuation schools till 16 or 17,[26] but none had passed – continuation schools cost money.

Disturbing figures were bandied about concerning the low take-up in apprenticeship and further education, and the proliferation of seductive dead-end jobs. For example, whereas in 1881 some 46,000 youths under 15 in England and Wales were recorded as being messengers, porters and watchmen for private employers, in 1901 nearly 134,000 were so recorded.[27] In 1909 85 per cent of adolescents between 14 and 17 were said to be receiving no further education at all.[28] Too many were drifting 'hob-jobbers', and in the post-Boer War economic recession, a worrying number of youths were seen among the unemployed. The irrelevance of much school work and the inadequate facilities for practical subjects, plus the readiness with which basic school skills were forgotten, were seen as contributory factors.[29] There was also a worrying correlation between dead-enders and delinquency. In Glasgow in 1906 84 per cent of the 14–21-year-olds charged with offences were messengers, street traders, carters, labourers and the like.[30] None the less the picture was not all black. Apprenticeships did not generally start till 15 or 16 and many school-leavers were 'filling in' in the meantime. Thus a survey among London boys in 1909 showed that at 14 years old 11.2 per cent entered skilled trades, but at 16, two years later, 16.8 per cent were in skilled trades. At 14, 30.5 per cent were errand and shop boys but at 16, this was down to 18.4 per cent.[31] School care committees were beginning to develop post-school guidance services, and some good employers like Cadbury's and Rowntree's, Lever Brothers and Vickers, Sons & Maxim, and the Post Office were either encouraging attendances at evening classes or offering day release as part of an apprenticeship training. Some progressive education authorities were actively promoting continuation classes. For example, at Runcorn, early exemptions under the 'Dunce's Pass' were made conditional upon attendance at evening schools for 2 years, and in the West Riding of Yorkshire school-leavers and their families were approached to encourage attendances and the results had been very gratifying. Sunday Schools, youth clubs and trade unions were being recruited to promote the evening school idea to their members.

Scotland had shown the way when an Act of 1908 obliged all Scottish education authorities to establish continuation classes and empowered them to make attendance compulsory between 14 and 17 provided their working hours were reduced correspondingly. In 1909 a Consultative Committee on Attendance at Continuation Schools reported in favour of extending the Scottish law to England. The English were lagging behind the Germans and the Swiss, who already had provision for compulsory further education. The committee believed that the youngsters' loss of pay due to attendance for 5 or 6 hours a week would only be marginal, and that they and the country would benefit from the alleged 'character-building' and 'efficiency' such courses would bring.

Between 1909 and 1914 there was a succession of private members' bills to make continuation classes compulsory but they all failed to get very far.[32] In introducing the bill of 1913 Sir Leo Chiozza Money MP contrasted the British provision with Germany's, warning that if Britain did not take heed

I believe it will go hard with the people of this country in competition with Germany in 20 years time ... If you contrast Munich with Manchester there is an extraordinary contrast between the one town which is training all its youths and the other town of almost the same size which is leaving nearly all its youth untrained.[33]

Despite the widespread support for continuation schools the government did nothing in England and Wales; there was no parliamentary debate on the Report of the Consultative Committee. All the bills were privately sponsored. One government bill did contain a provision: the Employment of Children Bill of 1913 would have allowed local authorities to make the grant of a licence for street trading conditional upon attending continuation classes, but the bill was dropped owing to opposition from newspaper interests.

It was not until the Fisher Education Act of 1918 that any provision was made for compulsory attendance till 18, but even this turned out to be a dead letter; employers complained about the cost of releasing young workers for schooling, and post-war economic stringencies killed off the scheme.[34]

21

EXPLOITATION, DISCIPLINE AND DUTY IN THE WORKING-CLASS HOME

The status of children as cynosures of family life is historically recent; one result of the fall in the birth rate and the relative scarcity of children. Today childhood is treated as a 'kind of holiday from life',[1] but in Victorian times, and even into Edwardian times, children were regarded as 'little adults', whose childish vices and mischiefs had to be repressed as early as possible.[2] Admittedly Victorian factory laws and correctional legislation, with the advent of industrial schools and reformatories, were a recognition that children needed special treatment, but in social matters they were regarded as objects rather than subjects. In large poor families their value was primarily economic, and in domestic workshops parents could be harder and more ruthless than a large factory employer. The Children's Employment Commission of 1843 commented: 'The evidence ... also abundantly shows that in too many cases the children are overworked by parents who have no need of such accession to their own earnings, but who only thereby acquire greater means of self-indulgence.'[3] A Midlands factory inspector pointed to the same thing in 1873, and gave a glaring example I have cited in Chapter 2.[4]

Mercenary parents were apt to take more advantage of their daughters. The Employment of Schoolchildren Inquiry of 1902 found that 'moonlighting' girls could expect a third less than the going rate for boys, irrespective of whether they were employed by strangers or their own parents.[5]

We must beware of making sweeping, generalized statements about working-class family relationships. Families varied according to their personalities and the pressures they were under. In many homes there was much love and warmth in a rough and ready way, in others drunkenness and brutality. But where there was a firm hand children were expected to know their place and authoritarian fathers were typical figures. The eagerness to see their children earning as soon as possible was often motivated not just by parental 'greed' or dire need but a lingering Puritan ethic that work was the best discipline for a child and the best way to make sons and daughters grow up and face their responsibilities as early as possible.[6]

Victorians saw the child as the chattel of the parents; only within the most restrictively interpreted limits, say, of criminal assault, would the law intervene. Even the early Poor Law provisions obliging parents to maintain their offspring were conceived with a view not to uphold children's rights *vis-à-vis* their parents, but to ensure that the child did not become a burden on the poor rates.[7] Inroads by the state on parental prerogatives, as with compulsory education in 1880, were looked on by many as an infringement of 'liberty' – adult liberty, that is. The Prevention of Cruelty to Children Act of 1889 was a great landmark in state intervention, for it gave children defined rights against their parents. Although this and various child correctional measures were to culminate in the grat 'Children's Charter' of 1908, John Gorst could still say in 1913: 'The independent rights of children are scarcely recognized or acknowledged by the governing classes. It has become customary to regard them as mere appendages of their parents; the idea that a child has any legal right of its own is startling and unacceptable.'[8]

There was little of a conversational relationship between parents and children; father was preoccupied by work, fatigue and the pub, and wanted peace from his brood when he returned to the cramped one- or two-room apartment; mother was work-worn, and perhaps expecting yet another baby. Children learned when to hold their tongues, to go to bed, or run an errand when told. At mealtimes father was usually served first as he was the wage-earner and had to keep his strength up; then it went down the line according to age, and girls were given smaller portions, as it was commonly believed that they needed less than boys. Meals had to wait until father returned home, and if there was as family paper no one dared touch it before father had read it.[9]

The mere threat of a thrashing was enough to make children toe the line, and in many working-class kitchens a cane or a strap was kept on display hanging by the fireplace as a warning. None the less, except where parents were vicious and drunken, there was an underlying warmth, however rough and ready those relationships might appear to an outsider, and ranks were closed to any threat from outside, like the law.[10] But many children accepted it if a stranger, like a policeman or neighbour, casually cuffed them for mischief, and their parents would give them no sympathy.[11]

One boyhood recollection of Oxford in the 1880s retailed: 'The policeman in our district generally had a stick with which he punished offenders on the spot. I dare say it was thoroughly illegal for this to be done but I cannot help thinking it did us more good than being brought before the ... court.'[12] None the less there were parents, who, though slack disciplinarians themselves, were ready to run to the courts if some teacher or other outsider 'assaulted' their child. Robert Holmes,[13] a probation officer, was a firm believer in the summary clip round the ear, and told the story of a judge who caught some boys scrumping apples in his orchard, caned them and then let them go: 'To his great astonishment a bevy of indignant parents came to his door a few hours later breathing threatenings of procedure for assault.'[14] Some parents gave up on discipline altogether and readily brought their children before the courts as 'beyond control', hoping that the law would take over their responsibilities. Working women, especially widows, had a hard time of it keeping their children in check. Some even felt that leniency was a way of compensating for their underprivileged conditions: Jane Ellice Hopkins, the Victorian purity campaigner and vigilante against child prostitution, quoted a working mother who defended her laxity: 'Well you see, ma'am, I haven't much to give 'em, poor things! so I give 'em their own way', an attitude she thoroughly disapproved of as heaping up problems for the future.[15] The strain in the home of an exhausted, deserted, or widowed mother was described by Ethel Williams in a report to the Royal Commission on the Poor Laws in 1910:[16]

> The children ... become wild and undisciplined, or worried and anxious, according to their circumstances and temperaments. When the mother comes home at night she often has her own housework to do and preparations for the morrow to make. This often takes her till late into the night, and in several cases in which children's appearance led me to think that they were not having enough sleep, I found that they were up till very late helping their mother with the belated housework.

A common form of laxity was to allow the children to knock about the streets till late at night to keep them out of the way. Even the superficial discipline of sending them off to Sunday School or the Band of Hope was just a pretext for the same reason, and attendances meant nothing when the parents were not churchgoers and were keen tipplers. Robert Sherard in 1905 told of a charitable lady who gave two youngsters 3*d* each for regular attendance at the Band of Hope: '"Well, children," they were asked at the next meeting, "and what did you do with your threepenny-bits?" "Took them home," they said, "and we all had gin in our teas."'

Drink was a serious cause of parental brutality towards children in the slums, but in the overcrowded tenements neighbours knew each other's business, and generally working-class folk instinctively knew the difference between permissible chastisement and brutality; indeed, the NSPCC depended on information from such people. Robert Roberts recalled:

> Whenever my mother heard of a heinous case, as with the woman who boasted in the shop, 'My master [husband] allus flogs 'em till the blood runs down their back!' she quietly put the Cruelty man on. In its city windows the NSPCC displayed photographs of beaten children and rows of confiscated belts and canes. Gallantly as it worked, the Society hardly touched the fringe of the problem.[17]

Whilst working-class youngsters could be rough and socially untamed, in other respects they were thrust prematurely into the world of adult responsibilities; as 'little mothers' and street traders, as errand-runners for their parents cadging credit from shopkeepers or a meal from the soup-kitchens, and as witnesses of drunken rows and brawls, they soon came to know the hard edge of real life. Death also became familiar to them early, with the high death rates in the slums. In some neighbourhoods children might knock on neighbours' doors and be allowed to see the body of their dead friend, and there was custom of letting the children touch the body before the funeral.[18]

Sons and daughters tended to have stereotyped roles within the family. Daughters were more closely controlled and were expected to help with domestic chores, while boys were freer to be out and about and might be spoilt more by their mothers. Charities which aimed at giving slum children outings and holidays, like the Children's Country Holiday Fund, found that parents were willing for their sons to go while daughters were kept back as they were 'needed' at home.[19] However, certain jobs were regarded as boys' within the home, such as helping father in whitewashing the yard walls and in cleaning out the privy.[20] Both boys and girls were expected to 'odd-job' to bring in extra funds. Parents were fiercely sensitive about their daughters' virtue, and even into their late teens girls had to be home by a certain time. Robert Roberts told of one neighbour's daughter, a 19-year-old, who was beaten when she returned home 10 minutes late from choir practice.[21] In rural areas, it seems, once a son had started earning a living he acquired a new status and his parents wanted to keep him at home, whereas girls were sent away to domestic service as soon as possible.[22] In the slums older children of either sex might be pressed to leave home to make way for new infant arrivals, so that 15- and 16-year-olds had to share rented rooms, or end up in the insalubrious common lodging-houses.[23] In some cases the departure of adolescent sons was due to friction with parents, where the youths were becoming wayward and defiant, staying out late and spending their earnings on beer, cigarettes and music-halls.[24]

What proprietary claim did parents have on their youngsters' earnings? It seems to have varied from home to home. It was not uncommon for girls to hand over all their earnings to their mothers and receive a pocket money allowance; girls living away in service might send all their money home.[25] Robert Sherard referred to Manchester parents who looked upon their large families as 'good capital' and said that mothers even *debited* their daughters when the mills were shut, and made them pay the arrears when they were earning again. However, there is evidence that quite a few Victorian girls kept back a significant part of their earnings. The Report of the Royal Commission on Employment of Children in 1864 mentions the weakness of girls in tailoring shops for spending their earnings on finery,[26] and the Band of Hope Annual Report of 1872–3 lamented the licence which independent earning power conferred on girls: 'Thousands of them now support themselves and they take their own wages, in a large number of instances, and spend them as they choose.' And it referred to girls of 14 to 17 earning up to 12s a week, squandering the money in pubs at the weekend and ending up in court for drunkenness.

Dutiful sons also gave up a substantial part of their earnings to their parents. Thomas Morgan, born in Blackfriars in 1892, earned 5s a week in his first job as a van boy at 13, and gave half to his mother; this he regarded as 'fair'. (He spent his half on beer.)[27] C. E. B. Russell said of 'Manchester Boys' in 1905 that a typical 17-year-old earning 14s a week would give 10s to his mother. Where job opportunities for youngsters were plentiful and earnings were good, they felt their independence and their bargaining power with their parents, and if dissatisfied were said in the early Victorian period to be prepared to walk out as young as 14 and set up for themselves in lodging-houses.[28] During the First World War the jobs boom for youngsters weakened family discipline in this way, and youngsters expected to be treated with special consideration at home once they were earning. A contemporary commented: 'Not infrequently the mother, to secure the boy's goodwill and to keep him attached to the home, makes him an absurdly generous allowance of pocket money. In other cases the boy hands to his mother just as much of his wages as he thinks fit.'[29]

The proportion of the earnings of younger children earned in odd-jobbing and street trading that parents took varied from home to home.[30] Where the earnings were essential to a poor family's subsistence it might all be taken, or snatched by greedy parents for drink. But where it was less essential the child had more chance to keep back a portion of it, and as in any case parents could have no accurate idea about their children's earnings in the streets, there was scope for deception. Children tended to squander their earnings on sweets, cigarettes, the music-hall and gambling; 'pitch and toss', a coin game, was an addiction of many a street boy, and cards and horses were other lures. The Victorian zeal for thrift was brought to bear on youngsters' earnings through the 'penny bank' schemes run through the ragged and elementary schools. Children were encouraged to bank their savings from odd jobs, and the scale of the scheme is a pointer to the retention of earnings from their parents. In 1880 in England and Wales there were 1,087 penny banks in elementary schools and by 1891 there were 2,498. In Liverpool alone in 1891 there were 25,114 individual school bank accounts containing £10,518 altogether. Within the London School Board in 1892 there were about 14,700 depositors whose savings stood at nearly £12,000 in December of that year. Even at the impoverished Johanna Street School in Lambeth 349 savers had accumulated over £27.[31] Admittedly penny bank funds may have included some allowance given by parents, especially after the progressive abolition of school fees from 1891; but 'pocket money' was then almost unheard of among the working classes, and the bulk must have come from their own earnings which they were suffered to keep by their parents.

22

UPBRINGING IN THE
UPPER-CLASS HOME

Whilst the crowding in the working-class homes enforced a physical (if not mental) intimacy between parents and children, the spaciousness of upper-class villas permitted the relegation of children to remote parts of the house, out of sight and sound; and the employment of staffs of servants to supervise them relieved parents of the need to play any part in their early upbringing. Fathers were too grand and busy, and mothers too elegant and superior, to attend to the feeding and nurture of their numerous progeny. From the moment of birth a wet-nurse, or patent brands of baby food of dubious nutritious value, would be the instinctive and customary answer to the problem of feeding; mother's figure and time to socialize took overriding precedence.[1] Many children, surrounded in the nursery by nurses and nannies, were raised to feel that physical distance from the parent was right and proper. Gwen Raverat recalled:

> I can never remember being bathed by my mother, or even having my hair brushed by her, and I should not at all have liked it if she had done anything of the kind. We did not feel it was her place to do such things.

However, there were many children, too, who keenly felt their parents' remoteness and suffered mental dereliction from cold and perhaps uncaring fathers and social butterfly mothers.[2] One psychological comfort was the sublimation of parents into idealized beings, idols to be worshipped from afar, who in children's fantasies would surely appear to rescue them from distress. The young Winston Churchill worshipped his socialite mother in this way: 'She shone for me like the Evening Star. I loved her dearly – but at a distance.' Little Rudyard Kipling's parents in India sent the boy home to England to be fostered for 5 years and when he saw his mother again after this time he found her 'as beautiful, as adored, as ideal as she was when she went away'.

To social grandees childhood was a tiresome phase of existence tht they must do their material duty by, with the minimum of disturbance to their own lives. *Punch* satirized this parental remoteness with a joke in 1892:

Visitor: What a sweet child! How old is she?
Mother: Well, really, if you are going to ask that sort of question I'd better send for the nurse.

In their early years children were segregated in the nursery suite at the top of the house, comprising a day nursery, a night nursery (a shared bedroom), the nanny's room, and perhaps a schoolroom. To the most distant parents this was foreign territory, to be visited only as a special treat and 'occasion' for the children, or when a child was ill.[3]

However wealthy the family might be, relatively little concession was made to children's comforts. Many memoirs of Victorian nurseries recall the spartan conditions. No real thought was given to furnishing them to suit children's tastes; they were 'Cinderella' areas, second only to the servants' quarters. The adult-sized furniture comprised 'left-overs' from other parts of the house; the wallpaper was drab, with perhaps the odd picture, say of royalty, or a map, though nursery-designed wallpapers and pictures illustrating nursery rhymes or fairy tales were becoming available. Often there was no carpeting, just bare boards to reduce the chore of cleaning. A medicine cupboard contained dreaded 'nanny's remedies', such as rhubarb for diarrhoea, Gregory's Powders and syrup of figs for constipation, calomel for fevers, and castor oil as an emetic. A bookshelf might contain only a limited range of books, perhaps 'moral' stories published by the Society for Promoting Christian Knowledge (SPCK) or the Religious Tract Society (RTS).[4] The bedrooms had no fires (though their parents' bedrooms were warmed), except perhaps when children were ill or convalescing. Marion Lochhead remarks: 'One of the signs, not always welcome, of a complete recovery was getting up in a cold bedroom.' The day nursery would have a fire, partially offset by the draughts, and passages and staircases were freezing. These physical miseries were often compounded by nannies' idiosyncratic ideas about health. Joanna Smith quotes one informant: 'Edwardians were great believers in fresh air. They thought you would die unless you had your bedroom window open at night.' Whilst Victorian fashion kept children cocooned under layers of under-clothing by day, they were underclad at night in winter – no bedsocks or hot water bottles were allowed in their cold, clammy beds, as this was considered unhealthy 'mollycoddling' of children.[5] In the early Victorian period children might still be washed in cold water – this was thought to harden them against ailments. Warm baths were thought to soften them, and strong sunlight was considered bad for health, so the blinds were pulled down keeping the nursery dark on bright summer days, though Florence Nightingale's *Notes on Nursing* criticized this practice. Many nurses and nannies believed in the efficacy of regular dosing of children with brimstone and treacle, and in the 1860s it seems children were still being bled with leeches.[6] The more tyrannical nannies expected children to perform their bowel movements at set times during the day; to fail was regarded as laziness or recalcitrance, to be remedied with a stiff dose of purgative or even a suppository.[7]

In contrast to the sumptuous fare of their elders in the dining-room below, children's diet was plain and monotonous. Gwen Raverat recalled breakfasts of porridge and salt, and buttered toast; jam was allowed on their toast only twice a week, and even then without butter. (She tasted bacon for the first time at 10, when staying away from home.) For tea she had bread, butter and milk, with sponge cake when visitors came. Sweets were generally not allowed. Eleanor Acland recalled of her late Victorian upbringing a similar diet for tea, and for breakfast 'we had a boiled egg each on Sundays, Tuesdays and Thursdays, bread and milk on the other four'; dinners comprised roast meat and boiled potatoes, with milk pudding in winter, followed by stewed fruit. Lord Curzon suffered from a martinet of a nanny who fed her charges on nothing but tapioca and rice pudding 'which we detested and which we used to drop into our caps when she was not looking and carry away and hide in chinks in the wall'.[8]

Whilst there was a varied and growing range of toys in the Victorian period the actual provision of toys varied from household to household. Rocking horses, Noah's Arks, board games and puzzles (including the 'dissected puzzle', the early jigsaw), alphabet and picture bricks, dolls and dolls' houses, archery games, toy theatres, tops and kaleidoscopes are just a selection of what was available. However, even in a well-stocked nursery the toys were locked away and rationed out carefully; many comfortable homes gave little thought to toys, and children had to improvise in play. Molly Hughes recalled how

> a large box of plain bricks was the foundation of all our doings. It served for railway stations, docks, forts, towers, and every kind of house .... A packing-case did for a shop, where goods of all kinds were sold for marbles or shells or foreign stamps. The whole room was occasionally the sea, where a chair turned upside down was the *Great Eastern*, well and truly launched on the floor, for laying the Atlantic cable.

Beatrix Potter's parents were wealthy but had no understanding of children; her only toys were a black wooden doll and a grubby stuffed pig which she was allowed to play with only on special occasions.[9] Little Winston Churchill seems to have been exceptionally well provided for in the 1870s with 'a real steam engine, a magic lantern and a collection of toy soldiers already nearly a thousand strong'.[10]

So prevalent was the depressing bleakness of nursery surroundings that in 1888 J. E. Panton's *From Kitchen to Garret* made a special point of advocating a brightening of nursery décor, with more comfortable furnishings and a good warm fire.[11] But the nursery regime needed lightening, too. Sunday was the most miserable day for the nursery in the strictest households. Jane Brough in 1857 characterized the effects of enforced church attendance, with its 'dull lifeless service with stinted truth, or truth told so sleepily that the children go to sleep', while all the children had to look forward to for the rest of the day was Sunday School heaviness and the company of adult visitors, the 'listless, idle lollings and loungings, the nothing-to-do, the tittle-tattle, the tale and slander and the early going to bed'.[12] Her recommendations of Sunday toys and games, like Scripture bricks and puzzles, and Sabbath day reading geared to juvenile audiences, like *Mama's Bible Stories*, the *Peep o' Day*, and *Infants' Pilgrim's Progress* were echoed by boys' author William H. G. Kingston in 1867. He had a good understanding of children – he had made many of his own children's toys himself – and felt strongly about the bleakness of so many nurseries. In his little work *Infant Amusements; or, How to Make a Nursery Happy* he urged a brightening up of nursery life with more toys and the encouragement of activity games; but even he believed in the virtues of plain food – tapioca, sago, ground rice and boiled mutton – and emphasized the religious structuring of the nursery regime; Sabbath day tedium should be enlivened with permissible toys like Noah's Arks and cardboard cut-outs of Bible scenes and characters, and there should be a well-stocked library of SPCK and RTS publications. A wide range of Sunday periodicals for the young was becoming available, such as *Good Words for the Young, Sunday at Home, Little Folks, Sunday Reading,* and *Boy's Own Paper* and the *Girl's Own Paper*,[13] while some children's authors like Charlotte Yonge and Hesba Stretton made a speciality of writing moral and 'pious' stories, like the latter's *Jessica's First Prayer*, suited to Sabbath day reading.

Nannies were the linchpin of nursery life, and memories of them figure prominently in so many memoirs. Emotionally and psychologically, nanny was mother-substitute for the children, and if good she was adored – a feeling of warmth that carried into adulthood.[14] Even into old age, Winston Churchill cherished devoted memories of his beloved nanny, Mrs Everest, who looked after him till he went to boarding-school at 8. One nanny might serve the same family many years, looking after a succession of new arrivals, but in other households there might be a rapid turnover of unsatisfactory nurses. For a child who had become deeply attached to nanny, her departure once he or she had grown beyond the nanny stage was heartbreaking. There were, however, many disliked or actively detested nannies, dragon-queens of their segregated domain at the top of the house. Jonathan Gathorne Hardy suggests that a good many nannies, lacking real families of their own, might have been emotionally unbalanced and liable to fly off the handle with children, or become over-severe and even sadistic. Lord Curzon recalled how his nanny used to slipper her charges on their bare backs and tie them to chairs for hours in uncomfortable positions, or lock them for hours in darkened rooms. In other cases the mistreatment was due to downright ignorance, as with the nurse who used to give children whiffs of coal gas to make them sleep. Compton Mackenzie, born in 1883, had one feared nanny he later on depicted fictionally in *Sinister Street*; she would threaten that the lions would get him or the coalman would take him away if he was naughty; he was roughly handled and slapped and told that he would be given nasty medicines if he did not eat all his meals up.

Parents in their remoteness remained ignorant of nannies'

excesses as children were so often too terrified to tell. Bertrand Russell's mother had to be told by other servants of the nurse's mistreatment of an older brother – he was starved and lied about – before she was dismissed.[15]

Nannies were often remembered vividly but neutrally for their idiosyncrasies, as, for example, in enforcing a strict etiquette in lavatory functions. Children on the WC had to wait to be 'fetched', and they must on no account call out when finished, or else they would be shamed for letting the whole house know where they were.[16] It was also bad etiquette to *tell* anyone they wanted to relieve themselves; they must contain themselves till the set times for going to the lavatory. This rule applied even more strictly to girls, who were taught never to admit to the lavatory functions and to go in secret after ensuring that there were no males about.[17]

Another idiosyncrasy might be their fund of macabre old wives' tales and superstitions, which they regaled and even deliberately frightened the children with. Children's heads were filled with fears and fantasies, compounded by the morbid surroundings of nursery life, and Magdalen King-Hall has remarked: 'One is struck, when reading Victorian memoirs, by the many obscure terrors that seemed to have haunted the children of that period.' The threat to one impressionable girl that the chimney sweep boy would take her away if she was naughty was enough to scare her every time she saw one, and the same girl was frightened by the shadows on the staircase of the great house she lived in. King-Hall cites the memoirs of Lady Sybil Lubbock whose upbringing in the 1880s was riddled with fears of 'the eye of God', burglars, penny-for-the-guy urchins, mad dogs and gipsy women. Deprived of the company of their own parents, children picked up many fanciful notions from contact with ignorant and superstitious servants. The mind of the sensitive young Edmund Gosse,[18] raised in isolation in a morbidly religious house, was filled with phantasmagoric images and invented superstitions. At night noises in his room sent him into hysterics – they turned out to be air currents rustling the text-cards on his bedroom wall.

Children needed to exercise their imaginations as a mental escape from the dreary confines of the nursery walls. High up in the house they were virtual prisoners, and lonely children, like girls whose brothers had been sent off to boarding-school, would pass time in gazing wistfully out of the windows onto the street life below. Where brothers and sisters shared the nursery, intelligent ones could compensate for a lack of toys with make-believe games, and even concoct their own sub-culture of a secret language that kept the adult world at bay. In Maurice Baring's nursery days the children infuriated the servants who had charge of them with a gibberish chant; thus, for instance, 'shartee' was 'yes', and 'quilquinino' was 'no'.[19]

The restrictions of nursery life inspired a minor genre of children's literature, expressing the boredom and wish to break free. In Annie Keary's *Blind Man's Holiday* (1860) Helen was a parson's daughter whose one release from the nursery was the stroll on the local common, and even then under the strict supervision of a nursemaid. She had to stay close by and avoid brushing her dress against some newly painted railings:

> The smell of paint made Helen's head ache, and when she passed the corner of a narrow street, and caught sight of a group of poor children playing at 'oranges and lemons' or making mud houses for their ragged dolls, she felt a great lump rising in her throat, and she would gladly have sat down on the next curbstone and cried for longing to be with them, as free from care about painting their clothes as they were.

J. M. Barrie's *Peter Pan*, with the Darling children's fantasy flight from the nursery, is the classic example and must have struck a responsive chord in many a child reader.

Contact with parents was highly formalized; children were carefully scrubbed and dressed and went down at set times in the day accompanied by the nursemaid to sit and talk politely with mama and papa. In the most formal upper-class households this was almost like a gracious audience, but in medium middle-class homes, where there were fewer intermediary servants, the contact was more spontaneous; father might allow himself a romp and a story-reading session with the children, but here too time was likely to be strictly rationed,[20] and there remained a definite framework of discipline.

Molly Hughes, growing up in a city businessman's home in the 1870s, enjoyed a warm relationship with her father, but the children soon knew it if they overstepped the mark: she would be put in the corner, and the boys would be threatened with a slippering:

When one of the boys had really annoyed Mother, she would address him, as 'Sir', and send him to have his hair cut. This does not sound so bad as it in fact was. Our only available hairdresser had a strange habit of keeping a customer waiting for a half to three-quarters of an hour. There was nothing to do but stare at a fern and a picture of Cromwell sitting at his daughter's death-bed.

Part of the job of nannies and governesses was to teach the children etiquette to prepare them for the transition from the nursery. As very young children they might be permitted to watch the arrival of guests to a dinner party through the banister rails on the landing, but the time would come when they would be allowed downstairs to be introduced to the adults, and perhaps as a privilege allowed to eat dessert with them.[21] They knew not to interrupt conversations and speak only when spoken to. One little girl around the turn of the century had this poem nailed to her cupboard door as a reminder:

In silence I must take my seat
And give God thanks for what I eat,
With knife or fork or napkin ring
I must not play, nor must I sing.
But for my meat in silence wait
'til I am asked to hand my plate.[22]

At around 12 to 14 children were considered grown up enough to join guests at the lunch table and take part in the conversation (indeed, total silence would now have been considered ill-mannered), always understanding that they must defer to adult speakers.[23] There was now more freedom to go on outings to zoos, the Crystal Palace, pantomimes and public exhibitions, but always chaperoned. Their lives remained bounded by strict etiquette training, like dancing and piano lessons, and girls were more restricted than boys. Girls were expected to be more passive and obedient by nature, while a little more latitude was given to male boisterousness. Grace, deportment and modesty were the most valued social accomplishments of a girl, for she was not expected to be clever or to achieve anything independently in life.[24] In the schoolroom she might have to wear a backboard or a 'training corset' to improve posture,[25] and dress was a miniature version of adult attire with little or no concession to her physical development. Around 1850 girls wore at least 7 layers of petticoats under their dresses, and though the crinoline of the 1860s gave them more freedom, the arrival of the bustle at the end of the decade, with the tight drawing of the skirt at the front, and the tight-corseting to achieve the achieve the ideal small waist, presented physical dangers to a growing girl.[26] The restrictive over-protectiveness towards girls was criticized in an anonymous pamphlet of 1843, *The Mothers of England*:

> It is indeed a matter of astonishment that girls should be so frequently cooped up in close rooms, scarcely permitted to breathe or walk lest the air should be impregnated with damp, or the ground a little moistened by some passing shower; that they should be forbidden to run lest they should heat themselves and thus bring on a delicacy of the chest; should be dressed in such a manner that they have to bear perpetually in mind the spoiling of their clothes; while the little remaining strength they have is supposed to be kept up by patent pills and tonics of every description.

Even 60 years later, when restrictions on girls were easing and sedate games of tennis, cricket and hockey were considered quite acceptable, Edwardian schoolgirls would wear woollen combinations, 'liberty' bodices, stockinette knickers, flannel petticoats and often high-necked woollen 'spencers' as underclothing in the summer.[27]

Children were expected to behave like little adults on social occasions among themselves. At children's parties there were strict conventions in dress and manners. H. C. Barnard remembered how as a boy guest at a Christmas tea he went in his Eton suit with white cotton gloves, carrying his sheet music to contribute to the entertainment. Children were expected to display their accomplishments, like piano-playing or singing. The dances, like the Sir Roger de Coverley, were adult and courtly, and the girls had cards with the names of their partners inscribed.[28]

In the same way children had to observe the same mourning rituals as adults; they had to wear special mourning clothes for prescribed periods on the death of a relation, and even on the death of the monarch.[29]

It would be misleading to think of every high Victorian father as the severe patriarch of popular image. It was perhaps in the most

religious households, especially among Evangelicals and Pres-
byterians, that the reality came closest to the image, an inheritance
of the Puritan ethic that saw in childish mischief and waywardness
a sign of devilish influence. When carried to extremes this outlook
was prepared to tolerate continued pain and suffering among
offspring as a divine infliction to test their faith. The young
Augustus Hare was adopted by a widowed aunt, a religious fanatic.
The delicate boy was in continual pain from a spinal defect but his
aunt gave him no comfort: 'There was no attempt at cure, for his
aunt-mother believed in the moral validity of pain; the boy *ought
to suffer*. Pain was sent by God . . . to draw its victim to heaven.
Physically he was starved, mentally fed upon tracts and
sermons.'[30]

In sterner homes the cane or birch was used, and into Edwardian
times there was a trade in birch rods.[31] Not only fathers but
mothers and (with parental permission) nannies would apply the
rod,[32] and where children were deemed incorrigible there was, it
seems, a demand for the services of professional flagellants. Ian
Gibson's *The English Vice* (1978) quotes numerous Victorian
newspaper advertisements offering and seeking such services
(though he cautions that some of these may have been 'coded' and
really intended for sexual deviants).

Whereas in the working-class home punishments were hot-
blooded and spontaneous, in some middle-class homes the
formalization and protraction of punishment in its crueller
applications added mental to the physical pain. Children might be
banished from the table and ostracized by parents for a time, or
they might be shamed by having to wear self-ridiculing placards
round their necks. Eleanor Acland's brother George was so
punished when he kicked a nurse; the legend ran 'Georgina, She
Kicks' – the use of the feminine gender was intended to humiliate
him. Deprivation of food, being locked in one's room or in a dark
cupboard, and being forced to take unpleasant medicines or wash
one's mouth out with soap and water, were other common
reprisals.[33]

Tentatively one can say that corporal punishment at home was
declining in the post-Edwardian period, paralleling the decline in
the public schools, if the comment in 1915 by Bishop Welldom, a
former headmaster of Harrow, is to be believed.[34] This would tend
to be supported by an observation by Edward H. Cooper in 1905.
He saw a relaxation in the Victorian upper- and middle-class

conventions regarding the upbringing of children. They were now less confined to their nurseries and seemed freer and more independently active. They were readier to talk to and question their elders; they were more outgoing and showed more initiative, and could be seen helping out at bazaars and charity concerts. And where once they went for walks in Belgravia gardens, he said, they were now seen cycling in the park.

23

THE CHILD PROTECTION MOVEMENT

I observed in Chapter 21 how the common law traditionally upheld the near-absolute authority of a parent over a child. The right to chastise was held inviolable, subject to manslaughter and murder, though the 1861 Offences Against the Person Act did specify offences of common and 'aggravated' assault.[1] In a rare success against a parent in 1869 a man named Griffin was convicted for so severely thrashing his $2\frac{1}{2}$-year-old daughter with an 18-inch strap when her crying annoyed him, that she died of shock. His defence that he had every right to 'correct' his child was rejected by the judge on the grounds that the chastisement must be appropriate to the age of the child.[2] And by the later 1880s it was established in principle that chastisement by teachers and parents must be 'reasonable' but it was still difficult to secure convictions before conservative-minded judges where no death resulted. Thus, when at that time a father was tried for stripping and beating his frail son when drunk till the boy was found a mass of bruises, the magistrate held that this was insufficient to amount to an 'aggravated assault'![3]

The common law recognized no liability for 'neglect' or 'desertion' by a parent, though by 1887 it seems the courts had come round to viewing cold-blooded, wilful neglect as chargeable.[4] However, Parliament had already imposed duties on parents to care for their children, not in a spirit of welfare but to prevent those chldren being foisted as a public burden on the poor rate. The Poor Law Act of 1834 required a parent to support a child to this end, and the 1868 Poor Law Act extended this by making wilful neglect by a parent of a child under 14 that threatened or resulted in *serious* injury to its health an offence liable to up to 6 months' imprisonment. Poor Law guardians were to be the prosecuting agencies, but in the event they could barely stir themselves to investigate case of domestic neglect, and if that neglect seemed likely to lead to the children's death then the Poor Law would be spared, so there was no incentive to prosecute.[5] In any case, what would the courts regard as 'serious' injury? And could the final state of the child, such as TB, be related specifically to the parental neglect? The law proved virtually a dead letter and was to be superseded in the the 1889 Prevention of Cruelty to Children Act.[6]

Under an Act of 1851, following the death of Jane Wilbred, as described in Chapter 5, former workhouse children put out as servants or apprentices were intended to be safeguarded from cruelty or neglect, and in 1861 it was made an offence for any master to endanger the life or injure the health of any apprentice or servant by neglect.[7] Statutory protection of neglected children was applied to another ulterior end of forestalling the descent into crime, under the industrial schools legislation, starting in 1857; children found begging, wandering, without a home or 'proper guardianship', or frequenting the company of known thieves were liable to be sent to an industrial school. The parents may have been morally neglectful, but this legislation did not punish them, except in so far as they might have to contribute towards the child's upkeep in the institution.

Again, it was statute not common law that was evolved to protect children from sexual abuse. The Offences Against the Person Act 1861 made it an offence to procure the defilement of a girl under 21 (to stop parents selling their daughters to procurers). Legislation culminating in the Criminal Law Amendment Act of 1885 raised the 'age of consent' for girls finally to 16, so extending the offence of carnal knowledge with under-age girls, but no specific offence of incest existed until the Incest Act of 1908. Prior to that a father, a brother or an uncle would have had to be charged with rape or unlawful carnal knowledge of an under-age girl.

But although there was sufficient body of laws to give children a rudimentary protection by the 1880s, the problem remained one of enforcement. Neither school boards, nor policemen, nor Poor Law authorities saw it as their particular province to institute proceedings, while philanthropists working in the slums and witnessing so much cruelty and neglect were deterred for fear of being rejected as snoopers by those they were seeking to help.[8] The 1880s were, however, a period of growing sensitivity to the problems of child cruelty and neglect. Revelations about child degradation and slum life, for example, in Andrew Mearns and W. C. Preston's *The Bitter Cry of Outcast London* (1883) and the work of the Royal Commission on the Housing of the Working Classes (1884–5), coupled with contemporary scandals of child prostitution and an associated campaign to raise the age of consent for girls, helped to focus attention on the vulnerability of children. The school system, too, was bearing witness to the extent of child deprivation, more starkly impressive since the advent of compulsory education in 1880. The growing interest was international. In 1882 at Paris there was held the first international conference of any significance dealing with child welfare issues, like those of orphans, the handicapped and children with unfit parents. Other conferences were to follow and in 1896 at Florence the International Congress for the Welfare and Protection of Children was formed, pledged to hold triennial conferences for the exchange of ideas.[9] In 1882 the enlightened American state of Massachusetts pioneered a law to protect children from cruelty and neglect, and this, originating in the 'land of the free', commented Samuel Smith MP, put the lie to the 'civil liberty' cry against state intervention in parent–child relations.[10]

Smith, nicknamed the 'Arabs' Member' for his advocacy of child welfare laws, was MP for Liverpool where the first moves towards establishing a child protection society in Britain were to be made. The city was notorious for its dockside urchins and clamorous young street traders; while its slumdom and drunkenness also impinged on the child welfare issue. In 1879 the Rev. Silas K. Hocking of Liverpool published a story, based on real-life characters, about two urchins and the brutality they suffered from their father; it was a best-seller in the city and helped to stimulate public awareness.[11] In 1881 a Liverpool businessman, T. Frederick Agnew, visited New York where he learned of a curious case of a mother who had been convicted for maltreating her child under a law against cruelty to animals. The prosecution had been brought by the New York Society for the Prevention of Cruelty to Animals. No equivalent law or society as yet existed to protect children there. On Agnew's return to Liverpool he found child abuse very much a live issue there following the publication of Hocking's book, and he in conjunction with other philanthropists formed the Liverpool Society for the Prevention of Cruelty to Children (SPCC) in 1883. In Britain, too, animal protection law predated any similar code for children; legislation to check cruelty to animals had been passed between 1822 and 1835, and the Society for the Protection of Animals, the forerunner of the RSPCA, had been formed in 1824.[12] The Liverpool SPCC found that the existing laws I have outlined were too weak, given the prejudice of magistrates against interference with parents' rights, and it had to rely on remonstrance and persuasion rather than threats to resort to law.[13] Its activities came to the attention of London philanthropists, like Baroness Burdett-Coutts, Benjamin Waugh, Doctor Barnardo, Lord Shaftesbury, Hesba Stretton, the children's author, and Mr Kegan Paul, the publisher. A correspondence in *The Times* early in 1884 led to a meeting at the Mansion House and the formation of a London SPCC.

By and large the churches were still blinkered to the problem, or unwilling to raise protests among their congregations at interference in the parental domain. Alfred Mayer wrote in 1886 of three starving orphan boys who went to Protestant and Catholic schools where 'the Parson passed them by, for their plight was only some degrees worse than the rank and file of the other scholars of his school. The Priest offered the wretched lads nothing but Mass and catechism, with the merciless alternative of stripes and starvation.' There were, however, outstanding exceptions, like Cardinal Manning, the Church of England's Bishop of Bedford, and, most famous and active of all, the Congregationalist minister Benjamin Waugh. In his parish work in Greenwich in the 1860s his philanthropy among the poor had made him acutely aware of the suffering of children. He became a member of the London School Board after the 1870 Act, and served as a 'police court missionary', the volunteer prototype probation officer, standing bail for pitiable young offenders and finding stop-gap work for them in waste-paper and shoeblack brigades. Waugh saw these young delinquents as victims of society's neglect, for whom prison was a gross injustice. His book *The Gaol Cradle – Who Rocks it?* (1875) was a plea for understanding and an alternative to jail, through a probation service. In 1884 he became the London SPCC's first Secretary.[14] In 1886 he wrote with Cardinal Manning an article entitled 'The child of the English savage' in the *Contemporary Review*, describing some of the horrific cases the society had to deal with.[15] There was, for example, the father who savagely beat his son for spending his school fee money on sweets. The attack went beyond 'reasonable chastisement', for after exhausting himself, the man went off to the pub, and returned to beat the boy's head with a hammer, leaving him unconscious. The father was jailed, but the SPCC had *illegally* to remove the boy from his father's reach (following his long recovery in hospital), for as the law then stood the boy would have passed back into his father's custody once he was out of prison. In another case an outwardly respectable stepmother systematically beat and starved her stepson who was found, a bag of bones, covered with severe lacerations, when rescued by the SPCC. She made him walk up and down the cottage stairs with 7-pound flat-irons in each hand for hours at a time, gave him 'hard labour' or beatings with a stick, trap, or thorn rod when he 'stole' crumbs and cat's meat, and even poured salt into his wounds. In a third case a woman who was *not* destitute kept her son from school by confining him in an orange box under the bed all day, sometimes drugged.

Drink and gambling lay behind much cruelty; but the theme of the article was that it was a profound mistake to equate cruelty invariably with social degradation. Many poor people did what they could for their children within their limits whilst prosperous and apparently educated people could perpetrate the most exquisite acts of cruelty. The *Child's Guardian* in 1887, for example, reported the case of the 3-year-old daughter of a doctor. He thrashed her for 20 minutes with the stock of a riding whip because she could not spell 'fox', and then made her drink port wine. The mother continued the whipping for a further half-hour, then the child was set to writing out copy with her hands swollen and bruised, and her eye blacked, till she fainted, vomiting port wine. The servants were horrified. But in court the parents were fined just £25 each, plus costs.

Where the SPCC did bring prosecutions it found itself hampered by the law of evidence. The child – perhaps the only witness – could not give evidence if it was shown not to understand the nature of the oath. One early victory for the society was the inclusion in the Criminal Law Amendment Act of 1885 of a provision exempting under-age victims of sexual intercourse from the need to testify under oath. Such a law needed widening, though there was still the practical problem of children's frequent reluctance to give evidence at all against their tormentors, out of a touching sense of loyalty. The law also precluded wives from giving evidence against their husbands, though paradoxically an unmarried co-habitee with an illegitimate child could give evidence against her lover.

In 1889 – the year in which English and Irish societies amalgamated to form the NSPCC – came the early crowning achievement of the passage of the Prevention of Cruelty to Children Act which provided penalties against those having custody of boys under 14 and girls under 16 who wilfully ill-treated, neglected, abandoned, or exposed them in a manner likely to cause them unnecessary suffering or injury to health. Other provisions related to causing or procuring children to beg or perform in the streets, and to performing or peddling in public houses at night. The definition of mistreatment was thus more widely drawn than under the 1868 Act, and it was open to anyone to bring a prosecution. Child victims no longer had to give evidence on oath, and wives could testify against their husbands. Children could be removed to a 'place of safety' pending the trial and upon the parent's conviction, and could be entrusted to a relative or other 'fit person' (which would include charitable institutions) for safety. The Act had a bearing on child labour, where the factory and workshops laws gave inadequate cover, for 'wilful ill-treatment' could include enslavement to a parent or guardian in domestic outwork. In the same year, 1889, the Poor Law was empowered to 'adopt' children under its care deserted by their parents; parental consent was not necessary (another step for state interventionism between parent and child) though a parent could appeal to the courts against the guardians' decision.

Children could only be legally removed from custody under the aforementioned Cruelty and Poor Law Acts. Doctor Barnardo got himself into legal and public relations difficulties between 1888 and 1891 over three children he had sent abroad without any legal authority to get them permanently out of reach of unworthy parents, who were none the less bitterly indignant.[16] His action was intended for the best though high-handed, but led in 1891 to the Custody of Children Act which gave the courts wide discretionary power to decide if a child should continue to be cared for by a fostering agency or be returned to its parent – a further inroad on the sanctity of parental rights.[17]

Even though armed with the new Cruelty Act, the NSPCC faced obstacles from a public that tended to look upon it as an interloper, and from magistrates still deeply imbued with the old prejudices. Loopholes in the Act, readily found by the courts, had to be closed. The 1894 Cruelty to Children Act more precisely defined the words 'suffering' and 'injury' and extended the definition of cruelty to cover wilful assault, as well as raising maximum ages for certain protected categories. An express recognition of the role of drunkenness in child cruelty was embodied in a provision allowing convicted parents the option of going to an Inebriates Home instead of prison.[18]

The 1904 Cruelty Act's most important additions were in relation to employment, as has already been discussed in the context of domestic employment and 'moonlighting'. The 1908 Children's Act, the great 'Children's Charter', a consolidating measure which also introduced Benjamin Waugh's dream of juvenile courts, extended the legal notion of neglect. This was defined as a failure to provide adequate food, clothing, medical aid, or lodging for the child, *or if unable, failing to procure this under laws for the relief of the poor*. Thus poverty was no longer a defence to a charge of neglect, and even if a child's suffering had been alleviated by others, parents or guardians could still be held liable for cruelty.[19]

One interesting legal question was the relationship between the protections provided by the Cruelty Acts and the industrial schools legislation. After all, the waifs and urchins picked up and committed under the latter were really the victims of neglect; while industrial schools might be thought to have been validly included among the 'fit persons' under the Cruelty Acts. The fact is, however, that the two sets of laws were almost mutually exclusive. Industrial schools were not classified as 'fit persons'; nevertheless, the 1894 Cruelty Act did provide that any child brought before the courts under the Industrial Schools Act could, at the court's discretion, be committed to a 'relation or person named by the court' instead of an industrial school.[20]

Having outlined the legal framework of emergent 'children's rights' we will look at aspects of the NSPCC's operations and policies. From the start the Metropolitan Police worked closely with the society but it also depended on building up confidence among the public that it was not a snooping busybody. It leaned over backwards not to usurp parental duties; it was loath to prosecute and relied overwhelmingly on persuasion and instruction of parents. Indeed, it shared the attitude of many magistrates in not wanting industrial schools or 'fit persons' orders to become a soft option for irresponsible parents eager to shuffle off their own duties.[21] Thus, the NSPCC opposed the public provision of school meals under the 1906 Act, on the grounds that the existing

Cruelty laws were sufficient to make parents do what they must.[22] In the area of feeble-minded children, however, the NSPCC did believe in more state paternalism. Robert Parr, Waugh's successor as director, believed that such children should be removed compulsorily and placed under state care.[23] The feeble-minded were considered particularly vulnerable to sexual abuse, and Parr's views fitted into a wider Edwardian interest in eugenics and the discouragement of reproduction among the defective. In fact the proportion of NSPCC cases involving mentally defective children was very small. Over a 4-year period from 1900, when the society was handling a case load of 35,000 to 40,000 a year, it had dealt with 1,113 such cases altogether, and prosecuted in 141 of these. The NSPCC, along with the National Vigilance Association, a 'purity' lobby concerned with issues like the white slave traffic and pornography, played a leading part in securing the passage of the Incest Act in 1908. From its early years the NSPCC had been acutely aware of sexual dangers to children within the family, and Victorian observers of slum life and its dire overcrowding had hinted at the prevalence of incest. In 1911 Robert Parr gave an address before a female audience on sexual assaults on young children, instancing cases of girls under 5 being assaulted by fathers or perverts in the streets; children were known to contract VD as a result.[24] Cases were hushed up, he said, when the rapist bribed parents not to report them; and wives might refuse to believe that the husbands were capable of such monstrosity, and even turn on their own daughters if they tried to complain. Steve Humphries cites the recollection of one subject who was raped by her uncle when she was 12: 'I've never forgot it. My mother laughed at me and my father gave me a good hiding and said I told lies. But neither of them took me to a policeman or to a doctor.'[25]

The NSPCC was no friend of the drink trade. Around 1900 various local branches of the society had given estimates of the proportion of their cases where drink was the underlying factor as ranging from 50 per cent to 90 per cent. In 1901, working with the Bishop of Hereford, the society produced a report, *The Children and the Drink*, describing numerous cases of outrageous brutality by drunken parents, and not only from among the poorer classes. For example, in 1895 a Jarrow surgeon with a history of drink-related acts of sadism to his wife and children was put on trial. His cruelties included setting light to his baby's hair, forcing his children out of bed at night to light his pipe or make him tea, knocking his pipe on their heads and generally beating them. He once put his 5-year-old son's hand in the fire 'saying that he would keep him out of mischief'. On another occasion he threw a son out of bed, knelt on his chest and forced the child, 'who had only his nightshirt on, [to] lie on the floor like a corpse for over an hour'. For all this he received only 3 months' jail (illustrating incidentally an abiding NSPCC grievance, that even when it did secure convictions the punishments were absurdly light). On the general social effects of drink on child welfare the report observed:

> The drink traffic is responsible for a great annual slaughter of infants and children; indirectly it works out into a stunted and under-grown physique and a lowered standard of health; it is largely responsible for neglect of educational chances; it helps to produce the wretchedness of the tramp-children and the workhouse 'ins and outs' and the juvenile street traders .... It fills unnumbered places in voluntary homes and reformatories and Industrial Schools. Scratch the surface of degradation anywhere, and you at once light upon the drink traffic ....

In 1907 George Sims's *The Black Stain* highlighted the role of drunken mistreatment in infant mortality (124,000 babies and under 1 were then dying each year). Babies were still being deliberately starved and maimed to make them more pitiful aids for professional beggars. Poverty, he said, was *not* necessarily the originating cause of cruelty and neglect; the poverty was itself caused by parents' addiction to drink. The NSPCC (exaggeratedly) related infant neglect and mortality to the widespread working-class practice of taking out burial insurance on babies' lives, and then allegedly spending the *post mortem* profits on a binge: 'small funeral, big drink' was a Birmingham saying according to Robert Sherard. Safeguards in the 1908 Children's Act, however, rapidly killed off suspected abuses associated with infant burial insurance.[26]

The NSPCC rapidly increased its activities in the early 1900s, as it expanded its organization and as growing public confidence saw more cases being referred to the 'Cruelty Man'.[27] In the administrative year 1895–6 it dealt with 20,739 cases and prosecuted in 2,107; in 1913–14 the figures were 54,772 and 2,349 respectively.[28] It can be seen that prosecution was only a last resort in a comparatively small hard core of cases, and the declining proportion of prosecutions to cases suggests that the growth of the NSPCC's reputation was enhancing its persuasive powers, and/or that the grosser forms of cruelty and neglect were diminishing. In 1905 C. E. B. Russell, in observing the improving physical condition of Manchester children, commented that cruelty in the form of physical violence was 'certainly diminishing' and he attributed this to the work of the NSPCC and the 'spread of education'.[29] In fact only 11 per cent of cases investigated by the society at this time involved active abuse and assault; the remainder were neglect and starvation cases.[30] The NSPCC reckoned that up to 0.4 per cent of all children in Britain suffered 'cruelty' (as distinct from 'neglect'), but George Sims mooted at least three times this figure in 1907.[31]

Indeed, like the police fight against crime, the NSPCC fight against child abuse was an ongoing struggle against some of the wickedest impulses in human nature. A society publication of 1909 entitled *The Ways of the Child Torturers Illustrated* contained a harrowing picture gallery of confiscated weapons for beating children – a shovel, a soldering iron, a thick knotted rope, a poker, a heavy brass-buckled belt, a table lamp and so on. It instanced cases of gross starvation and maiming, like the child who lost an eye and had to have an arm amputated through maltreatment; for which the father received just 2 months in jail with hard labour! The experiences of a 'Cruelty Man' published by the society in 1912 showed that the sale of children to professional tramp-beggars, itinerant performers and bargees was perhaps not yet extinct. It also illustrated the plight of unwanted stepchildren: Alfred was the son of a prosperous baker; his stepmother looked after the older children, who helped in the shop, but marked out Alfred, who was strapped and starved, and even tied to a swing for a whole day. He was reduced to an animal existence – eating swill from the hog tub and scraps that the family threw on the floor for him to eat. One witness saw the boy once ducked in a rain-water butt and left to shiver in a cold stable. Then there was Nellie; her stepmother treated her natural children well, but Nellie was used as a drudge, beaten and reduced to rags. Her father was a drunken labourer. Nellie's bed 'was a potato sack filled with filthy straw in a space 30ins square'. The pages of the NSPCC's journal, the *Child's Guardian*, were replete with similar shocking stories, yet there were signs of progress. As already seen, the proportion of prosecutions to cases investigated was declining prior to the First World War.

During the war itself there was a fall in cases and prosecutions, which one might be tempted to attribute to wartime diversions, but even after the war the figures remained down on pre-war levels. Thus in the year 1922–3 the society handled 38,027 cases and prosecuted in only 922. This improvement was borne out by the report of the Children's Branch of the Home Office in 1923:

> The children of the poorest classes are better cared for than they used to be, and it is now unusual to see dirty and ragged children in the streets of our great cities. Cases of extreme brutality, which were all too common not so many years ago, are becoming less frequent.[32]

This was attributed to an improvement in public welfare provision, the work of the NSPCC and other voluntary societies, and a decrease in drunkenness. The war had proved a climacteric in the nation's drinking habits. Alcohol consumption, most notably in spirits, dropped sharply, and remained at a moderate level throughout the inter-war period. Whereas before 1914 there were about 200,000 persons annually proceeded against for drunkenness offences in England and Wales, this figure had fallen to 29,000 in 1918, and though it rose to 100,000 in 1920 it fell away to 30–40,000 annually in the 1930s.[33] Another factor which may have eased the child's lot was the decline in the birth rate and the spread of birth control. Long-term marriages (covering all classes) contracted in the 1860s produced an average of just over 6 children per family; by the 1890s the average was just over 4 children, but in 1915 this was down to under 2.5.[34] One may conclude, therefore, that children being born from the Edwardian period were more 'expected' and therefore on the whole more wanted than before.

CONCLUSION

The lot of the child at the end of the First World War was a striking improvement on that of the child of the 1860s. Among the middle and upper classes there was less distance, awe, or repression in relationships with parents, and with the decline in religious observance the morbid austerities of extreme religiosity were not inflicted on them. Girls had greater preparation for independence, and doubtless their health was improved by the relaxation of dress conventions.

Among the working classes the main social agents for the relief of childhood were changing technology, which modified the pattern of demand for child labour, the advent of public schooling (not just for its own sake but because school gave public visibility to children's deprivations and sufferings), the fall in the birth rate, and latterly the decline in parental drunkenness. The slum child of 1918 was less ill-fed and better clothed, less maltreated and more endowed with time to enjoy the early years of irresponsibility than the Victorian urchins described by Mayhew and picked up off the streets by Dr Barnardo.

NOTES

ABBREVIATIONS

ch.	chapter (of statute)
LCC	London County Council
LSE	London School of Economics
PP	Parliamentary Papers
PRO	Public Record Office
Q	question
SPCK	Society for Promoting Christian Knowledge

1 CHILDREN WITHOUT CHILDHOOD: AN INTRODUCTION

1 Reported in the *Times Educational Supplement*, 11 September 1987.
2 Elias Mandelievich (1979).
3 Donald Read (1979).
4 10.5 million out of 32.5 million in 1901. For family sizes in different social classes, see Richard A. Soloway (1982) and John R. Gillis (1981).
5 F. Musgrove (1964).
6 Angus McLaren (1978); J. A. Banks (1981); J. Udney Yule (1920).
7 Chapter by Helen Dendy, in B. Bosanquet (1895).
8 See the Registrar-General's Annual Report for 1888, PP (1889), vol. 25.
9 James Samuelson (1911).
10 Adam Henry Robson (1931).
11 1861 census, England and Wales, vol. 2, table XVIII, p. xl *et seq.*, ibid., table XIX, p. xlii *et seq.*
12 Cited in J. S. Hurt.
13 1881 census, England and Wales, General Report, p. 18.
14 1901 census, England and Wales, vol. 1, appendix A, tables 32 and 34.
15 See Cyril Jackson (1908) Report to the Royal Commission on the Poor Laws (1905–9).
16 1911 census, England and Wales, volume of Preliminary Report and summary tables, pp. 150–8, and diagram 34 opposite p. 163.
17 1911 census, England and Wales, Preliminary Report, p. 164.

18 Robson (1931); Musgrove (1964).
19 PP (1868–9), vol. 14, report of Liverpool factory sub-inspector; quoted by Robson.
20 National Association for the Promotion of Social Science, address, 1867; cited by Musgrove.
21 Geoffrey Sherington (1981); Irene Osgood Andrews and Magarett A. Hobbs (1918).

2 FACTORIES AND MINES LEGISLATION

1 Marjorie Cruickshank (1981).
2 PP (1873), vol. 13, report of Robert Baker, inspector of factories.
3 Legislation 1833–53: 3/4 Will. IV ch. 103; 7/8 Vict. ch. 15; 10/11 Vict. ch. 29; 13/14 Vict. ch. 54; 16/17 Vict. ch. 104. See James Walvin (1982), Cruickshank (1981) and A. H. Robson (1931) for discussion of child factory labour.
4 J. R. Clynes (1937), vol. 1.
5 Fred Blackburn (1954).
6 Robson (1931); Edmund Frow and Ruth Frow (1970).
7 Robson (1931); Eric Forster (1978); *Children Working Underground* (1979); J. S. Hurt.
8 The 1842 Act applied only to coal mines; the 1860 Act took in ironstone mines as well.
9 Hansard, 1861, vol. CLXIV, cols 1875–9.
10 See the bibliography for the PP volume nos.
11 Jennie Kitteringham (1975).
12 Royal Commission on Employment of Children (1860–7), 3rd Report (1864).
13 ibid., interviews 681 and 682, p.67.
14 ibid., evidence of W. Tetler.
15 Royal Commission on Employment of Children (1863–7), 4th Report (1865), pp. vii–viii, paras 59–60.
16 Royal Commission on Employment of Chldren (1863–7), 1st Report (1863).
17 ibid., p. xxxi.
18 Royal Commission on Employment of Children (1863–7), 5th Report (1866), p. xxvi.
19 30/31 Vict. ch. 103.
20 F. Musgrove (1964).
21 Maurice W. Thomas (1945).
22 Royal Commission on Factories and Workshop Acts (1876), appendix D, Dr Charles Roberts's study.
23 41 Vict. ch. 16.
24 John E. Gorst (1906).
25 3 Edw. VII ch. 45.
26 Select Committee on Home Work (1907); see Q74 *et seq.* and appendix 1.
27 Gorst (1906).
28 Departmental Committee on Partial Exemption ... (1909).
29 Cruickshank (1981).

30 Hansard, 7 May 1909, col. 1415, and 14 June 1909, cols 715–22.
31 35/36 Vict. ch. 76 – Coal Mines Regulation Act 1872; 35/36 Vict. ch. 77 – Metalliferous Mines Act 1872; 50/51 Vict. ch. 58 – Coal Mines Act 1887.
32 Gorst (1906).
33 PP (1873), vol. 13, report of Robert Baker, inspector of factories.
34 See Frederic Keeling (1914).
35 Departmental Committee on Physical Deterioration (1904), Report.
36 Thomas (1945), citing Dr Scott's evidence before the Departmental Committee on Physical Deterioration.
37 *Child's Guardian*, April 1891, p. 30.

3 SWEATSHOPS, COTTAGE LABOUR AND MOONLIGHTING UP TO THE FIRST WORLD WAR

1 Ronald Fletcher (1966).
2 B. L. Hutchins and A. Harrison (1926).
3 Raphael Samuel (1975).
4 Cited in Lilian Birt (1913).
5 David Rubinstein (1969).
6 Royal Commission on Employment of Children (1863–7), 2nd Report (1864).
7 Select Committee on Home Work (1907), evidence of Gertrude Tuckwell at Q2351; Edith Hogg (1897a).
8 30/31 Vict. ch. 146.
9 Hutchins and Harrison (1926); Maurice W. Thomas (1945). Royal Commission on Factories and Workshops Acts (1876).
10 PP (1888), vol. 20, and PP (1889), vol. 14, parts 1 and 2.
11 Gertrude M. Tuckwell (1894).
12 Frederic Keeling (1914).
13 Edith Hogg (1897b).
14 John E. Gorst (1906).
15 Clementina Black (1907); Mrs Archibald Mackirdy (1907).
16 Rubinstein (1969).
17 Royal Commission on Reformatories and Industrial Schools (1884); Keeling (1914).
18 Gorst (1906).
19 Joseph Stamper (1960); Royal Commission on the Poor Laws (1905–9), Cyril Jackson citing Nettie Adler (1906); Robert H. Sherard (1905).
20 Sherard (1905); Elizabeth Roberts (1975).
21 Sherard (1905).
22 Black (1907).
23 Sherard (1905); Recollections of Clifford Mills, in Thea Thompson (1982); J. S. Hurt; (Inter)Departmental Committee on the Employment of School-children (1902).
24 Hogg (1897a).
25 Sherard (1905).
26 *Band of Hope Review*, 1 December 1859, p. 190.
27 Grace M. Paton (1915).
28 Mackirdy (1907).
29 Frank Hird (1898).

30 Hogg (1897b) on fur-pullers.
31 See, for example, *Child's Guardian*, September 1898, p. 110.
32 (Inter)Departmental Committee on the Employment of Schoolchildren (1902); Rubinstein (1969).
33 3 Edw. VII ch. 45.
34 PP (1907), vol. 6, and PP (1908), vol. 8, appendix 1, Select Committee on Home Work.
35 Hurt.
36 Paton (1915).
37 Dr Thomas's report to the LCC Education Committee, cited by Black (1907); Margaret McMillan (1907).
38 Black (1907).
39 See Departmental Committee on Physical Deterioration (1904), evidence of Sir Lambert Ormsby.
40 Select Committee on Home Work (1907), evidence at Q2351.
41 Roberts (1975).
42 Keeling (1914).
43 Children's Branch of the Home Office, 1st Report (1923).

4 CHILDREN ON THE LAND AND CHILDREN AT SEA

1 Royal Commission on Employment of Children (1863–7), 6th Report (1867).
2 Also found among cocklers on the Lancashire coast (Raphael Samuel (ed.) (1975)). The authenticity of juvenile pregnancies among girls as young as 13 must be vitiated by the later onset of menstruation in Victorian times.
3 Royal Commission on Employment of Children (1863–7), 6th Report (1867), F. D. Longe's report.
4 ibid., J. E. White's report.
5 Royal Commission on Employment of Children, Young Persons and Women in Agriculture (1868–70), 3rd Report (1870).
6 Pamela Horn (1974).
7 Sally Livingstone (1978); F. Musgrove (1964); Samuel (1975).
8 Frederic Keeling (1914).
9 Robert Roberts (1971); William Chance (1897), chapter 9.
10 Robert Sherard (1905).
11 Nigel Middleton (1971).
12 W. Cunningham Glen and R. Cunningham Glen (1887).
13 Departmental Committee on the Supply and Training of Boy Seamen ... (1907), evidence of Captain Thomas Sargent and W. H. G. Deacon at Q1164.

5 YOUNG SLAVES – CHILDREN IN DOMESTIC SERVICE

1 Apart from censuses for England and Wales, see also Carol Dyhouse (1981) for statistics.
2 See 1881 census, England and Wales, General Report, p. 18.
3 Theresa McBride, 'The Victorian nanny', in Anthony S. Wohl (1977).
4 Flora Thompson (1945); Pamela Horn (1974); Sally Livingstone (1978).
5 Recollections of Miss Renshaw, in Jeremy Seabrook (1982).
6 As told in Margaret Llewelyn Davies (1931).
7 Charles Booth (1896), vol. 8.

8 Memoir of Lilian Westall, in John Burnett (1974).

9 John Burnett (1982).

10 In Davies (1931).

11 Lionel Rose (1986); Steve Humphries (1988); Kellow Chesney (1970); Henry Mayhew (1851); McBride, in Wohl (1977).

12 Margaret Leonora Eyles (1953).

13 Ellen Barlee (1863).

14 Cited in Iona Opie and Peter Opie (1985).

15 Norman Longmate (1974).

16 Trial of George and Theresa Sloane: December 1850, police court case; January–February 1851, Old Bailey; see *The Times* (1850) 7 December at 7b, 14 December at 3a, 21 December at 5d, 28 December at 5c, and 31 December at 5d, all listed under 'Police' in *The Times* Index, and (1851) 9 January at 6e, 6 February at 7a, and 7 February at 7f, all listed under 'Crime' in *The Times* Index.

17 14/15 Vict. ch. 11.

18 Florence Davenport Hill (1889); A. M. Ross (1955); see Menella B. Smedley (1875) for the report of Mrs Nassau Senior (1874).

19 24/25 Vict. ch. 16.

20 *Child's Guardian*, October 1891, p. 103.

21 ibid., June 1892, p. 80.

22 ibid., September 1907, 'Little white slave'.

23 Barlee (1863).

24 As told to Joanna Smith (1983).

25 Quoted in June Rose (1987).

26 See Booth (1896).

27 Irene Osgood Andrews and Margarett A. Hobbs (1918). Dyhouse (1981).

28 John E. Gorst (1913).

29 Samuel Smith (1885).

30 Select Committee (Lords) on Sweating (1888), evidence of Rev. William Anderson.

31 Henrietta O. Barnett (1918).

32 Nigel Middleton (1971).

33 Longmate (1974); Select Committee on Poor Relief (1861), evidence of Mrs Emmeline Way at Q12,224.

34 Barlee (1863).

35 See note 32.

36 See Smedley (1875) where the report is reproduced.

37 ibid., appendix F, Mrs Senior's report. Of course I cannot vouch for her sampling techniques, e.g. we do not know how long each of the subjects spent in the respective schools.

38 See William Chance (1897), esp. chapters 4, 9 and 13.

39 PP (1908), vol. 92, Children under the Poor Law.

40 Dorothy Hatcher (1988).

41 Chance (1897); Tom Percival (1912); Mary G. Barnett (1913); Alicia C. Percival (1951); Dyhouse (1981). Different authors have given different dates for the founding of the Girls' Friendly Society; as various as 1874 (Dyhouse), 1875 (Alicia Percival) and 1877 (Tom Percival).

42 Middleton (1971).

43 Royal Commission on the Care and Control of the Feeble-Minded (1908), evidence of Maria Poole at Q13,544 *et seq.*

6 BRICKYARD AND CANALBOAT CHILDREN AND CHIMNEY SWEEPS

1 Quoted in Edwin Hodder (1896).
2 Royal Commission on Employment of Children (1863–7), 5th Report (1866).
3 Sally Livingstone (1978); memoir of Mrs Quick, in Raphael Samuel (1975).
4 Cited in Hodder (1896), speech in Lords, 11 July 1871.
5 F. Musgrove (1964).
6 Samuel (1975).
7 Clementina Black (1907).
8 Hodder (1896); George Smith (1879).
9 PP (1898), Report of Committee on Council for Education for 1897–8.
10 See canal boat inspectors' Annual Reports; A. C. O. Ellis (1973).
11 Robert Parr (1910b).
12 See Charles Henry Wyatt (1903), but *contra* this see Ellis (1973), Parr (1910b), Hodder (1896).
13 Gillian Avery (1965) refers to a children's story, 'Over there', published in 1890, about bargees' cruelty.
14 See Frank Hird (1898); Robert H. Sherard (1905).
15 There may have been a bill in 1923. For the 1928 bill see PP (1928/9), vol. 1, and for the 1929 bill see PP (1929/30), vol. 1.
16 Steve Humphries *et al.* (1988).
17 For sweeps' history, see Kathleen H. Strange (1982); E. S. Turner (1950); Frederic Keeling (1914).
18 Livingstone (1978).
19 Royal Commission on Employment of Children (1863–7), 1st Report (1863). See also the 5th Report (1866).
20 ibid., 5th report, Mr Ruff's evidence.
21 ibid., and W. Clarke Hall (1897).
22 Turner (1950).
23 Charles Booth (1896), vol. 8, p. 282 *et seq.*

7 THEATRICAL, CIRCUS AND FAIRGROUND CHILDREN

1 *Nicholas Nickleby*, chapter 23.
2 Giles Playfair (1967).
3 Hansard (Commons), 10 July 1889, Mr Jennings MP, col. 10, debate on the Prevention of Cruelty to Children Bill.
4 PP (1887), vol. 30. Royal Commission on Education (1887), evidence of Mrs Henry Fawcett at Q50,444.
5 ibid., evidence of Mrs Henry Fawcett at Q50,445 *et seq.*, and evidence of Charles T. Mitchell at Q50,647 *et seq.*
6 ibid., evidence of Mrs H. Fawcett at Q50,513–1.
7 Rosa Waugh (1913).
8 Quoted in the *Child's Guardian*, September 1888, p. 31.
9 John E. Gorst (1906), and Mr Jennings MP in 1889 in the debate on the Prevention of Cruelty to Children Bill.

10 Edith Craig and Christopher St John (1933).
11 See Hansard, 1889: 26 June at cols 806–21, 10 July at cols 6–38, 22 July at cols 951–68, 5 August at cols 280–92, 8 August at cols 718–20, 14 August at cols 1284–7.
12 Quoted by Mr Jennings MP in Hansard (Commons), 10 July 1889, cols 10–11.
13 ibid., col. 12.
14 Hansard (Commons), 5 August 1889, cols 281–2.
15 Frederic Keeling (1914); Gorst (1906).
16 3/4 Geo. V. ch. 7.
17 Children's Branch of the Home Office, 1st Report (1923).
18 *Tempted London*: reprinted from articles in the *British Weekly*, October 1887 to April 1888; article 10, 'Variety theatres'.
19 See *Child's Guardian*, July 1889, p. 113, and December 1889, p. 222.
20 Keeling (1914). 42/43 Vict. ch. 24.
21 For the 'Human Serpent' case see *The Times*, 2 August 1883, p. 2, col. 5; Hansard, 26 July 1883, cols 521–2. See also W. Clarke Hall (1897); Ellen Barlee (1884).
22 *Child's Guardian*, October 1892, p. 130, and May 1894, p. 66. The 'Belgian' case may have been the same one reported in the 1892 issue.
23 ibid., May 1890.
24 57/58 Vict. ch. 41 sections 2 and 3.
25 60/61 Vict. ch. 52.
26 'Lord' George Sanger (1952).
27 See Charles Dickens, *Sketches by Boz*, on the freak show at Greenwich Fair; Michael Howell and Peter Ford (1983).
28 Raymund Fitzsimons (1969).
29 Henry Ashby and G. A. Wright (1892).
30 Howell and Ford (1983).
31 George M. Gould and Walter M. Pyle (1901).
32 Sanger (1952), introduction by Kenneth Grahame (1925).

8 JUVENILE STREET TRADERS

1 Henry Mayhew (1851), p. 468 ff.
2 See Lionel Rose (1988).
3 'I'm a little Flow'r Girl' (1854), composer George Linley. BM Music Catalogue at H. 1296 (19).
4 Henry Mayhew and John Binny (1862).
5 Rose (1988); Helen Bosanquet (1914).
6 C. E. B. Russell and E. T. Campagnac (1902).
7 Third International Congress for the Welfare and Protection of Children, 1902.
8 Edwin Hodder (1894); Rose (1988).
9 Henrietta O. Barnett (1918).
10 John Urquhart (1900).
11 Mary Carpenter (1857).
12 Hodder (1894).
13 June Rose (1987).

14 C. J. Montague (1904).
15 Urquhart (1900).
16 James Samuelson (1911).
17 J. S. Hurt.
18 Samuelson (1911). Departmental Committee on the Employment of Children Act of 1903 (1910), appendices 1ᶜ(4) and 16.
19 Gertrude M. Tuckwell (1894).
20 Maddison's address at the Third International Congress for the Welfare and Protection of Children, 1902.
21 John Stuart (1907).
22 J. H. Whitehouse (1908).
23 Departmental Committee on Physical Deterioration (1904), evidence of Josceline Bagot at Q4519 *et seq.*; she thought that the Newsboys Brigade was 'still in its infancy'.
24 J. G. Cloete's chapter, in E. J. Urwick (1904).
25 See note 20.
26 Arthur Greenwood (1911); Whitehouse (1908).
27 Tuckwell (1894).
28 Royal Commission on Reformatories and Industrial Schools (1884).
29 ibid. This leaves out of account the Pedlars Act of 1871, which confined pedlars' licences to the over-17s. But this empowered holders to sell from door to door, not just in the street.
30 Frederic Keeling (1914).
   Robert Peacock's address at the Third International Congress for the Welfare and Protection of Children, 1902.
31 *Nineteenth Century*, August 1897.
32 Samuel Smith (1883); Thomas Burke (1900); Charles Henry Wyatt (1903).
33 Samuelson (1911).
34 The first licensing measure appears to have been in Scotland under the Burgh Police Act 1892.
35 Burke (1900).
36 Chief Constable Nott-Bower, quoted in Wyatt (1903).
37 Robert H. Sherard (1905); Cyril Jackson (1908).
38 *Child's Guardian*, October 1911, pp. 115–16; Grace M. Paton (1915); Jackson (1908) (this reduction appears to have been associated with a transfer of policing from the Public Control Committee to the Education Committee).
39 For England and Wales alone; census, vol. 10, part 2, table 13.
40 Home Office circular following the 1903 Act; reproduced in Keeling (1914).
41 3 Edw. VII ch. 45.
42 See Keeling (1914).
43 See, e.g. Rose (1988); Sherard (1905); *The Children and the Drink* (1901); Burke (1900).
44 ibid. (Inter)Departmental Committee on the Employment of Schoolchildren (1902), appendix 43.
45 Departmental Committee on the Employment of Children Act of 1903 (1910), evidence of L. J. Phenix at Q6386.
46 ibid., evidence of R. S. Allan at Q4432 and of Canon Pinington at Q7669.
47 ibid., evidence of R. S. Allan at Q4432.

48 ibid., appendix 7, evidence of Miss Reith.
49 Margaret McMillan (1904).
50 Departmental Committee on the Employment of Children Act of 1903 (1910), evidence of Olive Hargreaves.
51 ibid., quoted.
52 C. E. B. Russell and L. M. Rigby. See Chamberlain's chapter, 'The station lounger', in J. H. Whitehouse (1912).
53 Cited in Keeling (1914).
54 Departmental Committee on the Employment of Children Act of 1903 (1910), evidence of R. S. Allan at Q4432.
55 C. E. B. Russell (1905). See also his evidence and that of Robert Peacock, Chief Constable of Manchester, to the Departmental Committee on the Employment of Children Act 1903 (1910).
56 Russell and Campagnac (1902).
57 Departmental Committee on the Employment of Children Act of 1903 (1910), appendix 3: survey produced by Committee on Wage-Earning Children et al.
58 See note 57.
59 John E. Gorst (1906).
60 Departmental Committee on the Employment of Children Act of 1903 (1910), appendix 1.
61 See Keeling 1914.
62 Children's Branch of the Home Office, 1st Report (1923).
63 Steve Humphries (1981).

9 WAIFS AND BEGGARS

1 Joseph Kay (1857).
2 Lionel Rose (1988), chapter 5.
3 Cited in David Rubinstein (1969); Kathleen Mallam, however, (1908) cites Barnardo's figure as applying to *England*.
4 *The Uncommercial Traveller*, chapter 35.
5 Henry Mayhew (1851), vol. 1, p. 418 ff.
6 *Child's Guardian*, March 1887.
7 T. N. Kelynack (1922).
8 Thomas Barnardo (1881).
9 Evelyn Sharp (1927).
10 Words by F. E. Weatherly, music by Frederic H. Cowen.
11 Words by A. W. French, music by G. W. Persley.
12 For Standard 2.
13 Arnold Freeman (1914).
14 James Samuelson (1911).
15 Henry Mayhew (1851).
16 Quoted in Kelynack (1922).
17 See Rose (1988) for beggars' dodges.
18 'Emma Smith' (1958).
19 Rose (1988); George Sims (1907a) article in the *Tribune*, 18 February; Steve Humphries, Joanna Mack and Robert Parks (1988).
20 Ellen Barlee (1884).

21 Sims (1907a).
22 David Burrows (n.d.).
23 *Child's Guardian*, June 1908, p. 7.
24 ibid., February 1910, p. 18.
25 Royal Commission on the Blind, Deaf and Dumb (1889).
26 See, e.g., Walter Greenwood (1967); Robert Roberts (1971); John Burnett (1982), introduction.
27 Barlee (1884).
28 Joseph Stamper (1960).
29 See Chapter 8 for significance of adding the word 'allows'.
30 *Child's Guardian*, May 1889, p. 85 and March 1980, p. 25.
31 M. M'Cullum's chapter on 'The protection of children', in B. Bosanquet (ed.) (1895).
32 Alfred W. Mager (1886).
33 Robert Parr (1910a).
34 See Mary G. Barnett (1913); Hilary Douglas Clerk Peper (1915); Steve Humphries (1981).
35 (Inter)Departmental Committee on Vagrancy (1906), evidence of R. J. Parr at Q10,957, and Report, para. 424; NSPCC Annual Reports.
36 Juvenile Organizations Committee of the Board of Education (1920), Report on Juvenile Delinquency.

10 VAGRANCY

1 Lionel Rose (1988), chapter 16.
2 Departmental Committee on Vagrancy (1906), para. 412.
3 See the Third International Congress for the Welfare and Protection of Children, 1902, debate following address by Rosa M. Barrett, remarks by R. E. Stuart. Pan Anglican Papers, 1908: Henrietta O. Barnett, 'Destitute, neglected and delinquent children'.
4 See Rose (1988), chapter 16.
5 *Child's Guardian*, November 1888.
6 Rose (1988), chapter 16.
7 *The Cruelty Man* (1912).
8 Rose (1988), chapter 16.
9 Rosa Waugh (1913).
10 Rose (1988), chapter 16; Robert Parr (1910a).
11 See references under George Smith in the bibliography.
12 Smith's account quoted in Gertrude M. Tuckwell (1894).
13 Smith (1889).
14 Smith (1888); Departmental Committee on Habitual Offenders, Vagrants, Beggars, etc. (Scotland) (1895).
15 ibid., evidence of Dr M'Cullum.
16 Third International Congress for the Welfare and Protection of Children, 1902; John Macdonald on tinker children.
17 Smith (1880, 1885, 1888 and 1889); Edwin Hodder (1896); Tuckwell (1894); 1885 Act, 48/49 Vict. ch. 72.
18 See Rose (1988).
19 J. W. Horsley in 1887, cited in Leslie George Housden (1955).

20 C. E. B. Russell (1905).
21 C. E. B. Russell and L. M. Rigby (1906); Rose (1988), chapter 17.
22 Hansard, 24 March 1908, A. Allen MP, cols 1274–5, and Atherley-Jones MP, col. 1276, debate on the Children's Bill.
23 1908 Children's Act, section 74.
24 PRO, MH 18/5, report of the Local Government Board inspector, Mr Hedley.
25 See Rose (1988).
26 Royal Commission on the Poor Laws (1905–9), Majority Report, vol. 1, part IV, chapters 5 and 9.
27 ibid., part IV, chapter 9.
28 See Rose (1988), chapter 16, p. 133. I wish to make a correction to the *Rogues and Vagabonds* here. It was the *children* who had to be maintained by the Poor Law, not the parents. The latter, of course, might be in jail.
29 Royal Commission on the Poor Laws (1905–9), Minority Report, chapter 4.
30 PRO, MH 57/60, Vagrant Children: Adoption and Maintenance Powers of Vagrancy Committees 1924–30. See Rose (1988) for Poor Law adoption history post 1918.
31 There was no provision for support of Poor Law adoptees out of the county rates under the 1908 Act either.

11   THE BLIND-ALLEY JOB PROBLEM

1 Spencer J. Gibb (1911).
2 Robert Roberts (1976).
3 J. H. Whitehouse (1912), quoted in Arnold Freeman (1914).
4 Cyril Jackson (1908).
5 James Greenwood, *Old People in Odd Places*, cited in Frank Dawes (1975).
6 Whitehouse (1912); chapter 2 by R. H. Tawney, in Arthur Greenwood (1911); Royal Commission on the Poor Laws (1905–9), Majority Report and Minority Report.
7 Consultative Committee on Attendance at Continuation Schools (1909), R. H. Tawney's report.
8 See, e.g., C. E. B. Russell (1905).
9 Arnold Freeman (1914); Barclay Baron (1911).
10 Pamela Horn (1974).
11 Spencer J. Gibb (1911).
12 Departmental Committee on Physical Deterioration (1904), evidence of A. Eichholz at Q560.
13 Ivy Pinchbeck and Margaret Hewitt (1973); Horn (1974).
14 Greenwood (1911); Nigel Middleton (1971), chapter 6; Royal Commission on the Poor Laws (1905–9), Majority Report.
15 Chapter 2 by Tawney, in Whitehouse (1912).
16 Departmental Committee on Hours and Conditions of Van and Warehouse Boys (1913).
17 Gertrude M. Tuckwell (1894).
18 Departmental Committee on Physical Deterioration (1904), evidence of A. Eichholz at Q562 *et seq.*
19 Middleton (1971).
20 Charles Booth (1892–7), vol. 8 (1896).

21 See Freeman (1914).
22 Grace M. Paton (1915); Greenwood (1911); Consultative Committee on Attendance at Continuation Schools (1909).
23 'The boy and his work', chapter by J. G. Cloete, in E. J. Urwick (1904).
24 Greenwood (1911).
25 M. E. Sadler (1907).
26 C. E. B. Russell and L. M. Rigby (1908).
27 Helen Bosanquet (1914).
28 Consultative Committee on Attendance at Continuation Schools (1909).
29 Paton (1915).
30 Irene Osgood Andrews and Margarett A. Hobbs (1918).

12 EMPLOYERS, EDUCATION AND THE PART-TIME SYSTEM

1 *Edinburgh Review* LIII (1831): 611–2.
2 Quoted in Adam Henry Robson (1931).
3 F. Musgrove (1964).
4 Anne Digby and Peter Searby (1981).
5 T. G. Rooper before the Third International Congress for the Welfare and Protection of Children, 1902.
6 Departmental Committee on School Attendance and Child Labour (1893–4).
7 A. C. O. Ellis (1973); Charles Henry Wyatt (1903); G. M. Edwardes Jones and J. C. G. Sykes (1904); Digby and Searby (1981).
8 J. S. Hurt; Consultative Committee on Attendance at Continuation Schools (1909).
9 Frederic Keeling (1914); Royal Commission on Physical Training (Scotland) (1903).
10 Departmental Committee on School Attendance and Child Labour (1893–4); this contains a full résumé of exemption law at that date.
11 Edmund Frow and Ruth Frow (1970), the hours of Ben Turner. See also Gertrude M. Tuckwell (1894); Steve Humphries, Joanna Mack and Robert Parks (1988).
12 Frow and Frow (1970).
13 Robson (1931); see the Royal Commission on Factories and Workshops Acts (1876).
14 See Frow and Frow (1970); Clement Dukes (1893 and 1899).
15 Samuel Smith (1885).
16 Hansard, 22 April 1909, cols 1781–3, debate on continuation schools.
17 Cited in the Royal Commission on Factories and Workshops Acts (1876).
18 PP (1873), vol. 13, report of Robert Baker, inspector of factories.
19 See Tuckwell (1894); Margaret McMillan (1904); Margaret McMillan (1896); Departmental Committee on Partial Exemption from School Attendance (1909).
20 Royal Commission on Physical Education (Scotland) (1903), Q13,204 *et seq.*
21 Departmental Committee on Physical Deterioration (1904), e.g. evidence of HM inspector of factories Harry James Wilson at Q1924 *et seq.* and of factory surgeon Dr A. Scott at Q1787 *et seq.*
22 Cited in Arthur Greenwood (1913).
23 Departmental Committee on Partial Exemption from School Attendance

(1909), appendix 15, evidence of Dr Alfred Greenwood, Medical Officer of Health for Blackburn.

24 Departmental Committee on Partial Exemption from School Attendance (1909). Wyatt (1903). There are some discrepancies between these two sources. The Departmental Committee also based its own absolute figures on a different statistical footing from the Board of Education's and its statistics are much lower. However, the *trends* indicated by the Board of Education's statistics seem broadly correct, so I have cited trends here, not absolute figures. A boom in the cotton industry from 1901 did check the long-term rate of decline.

25 Frow and Frow (1970).

26 ibid; Hansard, 19 June 1914, cols 1433 *et seq*. See Departmental Committee on Partial Exemption from School Attendance (1909) for references to ballots.

27 See also Grace M. Paton (1915).

28 PP (1914), vol. 1, 'Children (Employment and School Attendance) Bill'; Hansard, 19 June 1914, cols 1433 *et seq*., debate.

29 Frow and Frow (1970).

13 SCHOOL CURRICULUM AND THE 'STANDARDS' 1862–1918

1 For general background see J. S. Hurt. Sir Graham Balfour (1898); Henry Bryan Binns (1908); Anne Digby and Peter Searby (1981); S. J. Curtis (1967); W. H. G. Armytage (1964).

2 J. S. Hurt considers the figures of the Royal Commission on Education (1858–61) to be exaggerated.

3 Cited in Joseph Kay (1857).

4 1861 census, England and Wales, vol. 2, tables XIX and XX.

5 Lawrence Stone (1969).

6 Royal Commission on Employment of Children (1863–7), 1st Report (1863), citing reports of factory inspector, 1859 and 1861.

7 Figures cited in Digby and Searby (1981).

8 *Morning Chronicle*, 1850: 25 March, 29 March, 22 April, 25 April; and see Henry Mayhew and John Binny (1862) where reference is made to the reaction to the articles.

9 Royal Commission on Education (1858–61), report of Cumin.

10 C. J. Montague (1904).

11 Royal Commission on Education (1887), evidence of Henry Reader Williams at Q53,742 *et seq*.

12 A. C. O. Ellis (1976).

13 Edmund Frow and Ruth Frow (1970).

14 N. Ball (1983).

15 See Mary Sturt (1967); Armytage (1964); J. Lawson and H. Silver (1981); David Rubinstein (1969).

16 PP (1884), vol. 61, J. G. Fitch, chief inspector of HMIs.

17 Lord Norton (1883).

18 A. B. Robertson (1972).

19 J. G. Fitch (see note 16); Sturt (1967).

20 George Sims (1889); Ellis (1976); Thomas Gautrey (1937); Greater London

Record Office, SBL 1466, Report of Special Committee on . . . Overpressure (1885).
21 Frow and Frow (1970); David Gwyn Pritchard (1963).
22 E. J. Eaglesham (1967); Ellis (1976); Charles Henry Wyatt (1903).
23 PP (1884), vol. 61, for Crichton-Browne's report and Fitch's reply.
24 Greater London Record Office, SBL 1466.
25 ibid.
26 Hugh B. Philpott (1904).
27 See also Mary Dendy's evidence in favour of moving duller children up for social reasons at Q805 in her evidence before the Royal Commission on the Care and Control of the Feeble-Minded (1908).
28 Pritchard (1963).
29 Report of the Royal Commission on the Care and Control of the Feeble-Minded (1908).
30 Gautrey (1937).
31 Pamela Horn (1974); Joseph Stamper (1960); Flora Thompson (1945).
32 James Runciman (1887).
33 Gautrey (1937). Sturt (1967).
34 James Runciman (1885).
35 Reproduced in G. M. Edwardes Jones and J. C. G. Sykes (1904).
36 Quoted in Sturt (1967). William Watson's Arithmetic Cards (1885).
37 H. Major was the author of many school texts and readers in the late nineteenth century.
38 Frow and Frow (1970); Departmental Committee on Physical Deterioration (1904), evidence of A. Eichholz at Q471.

14 TEACHING METHODS 1860–1918

1 Royal Commission on Education (1858–61), p. 255.
2 ibid., p. 251.
3 Alison Uttley (1937).
4 Pamela Horn (1974).
5 H. C. Barnard (1970); Margaret Leonora Eyles (1953).
6 See Barnard (1970); Winifred Peck (1952).
7 Henry Mayhew and John Binny (1862), p. 421.
8 See J. H. Whitehouse (1912), chapter 4; Spencer J. Gibb (1911).
9 C. E. B. Russell and E. T. Campagnac (1902).
10 See William Bousfield (1890), preface.
11 David Rubinstein (1969); Mary Sturt (1967).
12 See references in note 8.
   Margaret McMillan, 'The ethical end in education', quoted in Walter D'Arcy Cresswell (1948).
13 Cited in Gillian Avery (1967); George Orwell's book was originally published by Christy & Moore.
14 Peck (1952).
15 R. Mangnall, *Historical and Miscellaneous Questions* (1869 edn).
16 Orwell, cited in Avery (1967).
17 Lord Norton (1883).
18 Memoir of Kate Taylor, in John Burnett (1982).

19 C. E. B. Russell; Robert Roberts (1971); Royal Commission on Education (1858–61).
20 John E. Gorst (1913).
21 Anne Digby and Peter Searby (1981).
22 Quoted in Rubinstein (1969).
23 Gillian Avery (1965).
24 Roberts (1971); Ruth Johnson (1974); Steve Humphries (1981).
25 Bousfield (1890), preface; Samuel Smith (1885).
26 Departmental Committee on Reformatories and Industrial Schools (1896), Report, p. 14.
27 Digby and Searby (1981).
28 Mary G. Barnett (1913).
29 Barnard (1970); J. Gathorne Hardy (1972); Marjorie Cruickshank (1981); Margaret McMillan (1896).
30 John E. Gorst (1906); Hansard, 21 April 1913, cols 30–1. The 1918 Education Act empowered local authorities to provide nursery classes from 2–5 years old.
31 Quoted in Gorst (1906). (For the NSPCC's view see *Child's Guardian*, October 1908.)
32 Chapter by Crichton-Browne, in Malcolm Morris (1883); Greater London Record Office, SBL 1466; Report of Special Committee on Overpressure (1885); chapter by George Ricks on 'hand and eye' training in Bousfield (1890).
33 Charles Booth (1892–7), vol. 3, part 2.
34 PP (1906), vol. 90, Reports on Children under Five.
35 Charles Henry Wyatt (1903).
36 PP (1906), vol. 90, Mrs Bathurst's report.
37 Johnson (1974).
38 Norton (1883); Lord Brabazon's letter to *The Times*, 1886, cited in Digby and Searby (1981).
39 Norton (1883).
40 Legge's address before the Third International Congress for the Welfare and Protection of Children, 1902.
41 Gorst (1913).
42 Henrietta O. Barnett (1918), chapter 23.
43 Bousfield (1890), preface.
44 Hugh B. Philpott (1904).
45 J. Lawson and H. Silver (1981).
46 Philpott (1904).
47 Consultative Committee on Attendance at Continuation Schools (1909), Report, p. 56; Barclay Baron (1911).
48 Mabel Ashby, quoted in Carol Adams (1982).
49 Memoir of Charles Cooper, born 1872, in Burnett (1982).
50 James Walvin (1975); Clement Dukes (1899).
51 Royal Commission on Physical Training (Scotland) (1903).
52 A. M. Ross (1955); Greater London Record Office, SBL 1578, LCC Report on Industrial Schools 1870–1904.
53 Ellen Barlee (1863); Carol Dyhouse (1977); Carol Dyhouse (1981).

54 Adams (1982); Burnett (1982); T. A. Spalding (1900), cited in Digby and Searby (1981); Lawson and Silver (1981).
55 Dyhouse (1981).
56 Wyatt (1903).
57 Dyhouse (1977); Spalding (1900), cited in Digby and Searby (1981); Dyhouse (1981).
58 Charles Booth (1892), vol. 3, part 2.
59 Dyhouse (1981); Dyhouse (1977).
60 Quoted in Rose Kerr (1976).
61 *Our Towns: A Close-Up*, 1944.

15 HEALTH AND SCHOOLING

1 A. B. Robertson (1972); Clement Dukes (1893).
2 See also A. C. O. Ellis (1976) for earlier views of David Donaldson and Dukes (1893).
3 ibid., and Dukes (1899).
4 Ellis (1976).
5 Robertson (1972).
6 Malcolm Morris (1883).
7 PP (1884), vol. 61.
8 Greater London Record Office, SBL 1466, Report of Special Committee on . . . Overpressure (1885); Thomas Gautrey (1937); PP (1906), vol. 90, Reports . . . on . . . Children under Five in Elementary Schools, for Effects of Excessive Amount of Needlework.
9 Carol Dyhouse (1981).
10 Cited in Pamela Horn (1974).
11 J. H. Whitehouse (1912), chapter 1.
12 John E. Gorst (1906).
   Royal Commission on Physical Training (Scotland) (1903).
13 Robert Roberts (1971).
14 Horn (1974).
15 W. H. Barrett (1965).
16 Gorst (1906).
17 For classroom fittings see Ellis (1976); Hugh B. Philpott (1904); J. Lawson and H. Silver (1981). For spinal curvature and rheumatism, see Marjorie Cruickshank (1981) and the Departmental Committee on Physical Deterioration (1904).
18 Mary Sturt (1967).
19 Cruickshank (1981).
20 J. S. Hurt; Gautrey (1937).
21 Charles Henry Wyatt (1903).
22 W. H. G. Armytage (1964).
23 Hurst.
24 F. B. Smith (1979); Ivy Pinchbeck and Margaret Hewitt (1973).
25 Helen Bosanquet (1914).
26 Hansard, 1906, vol. 152, col. 1420.
27 Roberts (1971).
28 Charles Booth (1892–7), vol. III, pp. 207–8, cited in *The Children and the*

Drink; Departmental Committee on Physical Deterioration (1904), evidence of A. Eichholz at Q454; Royal Commission on the Poor Laws (1905–9), Minority Report, citing a Liverpool medical officer; Bill Harding's story as told to Steve Humphries (1981).

29 Hurt; (Inter)Departmental Committee on Medical Inspection and Feeding Schoolchildren (1906), PP, vol. 47, para. 238; Leslie George Housden (1955).

30 Philpott (1904).

31 Hurt; Housden (1955).

32 Walter D'Arcy Cresswell (1948); Grace M. Paton (1915); M. E. Bulkley (1914).

33 ibid.; Hurt; Flora Thompson (1945); Horn (1974).

34 Gorst (1906); Royal Commission on Physical Training (Scotland) (1903), appendix 7.

35 Samuel Smith (1885). See Gautrey (1937) for the London School Board's earlier attitude.

36 Hansard, 1906, vol. 152, col. 1420.

37 Bosanquet (1914).

38 Hurt; Departmental Committee on Physical Deterioration (1904), evidence of A. Eichholz at Q475 *et seq.*

39 This corresponds roughly with a figure of 133,000 out of 763,000 London children given by Dr Macnamara in a *Daily Mirror* article, cited by Robert H. Sherard (1905).

40 See, e.g., address by Sir Charles Elliott of the International Committee for Underfed Children in London, to the International Congress for the Welfare and Protection of Children, 1906.

41 Departmental Committee on Physical Deterioration (1904), evidence of A. Eichholz at Q435.

42 Bosanquet (1914).

43 Hurt; Gorst (1906); Royal Commission on the Poor Laws (1909), Minority Report, pp. 160–1; Pinchbeck and Hewitt (1973); *Child's Guardian*, September 1906.

44 6 Edw. VII ch. 57.

45 Chapter 12, by W. H. H. Elliott, in Whitehouse (1912).

46 Pinchbeck and Hewitt (1973), vol. 2.

47 *Child's Guardian*, September 1906, p. 103; Robert Parr (1910a).

48 Royal Commission on the Poor Laws (1905–9), Minority Report.

49 Hilary Douglas Clerk Pepler (1912) (1914 edn).

50 ibid.

51 Memoir of Thomas Morgan, in Thea Thompson (1982); Bulkley (1914); Margaret McMillan (1904) also for early feeding arrangements.

52 Royal Commission on the Poor Laws (1905–9), Minority Report.

53 PP (1911), vol. 18.

54 Pepler (1912) (1914 edn).

55 Paton (1915); Arthur Greenwood (1913).

56 Paton (1915).

57 ibid.; Greenwood (1913).

58 Jean Rennie (1955).

59 Hurst.

60 Hurst; David Gwyn Pritchard (1963); David Rubinstein (1969).
61 Cresswell (1948).
62 Sturt (1967).
63 Margaret McMillan (1907).
64 Departmental Committee on the Medical Inspection and Feeding of Schoolchildren (1906); Wyatt (1903); Gorst (1906).
65 7 Edw. VII ch. 43.
66 9 Edw. VII ch. 13.
67 Greenwood (1913).
68 Robert Roberts (1976); Robert Roberts (1971).

16 SCHOOLING AND THE UPPER CLASSES

1 Anne Digby and Peter Searby (1981); J. Lawson and H. Silver (1981).
2 Royal Commission on Education (1861).
3 John R. Gillis (1981); Steve Humphries, Joanna Mack and Robert Parks (1988).
4 F. Musgrove (1964).
5 *British Quarterly Review*, 1868, pp. 34–69: article on Eton and the Taunton Commission.
6 H. Salt (1910).
7 See note 5; Clement Dukes (1905b).
8 Gillis (1981).
9 Digby and Searby (1981).
10 ibid.
11 Thea Thompson (1982).
12 Winston S. Churchill (1947).
13 Maurice Baring (1922).
14 Quoted in Mary Sturt (1967).
15 Cited in Josephine Kamm (1965).
16 Marion Lochhead (1959).
17 Harley Williams (1973).
18 Joanna Smith (1983).
19 Gwen Raverat (1952).
20 Lilian Boys Behrens (1953).
21 H. C. Barnard (1970).
22 Jane Brough (1856).
23 Lochhead (1959).
24 Barnard (1970).
25 Vera Brittain (1933).
26 Carol Adams (1982).
27 Winifred Peck (1952).
28 Lawson and Silver (1981).
29 Digby and Searby (1981).
30 Carol Dyhouse (1981).
31 Raverat (1952).
32 Molly Hughes (1981).
33 Sir Graham Balfour (1898); Lawson and Silver (1981); PP (1911), vol. 18, Report of Imperial Education Conference, p. 104.

34 See Cyril Jackson; Balfour (1898); Consultative Committee on Attendance at Continuation Schools (1909).
35 HMI Rev. J. P. Norris, before the Taunton Commission, cited in S. J. Curtis (1967).
36 Chapter by Crichton-Browne, in Malcolm Morris (1883).
37 Clement Dukes (1905a).

17 PUPIL SOCIETY AND SCHOOL DISCIPLINE

1 Cited in John Burnett (1982).
2 Memoir of Fred Boughton, in ibid.
3 Steve Humphries (1981).
4 Burnett (1982).
5 C. Shaw (1903).
6 Dorothy Hatcher (1988).
7 See the Departmental Committee on Partial Exemption from School Attendance (1909).
8 Adam Rushton (1909).
9 C. S. Bremner (1897). For a relatively well-run dame school see George Smith's memoir in Edwin Hodder (1896).
10 Cited in Adam Henry Robson (1931).
11 James Walvin (1982); Henry Bryan Binns (1908).
12 Cited in C. J. Montague (1904).
13 Carol Adams (1982); Hugh B. Philpott (1904).
14 Charles Booth (1892–7), vol. 3, part II, p. 211.
15 By Thomas Hughes.
16 Peter Parker (1987).
17 From Augustus Hare, *The Story of My Life*, cited in Gillian Avery (1967).
18 Ronald Pearsall (1975).
19 Clement Dukes (1905a).
20 Cited in Joanna Smith (1983).
21 Ian Gibson (1978).
22 John E. Gorst (1906).
23 Quoted in Thomas Gautrey (1937).
24 Quoted in H. S. Salt (1916).
25 Gibson (1978).
26 Thea Vigne (1975); Flora Thompson (1945); Humphries (1981).
27 S. Humphries (1981); Thompson (1945); Memoir of Kate Taylor, in Burnett (1982); Gorst (1906).
28 Memoir of Charles Cooper, in Burnett (1982).
29 James Runciman (1887).
30 James Crichton-Browne's chapter on 'Education and the nervous system', in Malcolm Morris (1883).
31 Richard Church (1955).
32 Humphries (1981); J. Gathorne Hardy (1972).
33 J. S. Hurt.
34 *Child's Guardian*, 1907.
35 Patrick Macgill (1914).
36 Humphries (1981).

37 Raphael Samuel (1975), part 4: 'Quarry roughs'.
38 Gibson (1978).
39 As related in Norman Longmate (1974).
40 Humphries (1981); Dave Marson's chapter on 'Children's strikes of 1911', in Martin Hoyles (1979).
41 See Hansard, 1 April 1909, col. 493.
42 Gautrey (1937).
43 Hansard, 1 April 1909, col. 493; *Child's Guardian*, 1896, p. 127; Charles Henry Wyatt (1903).
44 Hurt; Walvin (1982); Hansard, 1 April 1909, col. 493; Hansard, 28 March 1900.
45 Hansard, 1 April 1909, col 493, says the board banned it in 1904 for girls and infants, but Gorst (1906) says the board merely disapproved of such use.
46 H. S. Salt (1912); Salt (1916).
47 Memoir of Bill Harding, in Humphries (1981).
48 Recollection of Clifford Hills, in Thea Thompson (1982).
49 Gautrey (1937).
50 Thomas Holmes (1900).
51 Quoted from Runciman (1887).
52 *Child's Guardian*, August 1888, p. 67.
53 Gibson (1978).
54 George Orwell's *A Clergyman's Daughter*, first published by Christy & Moore, quoted in Gillian Avery (1967).
55 Quoted in Salt (1912).
56 Cited in Gibson (1978).
57 Crichton-Browne's chapter in Morris (1883).
58 L. E. Jones (1955).
59 These incidents are from Gibson (1978). But Pearsall (1975) dates the William Gibbs case as 1887.
60 *Child's Guardian*, March 1894.
61 C. S. Lewis (1955).
62 Winston S. Churchill (1947).
63 Gibson (1978), quoting Roger Fry.
64 Maurice Baring (1922).

18 SCHOOL ATTENDANCE

1 Recollection of Mr Baines, in Jeremy Seabrook (1982).
2 Anne Digby and Peter Searby (1981); Marjorie Cruickshank (1981).
3 A. C. O. Ellis (1973).
4 David Rubinstein (1969) gives detailed figures of attendance rates, but he cautions that they are based on unreliable returns given by the schools, as teachers were tempted to inflate attendance figures to sustain their incomes under 'Payment by Results'. See Rosa M. Barrett (1900) and her address on young criminals before the Third International Congress for the Welfare and Protection of Children, 1902, for other figures; J. Lawson and H. Silver (1981) for statistics of absenteeism.
5 Rubinstein (1969); Charles Booth (1892–7), vol. 3, part 2.
6 William Mitchell (1886).

7 See John Springhall (1986), for example.
8 Booth (1892–7), vol. 3, part 2; William Bousfield (1890), preface.
9 Mrs Archibald Mackirdy (1907).
10 Hugh B. Philpott (1904).
11 Quoted in Rubinstein (1969).
12 Flora Thompson (1945).
13 Pamela Horn (1974).
14 Robert Roberts (1976).
15 William Mitchell (1886).
16 Booth (1892–7), vol. 3, part 2; Robert Roberts (1971).
17 Departmental Committee on Physical Deterioration (1904), evidence of A. Eichholz at Q440 *et seq.*
18 Ellis (1973).
19 Digby and Searby (1981).
20 Consultative Committee on Attendance at Continuation Schools (1909); Departmental Committee on Partial Exemption from School Attendance (1909).
21 Sally Livingstone (1978).
22 Rubinstein (1969); Lawson and Silver (1981).
23 Carol Adams (1982); Rubinstein (1969); Carol Dyhouse (1981).
24 Jerry White (1980).
25 Ellis (1973); Rubinstein (1969); G. A. Christian (1922); John Reeves (1913).
26 Christian (1922); Philpott (1904); Rubinstein (1969).
27 Greater London Office, SBL 152.
Royal Commission on Education (1887), evidence of Henry Reader Williams at Q53,756.
28 John E. Gorst (1906).
29 Joseph Stamper (1960); Thea Vigne (1975); Thea Thompson (1982); Rubinstein (1969).
30 Robert H. Sherard (1905).
31 Horn (1974); Departmental Committee on Medical Inspection and Feeding of Schoolchildren; Thompson (1945); W. H. Barrett (1965); Livingstone (1978).
32 John E. Gorst (1913).
33 'East End underworld . . . life of Arthur Harding', in Raphael Samuel (1975).
34 Booth (1892–7), vol. 3, part 2.
35 See George Sims (1889) for a description of an attendance panel meeting. Mary Sturt (1967); Ellis (1973); Philpott (1904); Lawson and Silver (1981).
36 See also Sturt (1967) on the London truant schools.

19 THE FORMATIVE RESULTS OF EDUCATION

1 Royal Commission on Employment of Children (1863–7), 3rd Report (1864).
2 Adam Henry Robson (1931).
3 Hugh B. Philpott (1904); see also J. S. Hurt on the inefficacy of board school education.
4 Lawrence Stone (1969); Anne Digby and Peter Searby (1981). For female literacy see Stone (1969) and Pamela Silver and Harold Silver (1974).
5 Henry Mayhew and John Binny (1862).
6 William Douglas Morrison (1895).

7 J. W. Horsley (1913).
8 See T. J. Macnamara (1905) for other examples of misspellings.
9 Memoir in John Burnett (1982).
10 Robert Roberts (1971).
11 Henry Mayhew (1851), vol. 1, p. 468 ff.
12 Mayhew and Binny (1862).
13 Samuel Smith (1885).
14 Consultative Committee on Attendance at Continuation Schools (1909).
15 Lord Norton (1883).
16 Chapter 1, by W. Lant Carpenter, in William Bousfield (ed.) (1890).
17 *Our Towns: A Close-Up* (1944).
18 See, e.g., Royal Commission on Education (1858–61) (the Newcastle Commission); Ellen Key (1909).
19 Gertrude M. Tuckwell (1894).
20 *British Quarterly Review*, 1868, pp. 34–69, on Eton and the Taunton Commission.
21 Steve Humphries (1981).
22 Jane Walsh, *Not Like Us*, cited in Carol Adams (1982).
23 Memoirs of Faith Ogersby and Jack Lanigan, in Burnett (1982); Dorothy Whipple (1936); Memoir of Annie Wilson, in Thea Thompson (1982).
24 John R. Gillis (1975), citing Aylward E. Dingle's *A Modern Sinbad*.
25 From *A Companion to the Catechism* (1885).
26 Quoted in Humphries (1981).
27 T. N. Kelynack (1922).
28 Band of Hope, Annual Reports, 1867–8, 1869–9, 1872–3.
29 Digby and Searby (1981); Marjorie Cruickshank (1981).
30 Steve Humphries, Joanna Mack and Robert Parks (1988).
31 C. E. B. Russell and L. M. Rigby (1908).
32 Arthur Greenwood (1911); Arnold Freeman (1914); J. H. Whitehouse (1912).

20   EDUCATION AND ECONOMIC MOBILITY

1 J. Lawson and H. Silver (1981); Josephine Kamm (1965).
2 Consultative Committee on Attendance at Continuation Schools (1909); S. J. Curtis (1967); Hugh B. Philpott (1904); Sir Graham Balfour (1898).
3 Lawson and Silver (1981); Curtis (1967). Pamela Silver and Harold Silver (1974).
4 John R. Gillis (1981).
5 ibid.
6 Henry Bryan Binns (1908) (appendix by Sidney Webb). Barclay Baron (1911). Pan-Anglican Papers, 1908: Mrs Creighton, 'The recreation for children of the poor' (these give figures for 1908). C. E. B. Russell (1917).
7 Silver and Silver (1974).
8 Stve Humphries (1981).
9 Binns (1908) (appendix by Sidney Webb).
10 Anne Digby and Peter Searby (1981).
11 Consultative Committee on Attendance at Continuation Schools (1909).
12 George Haw (1911).
13 J. R. Clynes (1937).

14 Ruth Johnson (1974).
15 Recollections of Annie Wilson, in Thea Thompson (ed.) (1962); Humphries (1981).
16 John Burnett (1982), part 2, 'Education'.
17 W. H. G. Armytage, (1964); Memoir of Charles Cooper, in Burnett (1982); Silver and Silver (1974); Margaret Leonora Eyles (1953); Departmental Committee on the Pupil-Teacher System (1896); Mary Sturt (1967); G. A. Christian (1922).
18 Henry Jones (1923); Caroline Louisa Timings (1954); Eyles (1953).
19 Owen's case cited in Sturt (1967).
20 Thomas Gautrey (1937).
21 Departmental Committee on the Pupil-Teacher System (1898).
22 Armytage (1964); Lawson and Silver (1981).
23 See also Joan Tomlinson (1977).
24 Consultative Committee on Attendance at Continuation Schools (1909).
25 Consultative Committee on Attendance at Continuation Schools (1909), appendix 1.
27 ibid.; Margaret McMillan (1904); Arthur Greenwood (1911).
28 Consultative Committee on Attendance at Continuation Schools (1909), appendix 1, and memo of R. H. Tawney to the committee.
29 See Hansard, 22 April 1909, cols 176 *et seq.*, Will Jones MP and Colonel Lockwood MP; Consultative Committee on Attendance at Continuation Schools, Report.
30 Consultative Committee on Attendance at Continuation Schools Report and memo of R. H. Tawney.
31 Reginald Bray (1911). This is also confirmed in R. H. Tawney's memo.
32 Hansard, 4 March 1909, at col. 1594, 11 February 1911, 9 May 1912, 16 April 1913, at cols 1967–9, 30 April 1914, at col. 1886 and see under Continuation School Bills in PP for those years. The Employment and School Attendance Bill of 1914 provided for the abolition of half-time schooling and would have made the right to leave early partly conditional upon attendance at continuation schools, but the bill failed owing to opposition from the cotton interests. (See Hansard, 19 June 1914, cols 1433 *et seq.*)
33 Hansard, 16 April 1913, col. 1969.
34 8/9 Geo. V ch. 39; Lawson and Silver (1981).

21 EXPLOITATION, DISCIPLINE AND DUTY IN THE WORKING-CLASS HOME

1 Jeremy Seabrook (1982).
2 J. Gathorne Hardy (1972).
3 Children's Employment Commission (1843), 2nd Report.
4 PP (1873), vol. 13, report of Robert Baker, inspector of factories.
5 Cited in J. S. Hurt.
6 Marjorie Cruickshank (1981).
7 W. H. Stuart Garnett.
8 John E. Gorst (1913).
9 Robert Roberts (1971); Michael Home (1967); Carol Dyhouse (1981); Recollections of Annie Wilson, in Thea Thompson (1982).

10 Mary G. Barnett (1913).
11 Paul Thompson (1975a).
12 Quoted in John R. Gillis (1975).
13 Robert Holmes (1923).
14 See also Thomas Holmes (1900).
15 Jane Ellice Hopkins (1882).
16 Ethel Williams *et al.* (1910), Report on the Condition of Children receiving Poor Relief in England and Wales, p. 65.
17 Roberts (1971).
18 Elizabeth Roberts (1975).
19 Grace M. Paton (1915).
20 Walter Greenwood (1967).
21 Roberts (1971).
22 Flora Thompson (1945).
23 Holmes (1900); Robert H. Sherard (1905).
24 C. E. B. Russell and L. M. Rigby (1906).
25 Thompson (1945); Departmental Committee on Physical Deterioration (1904), evidence of M. Stanley at Q13,367 *et seq.*; Sally Livingstone (1978).
26 Royal Commission on Employment of Children (1863–7), 2nd Report (1864).
27 Memoir of Thomas Morgan, cited in Thompson (1892). Rowntree's studies in York in 1901 showed that adolescents paid for food and lodgings only, and kept the rest.
28 F. Musgrove (1964).
29 J. J. Findlay (1918).
30 See Departmental Committee on the Employment of Children Act of 1903 (1910), e.g. appendix 7; Departmental Committee on the Employment of Schoolchildren (1902).
31 Charles Booth (1892–7), vol. 3, part 2; Greater London Record Office, SBL 249, pp. 18 and 25.

22   UPBRINGING IN THE UPPER-CLASS HOME

1 See Lionel Rose (1986).
2 J. Gathorne Hardy (1972).
3 Ethel, Lady Thomson (1955); Eleanor Acland (1935).
4 Mary Ann Gibbs (1969); Marion Lochhead (1956).
5 Acland (1935); Lilian Boys Behrens (1953).
6 Gibbs (1969); William H. G. Kingston (1867) includes a leech glass in the nursery medicine cupboard.
7 Hardy (1972).
8 Quoted in ibid.
9 Gibbs (1969).
10 Winston S. Churchill (1947).
11 Cited in Gibbs (1969).
12 Jane Brough (1856).
13 Lochhead (1956).
14 Hardy (1972).
15 Chapter 10, by Priscilla Robertson, in Lloyd de Mause (ed.) (1976).
16 Acland (1935).

17 Carol Dyhouse (1981, citing Ursula Bloom.
18 Edmund Gosse (1907).
19 Maurice Baring (1922). See also Eleanor Farjeon (1935) for nursery incantations.
20 Dorothy Whipple (1936); Eileen Baillie (1958); Steve Humphries, Joanna Mack and Robert Parks (1988); Hardy (1972); Alison Uttley (1937); Mary Howitt (1847).
21 Joanna Smith (1983); Lochhead (1956).
22 Thea Vigne (1975).
23 Smith (1983).
24 See, e.g., Mary Isabella Ogilvie (1952).
25 Lochhead (1956); K. Fawdry and M. Fawdry (1979).
26 James Laver (1951).
27 Vera Brittain (1933).
28 Smith (1983).
29 James Walvin (1982); Edward H. Cooper (1905).
30 Marion Lochhead (1959).
31 Robertson in de Mause (1976); Ian Gibson (1978).
32 Baring (1922); Caroline Louisa Timings (1954); Hardy (1972).
33 See Walvin (1982) on obedience; Gillian Avery (1965); Brittain (1933); Hardy (1972); Gwen Raverat (1952); Acland (1935).
34 H. S. Salt (1916).

23   THE CHILD PROTECTION MOVEMENT

1 C. C. M. Baker (1885); 24/25 Vict. ch. 100 s.42.
2 Cited in Leslie George Housden (1955). *Child's Guardian*, February 1887.
3 Case cited in W. Clarke Hall (1897).
4 *Child's Guardian*, September 1887.
5 Royal Commission on the Poor Laws (1905–9), Minority Report; Benjamin Waugh's evidence before the Select Committee (Lords) on Poor Relief (1888).
6 Section 18 of the 1889 Act.
7 24/25 Vict. ch. 16 s.26.
8 Alfred W. Mager (1886).
9 Third International Congress for the Welfare and Protection of Children, 1902.
10 Samuel Smith (1883).
11 Alan Brack (1983).
12 Acts: 1822 (3 Geo. IV ch. 71); 1833 (3/4 Will. IV ch. 19); 1835 (5/6 Will. IV ch. 59). Ann Stafford (1964); Rosa Waugh (1913).
13 Housden (1955).
14 Waugh (1913).
15 Benjamin Waugh and Cardinal Henry E. Manning (1886).
16 See Gillian Wagner (1979), chapter 13, for a full account of this.
17 John E. Gorst (1913).
18 57/58 Vict. ch. 41. Ivy Pinchbeck and Margaret Hewitt (1973).
19 8 Edw. VII ch. 67 s.12.
20 Prevention of Cruelty to Children Act, s.9. This corrects a statement I made in my book *Rogues and Vagabonds* in which I stated that the Cruelty and

Industrial Schools laws were completely mutually exclusive. Mary Hopkirk's statement that industrial schools were 'fit persons' under the 1889 Act is wrong.

21 See Hansard, 1 January 1908, cols 560 *et seq.*, debate on Children's Bill, where such attitudes are described.

22 *Child's Guardian*, April 1906, p. 41.

23 Robert Parr (1909).

24 *Child's Guardian*, January 1911, p. 5; Victor Bailey and Sheila Blackburn (1979).

25 Steve Humphries (1981).

26 See Lionel Rose (1986), for the story of infant life insurance and the effects of the 1908 Act.

27 See John R. Gillis (1975), pp. 117–18, for the increase in reported cases to the NSPCC by the public in Oxford.

28 Source for statistics: Annual Report of NSPCC for 1935–6.

29 C. E. B. Russell (1905).

30 *Child's Guardian*, May 1906.

31 George Sims (1907b).

32 Children's Branch of the Home Office, 1st Report (1923), pp. 69–70.

33 Gwylmor Prys Williams and George Thompson Brake (1979).

34 Angus McLaren (1978). See J. A. Banks (1981) for statistics showing how the decline in the birth rate affected all classes.

BIBLIOGRAPHY

Acland, Eleanor (1935) *Goodbye for the Present: The story of two childhoods*, London: Hodder & Stoughton.

Adams, Carol (1982) *Ordinary Lives a Hundred Years Ago*, London: Virago.

Anderson, Michael (1972) *Family Structures in Nineteenth Century Lancashire*, London: Cambridge University Press.

Andrews, Irene Osgood and Hobbs, Margarett A. (1918) *Economic Effects of the War upon Women and Children in Great Britain*, Washington, DC: Carnegie Endowment for International Peace.

Armytage, W. H. G. (1964) *Four Hundred Years of English Education*, Cambridge: Cambridge University Press.

Ashby, Henry and Wright, G. A. (1892) *The Diseases of Children, Medical and Surgical*, London: Longman, second edition.

Avery, Gillian (1965) *Nineteenth-Century Children. Heroes and Heroines in English Children's Stories, 1780–1900*, London: Hodder & Stoughton.

—— (ed.) (1967) *School Remembered. An Anthology*, London: Gollancz.

Bailey, Victor and Blackburn, Sheila (1979) 'The Punishment of Incest Act 1908', *Criminal Law Review*: 709 ff.

Baillie, Eileen (1958) *The Shabby Paradise*, London: Hutchinson.

Baker, C. C. M. (1885) *The Laws Relating to Young Children*, London: Waterlow.

Baldry, George ([1939] 1950) *The Rabbit Skin Cap*, London: Collins, second edition.

Balfour, Sir Graham (1898) *The Educational Systems of Great Britain and Ireland*, Oxford: Clarendon.

Ball, N. (1893) *Educating the People*.

Banks, J. A. (1981) *'Victorian Values': Secularism and the size of families*, London: Routledge & Kegan Paul.

Baring, Maurice (1922) *The Puppet Show of Memory*, London: Heinemann.

Barlee, Ellen (1863) *Friendless and Helpless*, London: Emily Faithfull.

—— (1884) *Pantomime Waifs*, London: Partridge.

Barnard, H. C. (1970) *Were Those the Days? A Victorian education*, Oxford, Pergamon.

Barnardo, Thomas (1881) 'Taken out of the Gutter', London: Haughton.

Barnett, Henrietta O. (1918) *Canon Barnett, His Life, Work and Friends*, London: John Murray.

Barnett, Mary G. (1913) *Young Delinquents: A study of reformatory and industrial schools*, London: Methuen.

271

Baron, Barclay (1911) *The Growing Generation*, London: Student Christian Movement.

Barrett, Rosa M. (1900) 'The treatment of juvenile offenders', *Journal of the Royal Statistical Society* (June).

Barrett, W. H. (1965) *A Fenman's Story*, London: Routledge & Kegan Paul.

Behrens, Lilian Boys (1953) *Echoes of a Turbulent Victorian Family*.

Binns, Henry Bryan (1908) *A Century of Education 1808–1908*, London: Dent.

Birt, Lilian (1913) *The Children's Home-Finder*, London: Nisbet.

Black, Clementina (1907) *Sweated Labour and the Minimum Wage*, London: Duckworth.

Blackburn, Fred (1954) *George Tomlinson*, London: Heinemann.

Booth, Charles (1892–7) *Life and Labour of the People in London* (10 vols), vol. 3 (1892), vol. 8 (1896), London: Macmillan.

Bosanquet, B. (ed.) (1895) *Aspects of the Social Problem*, London: Macmillan.

Bosanquet, Helen (1914) *Social Work in London, 1869 to 1912. A History of the Charity Organisation Society*, London: John Murray.

Bousfield, William (ed.) (1890) *Elementary Schools: How to Increase their Utility*, London: Percival.

Brack, Alan (1983) *All They Need is Love: The story of the Liverpool SPCC*, Neston: Gallery Press.

Bray, Reginald (1911) *Boy Labour and Apprenticeship*, London: Constable.

Bremner, C. S. (1897) *Education of Girls and Women in Great Britain*, London: Swan Sonnenschein.

Bristow, E. J. (1977) *Vice and Vigilance*, Dublin: Gill & Macmillan.

Brittain, Vera (1933) *Testament of Youth*, London: Gollancz.

Brough, Jane (1856) *Common Things Regarding the Bringing Up of Our Girls*, London: Sampson Low.

—— (1857) *How to Make the Sabbath a Delight*, London: Wertheim & Macintosh.

Bulkley, M. E. (1914) *The Feeding of Schoolchildren*, London: LSE.

Burke, Thomas (1900) 'The street-trading children of Liverpool', *Contemporary Review* (November).

Burnand, Mr, articles on child entertainers in *Nineteenth Century* (May 1882) and *Fortnightly Review* (January and September 1885).

Burnett, John (1974) *Useful Toil*, London: Allen Lane.

—— (ed.) (1982) *Destiny Obscure: Autobiographies of childhood, education and family from the 1820s to the 1920s*, London: Allen Lane.

Burrows, David (n.d.) unpublished ms on the Invalid Children's Aid Association, held at their headquarters.

Carpenter, Mary (1857) 'Juvenile delinquency in its relation to the educational movement', in Alfred Hill (ed.) *Essays upon Educational Subjects, read at the Educational Conference*, London.

Chance, William (1897) *Children under the Poor Law*, London: Swan Sonnenschein.

Chesney, Kellow (1970) *The Victorian Underworld*, London: Temple Smith.

The Children and the Drink (1901) (the results of an inquiry conducted by the Bishop of Hereford's Committee on temperance reform), London: R. B. Johnson.

Children Working Underground (1979) the National Museum of Wales.

Children's Branch of the Home Office, 1st Report (1923).

Children's Employment Commission, 2nd Report (1843) PP, vol. 13.

Christian, G. A. (1922) *English Education from Within*, London: Wallace Gandy.

Church, Richard (1955) *Over the Bridge*, London: Heinemann.

Churchill, Winston S. (1947) *My Early Life*, London: Collins.

Clynes, J. R. (1937) *Memoirs* (2 vols), London: Hutchinson.

Collier, D. J. (1918) *The Girl in Industry*, London: Bell.

Consultative Committee on Attendance at Continuation Schools (1909) PP, vol. 17.

Cooper, Edward H. (1905) *The Twentieth Century Child*, London: John Lane.

Craig, Edith and St John, Christopher (1933) *Ellen Terry's 'Memoirs'* (revised edition of Ellen Terry, *The Story of My Life*), London: Gollancz.

Cresswell, Walter D'Arcy (1948) *Margaret McMillan. A Memoir*, London: Hutchinson.

Crichton-Browne, James (1884) Report to the Education Department on Alleged Overpressure in Elementary Schools, PP, vol. 61.

The Cruelty Man (1912) (experiences of a NSPCC inspector), London: NSPCC.

Cruickshank, Marjorie (1981) *Children and Industry*, Manchester: Manchester University Press.

Curtis, S. J. (1967) *History of Education in Great Britain*, London: University Tutorial Press, seventh edition.

Cuthbert, V. I. (compiler) (1937) *Where Dreams Come True. A record of 95 years* [of the National Refuges, later the Shaftesbury Homes, and the *Arethusa* training ship], London.

Davies, Margaret Llewelyn (ed.) (1931) *Life As We Have Known It*, London: Leonard and Virginia Woolf.

Davies, Maud F. (1909) *School Care Committees. A Guide To Their Work*, London: Thomas Burleigh.

Dawes, Frank (1975) *A Cry from the Streets: The Boys' Club Movement in Britain from the 1850s to the present day*, Hove, Sussex: Wayland.

Dendy, Helen (*see also* Bosanquet, Helen) (1895) 'The children of working London', in B. Bosanquet (ed.) *Aspects of the Social Problem*, London: Macmillan.

Departmental Committee on School Attendance and Child Labour (1893–4) PP, vol. 68.

Departmental Committee on Habitual Offenders, Vagrants, Beggars, etc. (Scotland) (1895) PP, vol. 37.

Departmental Committee on Reformatories and Indudstrial Schools (1896) PP, vol. 45.

Departmental Committee on the Pupil-Teacher System (1896) PP, vol. 26.

Departmental Committee on Defective and Epileptic Children (1898) PP, vol. 26.

(Inter)Departmental Committee on the Employment of Schoolchildren (1902) PP, vol. 25.

Departmental Committee on Physical Deterioration (1904) PP, vol. 32.

(Inter)Departmental Committee on Medical Inspection and Feeding of Schoolchildren (1906) PP, vol. 47.

(Inter) Departmental Committee on Vagrancy (1906) PP, vol. 103.

Departmental Committee on the Supply and Training of Boy Seamen for the Merchant Marine (1907) PP.

Departmental Committee on Partial Exemption from School Attendance (1909) PP, vol. 17.

Departmental Committee on the Employment of Children Act of 1903 (1910) PP, vol. 28.

Departmental Committee on Hours and Conditions of Van and Warehouse Boys (1913) PP, vol. 33.

Departmental Committee on Reformatories and Industrial Schools (1913) PP, vol. 39.

Departmental Committee on Vagrancy in Scotland (1935–6) PP, vol. 14.

Dickens, Charles (1865) *The Uncommercial Traveller*, chapter 35, 'On an amateur beat', London: Chapman & Hall.

Digby, Anne and Searby, Peter (1981) *Children, School and Society in Nineteenth-Century England*, London: Macmillan.

Douglas, Norman (1916) *London Street Games*, London: St Catherine Press.

Drimmer, Frederick (1976) *Very Special People*, London: Bantam.

Dukes, Clement (1893) *Work and Overwork in Relation to Health in Schools*, London: Percival.

—— (1899) *Remedies for the Needless Injury of Children Involved in the Present System of School Education*, London: Rivingtons.

—— (1905a) *Health at School*, London: Rivingtons, fourth edition.

—— (1905b) *The Use of Alcohol in Youth and its Results in Our Public Schools*, Westminster: Church of England Temperance Society.

Dyhouse, Carol (1977) '"Good wives and little mothers" – the Schoolgirls' Curriculum 1890–1920', *Oxford Review of Education* 3.

—— (1981) *Girls Growing Up in Late Victorian and Edwardian England*, London: Routledge & Kegan Paul.

Eagar, Waldo McGillycuddy (1953) *Making Men: The history of boys' clubs and related movements in Great Britain*, London: University of London Press.

Eaglesham, E. J. R. (1967) *The Foundations of Twentieth-Century Education in England*, London: Routledge & Kegan Paul.

Ellis, A. C. O. (1973) 'Influences on school attendance in Victorian England', *British Journal of Educational Studies* 21: 313 ff.

—— (1976) 'The structure and organization of Victorian elementary schools', Occasional Paper no. 2 (Summer), History of Education Society.

Eyles, Margaret Leonora (1953) *'The Ram Escapes': The story of a Victorian childhood*, London: Peter Nevill.

Fagan, F. W. C. (n.d.; c. 1900) *A Plea for our Street Arabs*.

Farjeon, Eleanor (1935) *A Nursery in the Nineties*, London: Gollancz.

Fawdry, K and Fawdry, M. (1979) *Pollock's History of English Dolls and Toys*, London: Benn.

Fiedler, Leslie (1978) *Freaks: Myths and images of the secret self*, Harmondsworth: Penguin.

Findlay, J. J. (1918) *The Young Wage Earner*, London: Sidgwick & Jackson.

Finn, Ralph (1963) *No Tears in Aldgate*, London: Robert Hale.

Fitzsimons, Raymund (1969) *Barnum in London*, London: Geoffrey Bles.

Fletcher, Ronald (1966) *The Family and Marriage in Britain*, Harmondsworth: Penguin.

Foley, Alice (1973) *A Bolton Childhood*, Manchester: Manchester University Press.

Forster, Eric (1978) *The Pit Children*, Newcastle upon Tyne: F. Graham.

Freeman, Arnold (1914) *Boy Life and Labour*, London: P. S. King.

Frow, Edmund and Frow, Ruth (1970) *A Survey of the Half-Time System in Education*, Manchester: E. J. Morten.

Garnett, W. H. Stuart (n.d., but pre-1911) *Children and the Law*, London: John Murray.

Gauldie, Enid (1974) *Cruel Habitations. A History of Working-Class Housing, 1780–1918*, London: Allen & Unwin.

Gautrey, Thomas (1937) *'Lux Mihi Laus': School Board Memories*, London: Link House.

Gibb, Spencer J. (1911) *The Boy and his Work*, London: Christian Social Union.

Gibbs, Mary Ann (1969) *The Years of the Nannies*, London: Hutchinson.

Gibson, Ian (1978) *The English Vice*, London: Duckworth.

Gillis, John R. (1975) 'The evolution of juvenile delinquency in England 1890–1914', *Past and Present* no. 67 (May).

—— (1981) *Youth and History: Tradition and change in European age relations, 1770–Present*, New York/London: Academic Press.

Glen, W. Cunningham and Glen, R. Cunningham (eds) (1887) *General Orders of the Poor Law Commissioners*, London: Knight, tenth edition.

Gomme, Alice Bertha (1894a) *The Traditional Games of England, Scotland and Ireland*, London: Knight.

—— (1894b) *Children's Singing Games*, London: Nutt.

Gorst, John E. (1906) *The Children of the Nation*, ed. C. W. Saleeby, London: Methuen.

—— (1913) *Education and Race-Regeneration*, London: Cassell.

Gosse, Edmund (1907) *Father and Son*, London: Heinemann.

Gould, George M. and Pyle, Walter M. (1901) *Anomalies and Curiosities of Medicine*, Philadelphia, Pa: W. B. Saunders.

Green, Henry (1940) *Pack my Bag*, London: Hogarth.

Greenwood, Arthur (1911) *Juvenile Labour Exchanges and After-Care*, London: P. S. King.

—— (1913) *The Health and Physique of Schoolchildren*, London: LSE.

Greenwood, James ([1866] 1884) *The Little Raggamuffins*, London: Ward Lock.

Greenwood, Walter (1967) *There Was a Time*, London: Cape.

Hall, W. Clarke (1897) *The Queen's Reign for Children*, London: Unwin.

—— (1926) *Children's Courts*, London: Allen & Unwin.

Harbinson, Robert (1959) *No Surrender: An Ulster childhood*, London: Faber & Faber.

Harding, Arthur (1981) *East End Underworld*, ed. Raphael Samuel, London: Routledge & Kegan Paul.

Hardy, J. Gathorne (1972) *The Rise and Fall of the British Nanny*, London: Hodder & Stoughton.

Hatcher, Dorothy (1988) *The Workhouse and the Weald*, Rainham: Meresborough.

Haw, George (1910) *A Lad of London*, London: Cassell.

—— (1911) *From Workhouse to Westminster: The life story of Will Crooks MP*, London: Cassell, second edition.

Hill, Florence Davenport (1889) *Children of the State*, London: Macmillan, second edition.

Hird, Frank (1898) *The Cry of the Children*, London: J. Bowden, second edition.

Hodder, Edwin (1894) *John Macgregor ('Rob Roy')*, London: Hodder.

—— (1896) *George Smith of Coalville*, London: Nisbet.

Hogg, Edith (1897a) 'Schoolchildren as wage earners', *Nineteenth Century* (August): 235–44.

—— (1897b) 'The fur-pullers of South London', *Nineteenth Century* (November).

Holmes, Robert (1923) *'Them That Fall'*, Edinburgh/London: Blackwood.

Holmes, Thomas (1900) *Pictures and Problems from London Police Courts*, London: Edward Arnold.

—— (1908) *Known to the Police*, London: Edward Arnold.

—— (1912) *London's Underworld*, London: Dent.

Home, Michael (1967) *Winter Harvest*, London: Macdonald.

Hopkins, Jane Ellice (1882) *On the Early Training of Boys and Girls: An appeal to working women*, London: Hatchards.

—— (1885) *God's Little Girl*.

—— (1899) *The Power of Womanhood*, London: Wells Gardner.

Hopkirk, Mary (1949) *Nobody Wanted Sam: The story of the unwelcomed child, 1530–1948*, London: John Murray.

Horn, Pamela (1974) *The Victorian Country Child*, Kineton: Roundwood Press.

Horsley, J. W. (1913) *How Criminals are Made and Prevented*, London: Fisher Unwin.

Horsley, Victor and Sturge, Mary D. (1907) *Alcohol and the Human Body*, London: Macmillan.

Housden, Leslie George (1955) *The Prevention of Cruelty to Children*, London: Cape.

Howell, Michael and Ford, Peter (1983) *The True Story of the Elephant Man* (the life of Joseph Carey Merrick), London: Allison & Busby.

Howitt, Mary (1847) *The Story of a Happy Home* (also known as *The Children's Year*), London.

Hoyles, Martin (ed.) (1979) *Changing Childhood*, London: Writers & Readers.

Hughes, Molly ([1946] 1981) *A London Family 1870–1900*, Oxford: Oxford University Press.

Humphries, Steve (1981) *Hooligans or Rebels?*, Oxford: Blackwell.

—— (1988) *A Secret World of Sex . . . The British Experience 1900–1850*, London: Sidgwick & Jackson.

——, Mack, Joanna and Parks, Robert (1988) *A Century of Childhood*, London: Sidgwick & Jackson.

Hurt, J. S. (n.d.) *Elementary Schooling and the Working Classes 1860–1918*.

Hutchins, B. L. and Harrison, A. (1926) *A History of Factory Legislation*, London: P. S. King.

Imperial Education Conference Report (1911) PP. vol. 18.

International Congresses for the Welfare and Protection of Children, reports of; the third was held in 1902.

Jackson, Cyril (1908) Report on Boy Labour, for the Royal Commission on the Poor Laws (1905–9), PP (Cd 4499), vol. 20, appendix.

Johnson, H. M. (1897) *Children and Public Houses*, Seacombe, Cheshire: Mrs Shilston, third edition.

Johnson, Ruth (1974) *Old Road: A Lancashire Childhood, 1912–26*; compiled and written by Alfred H. Body, Manchester: E. J. Morten.

Jones, G. M. Edwardes and Sykes, J. C. G. (1904) *The Law of Public Education in England and Wales*, London: Rivingtons.

Jones, Sir Henry (1923) *Old Memories*, London: Hodder & Stoughton.

Jones, L. E. (1955) *A Victorian Boyhood*, London: Macmillan.

Juvenile Organizations Committee of the Board of Education (1920) Report on Juvenile Delinquency.

Kamm, Josephine (1965) *Hope Deferred: Girls' education in English history*, London: Methuen.

Kay, Joseph (1857) *On the Comparative Condition of Children in English and Foreign Towns*.

Keary, Annie (1860) *Blind Man's Holiday; or, Short Tales for the Nursery*, London: Griffith & Farran.

Keeling, Frederic (1914) *Child Labour in the United Kingdom*, London: P. S. King.

Kelynack, T. N. (1922) *The Progress of Child Welfare: A consideration of service for children during the last half century, with special reference to the share taken by Sir John Kirk and the Shaftesbury Society and the Ragged School Union*, London: John Kirk House.

Kerr, Rose (1976) *The Story of the Girl Guides, volume 1, 1908–38*, London: Girl Guides Association.

Key, Ellen (1909) *The Century of the Child*, New York/London: Putnam.

King-Hall, Magdalen (1958) *The Story of the Nursery*, London: Routledge & Kegan Paul.

Kingsley, Charles (1863) *The Water Babies*, London/Cambridge.

Kingston, William, H. G. (1867) *Infant Amusements; or, How to Make a Nursery Happy*, London.

Kitteringham, Jennie (1975) 'Country work girls in nineteenth-century England', in R. Samuel (ed.) *Village Life and Labour*, London: Routledge & Kegan Paul.

Laver, James (1951) *Children's Fashions in the Nineteenth Century*, London: Batsford.

Lawson, J. and Silver, H. ([1973] 1981) *A Social History of Education in England*, London: Methuen.

Lewis, C. S. (1955) *Surprised by Joy*, London: Geoffrey Bles.

Livingstone, Sally (1978) *A Penny a Boy*, Ipswich, Suffolk: Boydell.

Lochhead, Marion (1956) *Their First Ten Years: Victorian childhood*, London: John Murray.

—— (1959) *Young Victorians*, London: John Murray.

Longmate, Norman (1974) *The Workhouse*, London: Temple Smith.

Macgill, Patrick (1914) *Children of the Dead End: The autobiography of a navvy*, London: Herbert Jenkins.

Mackirdy, Mrs Archibald (Olive Christian Malvery) (1907) *Baby Toilers*, London: Hutchinson.

McLaren, Angus (1978) *Birth Control in Nineteenth-Century England*, London: Croom Helm.

McMillan, Margaret (1896) *Child Labour and the Half-Time System*, London: Clarion Pamphlet no. 15.

—— (1904) *Education through the Imagination*, London: Swan Sonnenschein.

—— (1907) *Labour and Childhood*, London: Swan Sonnenschein.

Macnamara, T. J. (1905) *School Room Humour*, Bristol: Arrowsmith.

Mager, Alfred W. (1886) *Children's Rights*, Bolton: Evening News.

Mallam, Kathleen (1908) *Destitute, Neglected, and Delinquent Children*, London: SPCK.

Mandelievich, Elias (ed.) (1979) *Children at Work*, Geneva: International Labour Office.

Mansbridge, Albert (1932) *Margaret McMillan, Prophet and Pioneer*, London: Dent.

Mason, Charlotte (1886) *Home Education*, London: Kegan Paul.

Massey, Victoria (1978) *One Child's War*, London: BBC.

Maugham, Somerset (1897) *Liza of Lambeth*, London: Fisher Unwin.

Mause, Lloyd de (ed.) (1976) *The History of Childhood*, London: Souvenir Press.

Mayhew, Henry (1851) *London Labour and the London Poor*, vol. 1, London.

—— (1949) *Mayhew's London*, selections from *London Labour and the London Poor*, ed. Peter Quennell, London: Pilot Press.

—— and Binny, John (1862) *The Criminal Prisons of London and Scenes of London Life*, London.

Mearns, Andrew and Preston, W. C. (1883) *The Bitter Cry of Outcast London*, London: James Clarke.

Middleton, Nigel (1971) *When Family Failed*, London: Gollancz.

Mitchell, William (1886) *Rescue the Children*, London: Isbister.

Montague, C. J. (1904) *Sixty Years in Waifdom: The Ragged School Movement in English History*, London: Chas Murray.

Morris, Malcolm (ed.) (1883) *The Book of Health*, London: Cassell.

Morrison, William Douglas (1895) *Juvenile Offenders*, London: Criminology Series.

The Mothers of England: Their influence and responsibility (1843), London: Fisher.

Musgrove, F. (1964) *Youth and the Social Order*, London: Routledge & Kegan Paul.

National Refuges for Homeless and Destitute Children, periodical *Our Work*.

Norton, Lord (1883) 'Middle-class education', *Nineteenth Century* (February): 229 ff.

Ogilvie, Mary Isabella (1952) *A Scottish Childhood*, Oxford: George Ronald.

Opie, Iona and Opie, Peter (1969) *Children's Games in Street and Playground*, Oxford: Clarendon.

—— (1985) *The Singing Game*, Oxford: Oxford University Press.

Oral History journal, esp. vol. 3 (1975).

Our Towns: A Close-Up (1944), Women's Group on Public Welfare, second edition.

Parker, Peter (1987) *The Old Lie: The Great War and the public school ethos*, London: Constable.

Parr, Robert (1909) *The Care and Control of the Feeble-Minded*, London: NSPCC.

—— (1910a) *The Seeds of Hope: How the NSPCC helps the State*, London.

—— (1910b) *Canal Boat Children*.

Paton, Grace M. (1915) *The Child and the Nation*, London: Student Christian Movement.

Pearsall, Ronald (1969) *The Worm in the Bud*, London: Weidenfeld & Nicolson.

—— (1975) *Night's Black Angels*, London: Hodder & Stoughton.

Pearson, Geoffrey (1983) *Hooligan: A history of respectable fears*, London: Macmillan.

Peck, Winifred (1952) *A Little Learning*, London: Faber & Faber.

Pepler, Hilary Douglas Clerk (1912) *The Care Committee*, London: Constable.

—— (1915) *Justice and the Child*, London: Constable.

Percival, Alicia C. (1951) *Youth Will Be Led*, London: Collins.

Percival, Tom (1912) *Poor Law Children*, London: Shaw.

Petrie, Glen (1971) *A Singular Iniquity*, London: Macmillan.

Philpott, Hugh B. (1904) *London at School: The story of the School Board 1870–1904*, London: Fisher Unwin.

Pinchbeck, Ivy (1930) *Women Workers and the Industrial Revolution 1750–1850*, London: Routledge.

—— and Hewitt, Margaret (1969–73) *Children in English Society*, vol. 1 (1969), vol. 2 (1973), London: Routledge.

Playfair, Giles (1967) *'The Prodigy': A study of the strange life of Master Betty*, London: Secker & Warburg.

Prevention of Cruelty to Children Acts:
1889 (52/53 Vict. ch. 44)
1894 (57/58 Vict. ch. 41)
1904 (4 Edw. VII ch. 15)
1908 (8 Edw. VII ch. 67)

Pritchard, David Gwyn (1963) *Education and the Handicapped 1760–1960*, London: Routledge & Kegan Paul.

Ragged School Union (1884) *The Dens of London. Forty Years' Missionary Work among the Outcast Poor of London.*

Raverat, Gwen (1952) *Period Piece: A Cambridge childhood*, London: Faber & Faber.

Read, Donald (1979) *England 1868–1914*, London: Longman.

Reeves, John (1913) *Recollections of a School Attendance Officer*, London: Arthur H. Stockwell.

Rennie, Jean (1955) *Every Other Sunday*, London: Arthur Barker.

Reports on Children under Five . . . in Elementary Schools (1906) PP, vol. 90.

Richards, Brinsley (n.d.) *Seven Years at Eton.*

Roberts, Alasdair (1980) *Out to Play*, Aberdeen: Aberdeen University Press.

Roberts, Elizabeth (1975) 'Socialization outside school', *Oral History 3.*

Roberts, Robert (1971) *The Classic Slum: Salford life in the first quarter of the century*, Manchester: Manchester University Press.

—— (1976) *A Ragged Schooling*, Manchester: Manchester University Press.

Robertson, A. B. (1972) 'Children, teachers and society: the overpressure controversy, 1880–1886', *British Journal of Education Studies 20.*

Robson, Adam Henry (1931) *The Education of Children Engaged in Industry in England 1833–1876*, London: Kegan Paul.

Rodaway, Angela (1960) *A London Childhood*, London: Batsford.

Rose, June (1987) *For the Sake of the Children*, London: Hodder & Stoughton.

Rose, Lionel (1986) *The Massacre of the Innocents*, London: Routledge & Kegan Paul.

—— (1988) *Rogues and Vagabonds*, London: Routledge.

Ross, A. M. (1955) 'The Care and Education of Pauper Children in England and Wales 1834–1896', unpublished PhD thesis, University of London.

Royal Commission on Education (Newcastle Commission) (1858–61) PP, vol. 21, part 1.

Royal Commission on Employment of Children (1863–7) PP:
1st Report (1863) vol. 18.
2nd Report and 3rd Report (1864) vol. 22.
4th Report (1865) vol. 20.
5th Report (1866) vol. 24.
6th Report (1867) vol. 16, part 1.

Royal Commission on Employment of Children, Young Persons and Women in Agriculture (1868–70) PP:
1st Report (1867–8) vol. 17.
2nd Report (1868–9) vol. 13.
3rd Report (1870) vol. 13.

Royal Commission on Factories and Workshops Acts (1876) PP, vol. 29.
Royal Commission on Reformatories and Industrial Schools (1884) PP, vol. 45.
Royal Commission on the Housing of the Working Classes (1884–5) PP, vol. 30.
Royal Commission on Education (1887) PP, vol. 30.
Royal Commission on the Blind, Deaf and Dumb (1889) PP, vols 19 and 20.
Royal Commission on Physical Training (Scotland) (1903) PP, vol. 30.
Royal Commission on the Poor Laws (1905–9) PP (Cd 4499), see (a) Jackson, Cyril (b) Williams, Ethel *et al.*
Royal Commission on the Care and Control of the Feeble-Minded (1908) PP, vols 36–9.
Rubinstein, David (1969) *School Attendance in London 1870–1904*, Hull: University of Hull.
Runciman, James (1885) *School Board Idylls*, London: Longman.
—— (1887) *Schools and Scholars*, London: Chatto & Windus.
Rushton, Adam (1909) *My Life: As farmer's boy, factory lad, teacher and preacher*, Manchester: S. Clarke.
Russell, C. E. B. (1905) *Manchester Boys*, Manchester: Manchester University Press.
—— (1917) *The Problem of Juvenile Crime*, Oxford: Barnett House Papers, no. 1.
—— and Campagnac, E. T. (1902) 'Memorandum on education, earnings and social condition of boys engaged in street-trading in Manchester; *see* appendix 45 in the (Inter)Departmental Committee on the Employment of School-children (1902). Also in PP, vol. 26, Special Papers on Educational Subjects.
—— and Rigby, L. M. (1906) *The Making of the Criminal*, London: Macmillan.
—— (1908) *Working Lads' Clubs*, London: Macmillan.
Sadler, M. E. (1907) *Continuation Schools in England and Elsewhere*, Manchester: Victoria University Publications, no. 1.
Salt, H. S. (1910) *Eton under Hornby.*
—— (1912) *The Case Against Corporal Punishment*, London: Humanitarian League.
—— (1916) *The Flogging Craze*, London: Humanitarian League.
Samuel, Raphael (ed.) (1975) *Village Life and Labour*, London: Routledge & Kegan Paul.
Samuelson, James (1911) *The Children of Our Slums*, London: Simpkin Marshall.
Sanger, 'Lord' George ([1910] 1952) *Seventy Years a Showman*, London: Dent.
Seabrook, Jeremy (1982) *Working-Class Childhood*, London: Gollancz.
Select Committee on Poor Relief (1861) PP, vol. 9.
Select Committee (Lords) on Sweating, PP (1888) vol. 20.
Select Committee (1889) vol. 14, parts 1 and 2.
Select Committee on Home Work (1907) PP, vol. 6.
Select Committee on Home Work (1908) PP, vol. 8.
Sewell, Mary, verses published in the 1860s on poverty, hardships of waifs and orphans, *see* British Library catalogues.
Sharp, Evelyn (1927) *The London Child*, London: John Lane.
Shaw, C. ('An Old Potter') (1903) *When I Was a Child*, London: Methuen.
Sherard, Robert H. (1905) *The Child Slaves of Britain*, London: Hurst & Blackett.
Sherington, Geoffrey (1981) *English Education, Social Change and War 1911–20*, Manchester: Manchester University Press.
Sherwell, Arthur (1891) *Life in West London*, London: Methuen.
Shiman, Lilian Lewis (1973) 'The Band of Hope movement: respectable recreation for working-class children', *Victorian Studies* (September).

Silver, Pamela and Silver, Harold (1974) *The Education of the Poor: The history of a National school*, London: Routledge & Kegan Paul.

Sims, George (1889) *How the Poor Live and Horrible London*, London: Chatto & Windus.

—— (1907a) 'The cry of the children', first published as six articles in *The Tribune* between 4 February and 21 February.

—— (1907b) *The Black Stain*

Smedley, Menella B. (1875) *Boarding Out and Pauper Schools, especially for Girls*, London.

'Smith, Emma' (1958) *A Cornish Waif's Story*, London: Odhams.

Smith, F. B. (1979) *The People's Health 1830–1910*, London: Croom Helm.

Smith, George (1871) *The Cry of the Children from the Brickyards of England*, London/Leicester.

—— (1879) *Our Canal Population*, London: Haughton.

—— (1880) *Gipsy Life*, London: Haughton.

—— (1881) *Canal Adventures by Moonlight*, London: Hodder & Stoughton.

—— (1885) *I've Been a-Gipsying*, London: Fisher Unwin.

—— (1888) *Our Canal, Gipsy, Van and Other Travelling Children*, London: privately printed.

—— (1889) *Gipsy Children; or A Stroll in Gipsydom*, London: Woodford Fawcett.

Smith, Joanna (1983) *Edwardian Children*, London: Hutchinson.

Smith, Samuel (1883) 'Social reform', *Nineteenth Century* (May).

—— (1885) 'The industrial training of destitute children', *Contemporary Review* (January).

Soloway, Richard A. (1982) *Birth Control and the Population Question in England 1877–1930*, Chapel Hill, NC: University of North Carolina Press.

Spalding, T. A. (1900) *The Work of the London School Board*, London: P. S. King.

Springhall, John (1986) *Coming of Age: Adolescence in Britain 1860–1960*, Dublin: Gill & Macmillan.

Stafford, Ann (1964) *The Age of Consent*, London: Hodder & Stoughton.

Stamper, Joseph (1960) *So Long Ago*, London: Hutchinson.

Stone, Lawrence (1969) 'Literacy and education in England 1640–1900', *Past and Present* 42.

Strange, Kathleen H. (1982) *Climbing Boys: A study of sweeps' apprentices 1773–1875*, London: Allison & Busby.

Strutt, Joseph (1875) *The Sports and Pastimes of the People of England*, London: Thomas Tegg.

Stuart, Dorothy Margaret (1941) *A Child's Day Through the Ages*, London: Harrap.

Stuart, John (1907) *Mr. John Kirk: The Children's Friend*, London: Partridge.

Sturt, Mary (1967) *The Education of the People*, London: Routledge & Kegan Paul.

Tempted London, reprinted from articles in the *British Weekly*, October 1887–April 1888; article on 'Variety theatres'.

Thomas, Maurice, W. (1945) *Young People in Industry 1750–1945*, London: Nelson.

Thompson, Flora (1945) *Lark Rise to Candleford*, London: Oxford University Press.

Thompson, Paul (1975a) 'The war with adults', *Oral History* 3.

—— (1975b) *The Edwardians*, London: Weidenfeld & Nicolson.

Thompson, Thea (1982) *Edwardian Childhoods*, London: Routledge & Kegan Paul.

Thomson, Ethel, Lady (1955) *Clifton Lodge*, London: Hutchinson.

Timings, Caroline Louisa (1954) *Letter from the Past*, London: privately printed.

Tomlinson, Joan (1977) *On a May Morning*, Richmond: Hickey.

Tuckwell, Gertrude M. (1894) *The State and its Children*, London: Methuen.

Turner, E. S. (1950) *Roads to Ruin: The shocking history of social reform*, chapter on boy chimney sweeps, London: Michael Joseph.

Urquhart, John (1900) *The Life Story of William Quarrier*, London: Partridge.

Urwick, E. J. (ed.) (1904) *Studies of Boy Life in Our Cities*, London: Dent.

Uttley, Alison (1931) *The Country Child*, London: Faber & Faber.

—— (1937) *Ambush of Young Days*, London: Faber & Faber.

Vigne, Thea (1975) 'Parents and children 1890–1918', *Oral History* 3 (2).

Wagner, Gillian (1979) *Barnardo*, London: Weidenfeld & Nicholson.

Walton, John and Walvin, James (eds) (1986) *Leisure in Britain 1780–1939*, Manchester: Manchester University Press.

Walvin, James (1975) *The People's Game: A social history of football*, London: Allen Lane.

—— (1978) *Leisure and Society 1830–1950*, London: Longman.

—— (1982) *A Child's World (1800–1914)*, Harmondsworth: Penguin.

Waugh, Benjamin and Manning, Cardinal Henry E. (1886) 'The child of the English savage', *Contemporary Review* (May).

Waugh, Rosa (1913) *The Life of Benjamin Waugh*, London: Fisher Unwin.

Weylland, John Matthias (1872) *The Man with the Book*, London.

Whetham, Catherine (1917) *The Upbringing of Daughters*, London: Longman.

Whipple, Dorothy (1936) *The Other Day*, London: Michael Joseph.

White, Jerry (1980) *Rothschild Buildings*, London: Routledge & Kegan Paul.

Whitehouse, J. H. (1908) *Report of an Enquiry into Working Boys' Homes in London*, London: P. S. King.

—— (1912) *Problems of Boy Life*, London: P. S. King.

Wiggin, Kate Douglas (1892) *Children's Rights*, London: Gay & Bird.

Williams, Ethel *et al.* (1910) Report on the Condition of Children Receiving Poor Relief in England and Wales, PP, vol. 52; *see* appendix, vol. 18 of the Royal Commission on the Poor Laws (1905–9) (Cd 5037).

Williams, Gwylmor Prys and Brake, George Thompson (1979) *Drink in Great Britain 1900–1979*, London: Edsall.

Williams, Harley (1973) *Requiem for a Great Killer: The story of TB*, London: Health Horizon for the Chest & Heart Foundation.

Wohl, Anthony S. (1977) *The Eternal Slum*, London: Edward Arnold.

—— (ed.) (1978) *The Victorian Family*, London: Croom Helm.

Wyatt, Charles Henry (1903) *Wyatt's Companion to the Education Acts 1870–1902*, Manchester: Thomas Wyatt.

Yule, G. Udney (1920) *The Fall of the Birth Rate*, Cambridge: Cambridge University Press.

INDEX